Shipbuilders, Sea Captains, and Fishermen

Also by Joe Follansbee

Get Streaming! Quick Steps to Delivering Audio and Video Online

Hands-On Guide to Windows Media

Hands-On Guide to Streaming Media

SHIPBUILDERS, SEA CAPTAINS, AND FISHERMEN

The Story of the Schooner Wawona

Joe Follansbee

iUniverse, Inc.
New York Lincoln Shanghai

Shipbuilders, Sea Captains, and Fishermen
The Story of the Schooner Wawona

Copyright © 2006 by Joseph G. Follansbee

iUniverse books may be ordered through booksellers or by contacting:

iUniverse
2021 Pine Lake Road, Suite 100
Lincoln, NE 68512
www.iuniverse.com
1-800-Authors (1-800-288-4677)

"Matt Peasley", © 1976, The Aberdeen Daily World. Used by permission
"Saga of the Wawona", © Northwest Seaport. Used by permission
Cover design by Robert Lasker.
Cover photo © 2006 Joseph G. Follansbee. The photo is of Wawona's fiddlehead, a simple type of figurehead.
For more information, visit www.wawonabook.com

4
CULTURE
KING COUNTY LODGING TAX

ISBN-13: 978-0-595-41833-6 (pbk)
ISBN-13: 978-0-595-86176-7 (ebk)
ISBN-10: 0-595-41833-3 (pbk)
ISBN-10: 0-595-86176-8 (ebk)

Printed in the United States of America

For Dave Wright and all the men who sailed in *Wawona*.

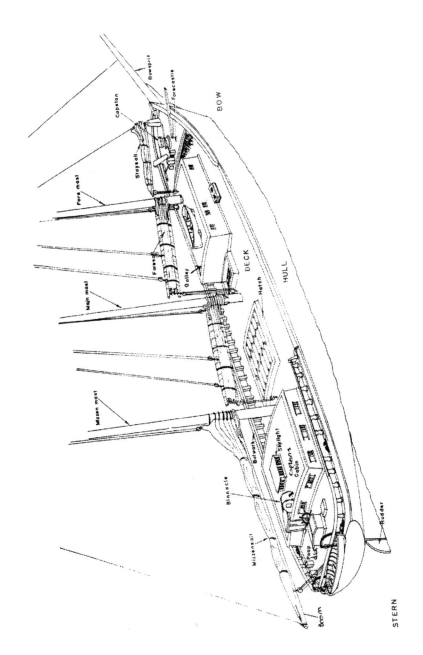

BOW

Bowsprit

Forecastle

Capstan

Staysail

Fore mast

Fore

Galley

DECK

Main mast

Hatch

HULL

Mizzen mast

Bulwarks

Skylight

Captain's
Cabin

Binnacle

Rudder

Mizzensail

Poop
deck

Boom

STERN

CONTENTS

▼

"*The history of Seattle and the Pacific Northwest is a maritime history. At the core of this history sails the Wawona. In telling the story of the three-masted schooner in* Shipbuilders, Sea Captains, and Fishermen, *Joe Follansbee captures a century of high-seas adventure, on-shore carousing, bottom-line commerce, and civic commitment. With skillful research and a flare for storytelling, Follansbee also delivers a great read. But perhaps most important, he reminds us of the terrible lose we incur if we lose the Wawona, one of the region's most important heritage landmarks.*"

—**Peter Donahue**, author of *Madison House* and editor of *Reading Seattle: The City in Prose*

"*Well-organized, well-documented, and written in a lively, appealing style.*"

—**William S. Hanable**, author of *A Maritime History of Alaska*

"*The value of this book cannot be overstated. Not only do we learn the history of the Wawona, we also get an insight into the hard-working people on board who contributed so much to the development of Washington State, and whose stories are rarely told.*"

—**Alan Stein**, HistoryLink, author of *Safe Passage: The Birth of Washington State Ferries*

Acknowledgements

The author would like to thank the following people for their invaluable help preparing this book: Flo Lentz, Charles Payton and the entire staff at 4Culture; Joe Shickich, Pat Hartle, Dave Clute, Dan Roberts and the volunteers at Northwest Seaport; Louise Shields; Jim Shields; the late Capt. Ed Shields; Capt. Harold Huycke; Dave Wright; Roger and Lily LaRue; Linda Haakenson; the librarians at the University of Washington Libraries, the Seattle Public Library, and the Aberdeen (Washington) Public Library; Catherine Mace and the Humboldt County (California) Historical Society; the Coos Bay (Oregon) Historical Society; the Andover (Massachusetts) Historical Society; the Anacortes (Washington) History Museum; Dan Sears and the Aberdeen (Washington) Museum of History; the Museum of History & Industry; the staff at Fern Hill Cemetery in Aberdeen, Washington; the editors at *Maritime Life & Traditions*, *The Seattle Times*, *The Seattle Post-Intelligencer*, *Humboldt Times-Standard*, *The Boston Globe*, *Pacific Northwest Quarterly*, *The Mariner's Mirror*, *Gastronomica*, *Columbia*, *Sea History*, and *Nostalgia*; HistoryLink; John C. Hughes; Graham L. Peaslee; Dave Barnes; Rick Boggs; Kay Bullitt; Priscilla Long; Diane Colson; Nick O'Connell; Janice Deweyert; Paul Douglas; Colleen Wagner; Jennifer Schile; Barbara Sjoholm; Peter Donahue; Alan Stein; William S. Hanable; Rex C. Browning; Nancy Wick.

The author also wishes to thank the many members of *Wawona*'s crews and their families for donating their memories to the *Wawona* Collection at Northwest Seaport. Their generosity made this book possible.

The author would like to express his deepest gratitude to his wife Edith and daughters Emily and Abbey for letting him stay focused in his cave.

Introduction

One day in 1999, I discovered 24 gray-blue archive boxes on a metal shelf in a closet. The boxes contained journals, diaries, personal letters, business letters, postcards, account books, logs, telegrams, framed and unframed photographs, bills of sale, government documents, and personal belongings. The inventory of the "*Wawona* Collection" pricked at old newspaper and radio journalism instincts. There was a story here.

A few weeks earlier, as I searched for a place to donate some time, I had walked the decks of the schooner *Wawona*, berthed in a decrepit industrial slip on Lake Union, just north of Seattle's downtown. The three-masted schooner and her boxes of archived records were owned by Northwest Seaport, which planned, it said, to restore the vessel. The ship certainly needed work. Tarps covered a large hole at the bow. New restoration work on the other side of the bow was unfinished. Paint peeled away everywhere, revealing wood bleached gray by repeated rains. I was captivated.

I knew almost nothing about boats, and little about Seattle's maritime history. A few faded display boards explained that *Wawona* was built in 1897, had carried lumber along the Pacific Coast, and fished in the Bering Sea during the 1930s. She was big, 165 feet long and 35 feet wide. Her masts were 110 feet tall. The volunteers talked about her builder, Bendixsen, and her captains, Peasley, Foss and Haugen, as if they were celebrities. And I learned *Wawona* took cod, not salmon, the fish most prized by fishermen and talked about by environmentalists, politicians, and chefs. She used dories, which I thought were a New England thing. And she made salt cod, a food as mysterious to me as whatever people ate in say, Bhutan. What's going on here? A big sailing ship from Puget Sound fishing for an east coast fish in Alaska using New England boats in the middle of the Depression?

Other than curiosity, I had no reason to be interested in *Wawona*. No one in my family worked in the timber or shipping industries. I was born in Seattle; my father wanted to be a firefighter. When I was four years old, Dad fell seriously ill, and our family moved to the eastern Washington town of Yakima to be near relatives while he recovered. However, I begged Dad and Mom to take me to Seattle for visits. When our car came down Snoqualmie Pass out of the Cascade Mountains, I could feel the rising moisture in the air and smell the sweetness of salt water. For me, Yakima was the visit. Seattle was home. My favorite destination was the central waterfront, with the cheesy tourist traps, the rusting train tracks that tripped the feet of unwary pedestrians, the working warehouses with undulating roof lines and moss-encrusted shingles, and the acrid smell of creosote protecting the pilings from worms.

After we moved back to Seattle, I got part-time jobs near the waterfront, and I often bought a lunch of fish and chips at Ivar's Acres of Clams at Pier 54. Most of the work done at the waterfront was retail: selling trinkets to Japanese tourists or meals to workers in downtown office buildings. The real maritime work, loading and unloading goods at the docks, or landing fish caught in the Pacific Ocean beyond the Olympic Mountains, was far away, at least from people's minds, because the shipping and fishing terminals were largely inaccessible. In years past, a visitor could pass the time by watching the work. Now, maritime work was as remote as the moon.

I moved away, working at newspapers and radio stations in Oregon, California and Minnesota. My career diverted into the Internet boom, which brought me back to Seattle. I did volunteer computer work for Northwest Seaport, and eventually started selling articles to local magazines and newspapers.

I cast about for book ideas. In 2003, I remembered the 24 boxes in the closet. I visited the office, opened each one, and I felt as Howard Carter must have felt when he opened Tutankhamun's tomb. The words in the documents were shouts from a century ago like the shouts of fishermen to companions lost in fog. The sailors, captains, fishermen, and ship owners in the photographs smiled at me as if I were a best friend they had not seen for years. I held their books, their wallets, even the buttons from their coats. They loved *Wawona* enough to offer her pieces of themselves, hoping that someone would tell their story.

CHAPTER 1

▼

THE STURDY DANE

Sunday, September 12, 1897
Fairhaven, Humboldt County, California

A fresh northwest breeze lifted the worsted wool lapel of Hans Ditlev Bendixsen's coat as he stepped out of his modest, well-furnished home on Fay Avenue[1] in Fairhaven, California, across Humboldt Bay from Eureka. The zephyr glided in from the North Pacific, up and over a low, thin peninsula that separated Humboldt Bay from the ocean, and it ruffled his gray hair, which was close-cropped above the ears and arranged in a pompadour on his high forehead. The blue of the late morning sky matched his eyes. "He was a Dane—very tall, slim," one of his men remembered. "He wore high top boots along with a stiff derby hat."[2] The sea air carried the sound of breakers on the ocean side of the peninsula. A good wind for seasoning the pine, he thought, and a good day for a launching.

Emma, his wife, came out the door cheerfully behind him, and she smiled warmly at her husband of 17 years.[3] She put her small, gloved hand in her mate's as he guided her to the street, and she adjusted her straw hat, topped with silk flowers that anticipated the coming fall colors of yellow and red, while shading her face from the late summer sun. A ship captain once called her "a dainty, little German woman, erect and spirited."[4] Man and wife paused while Emma smoothed out her petticoats. In the distance, toward the bay, they could see a ship's pennant fluttering from the second of three masts towering above the houses and trees. Emma put her hand under her husband's arm as they walked to the shipyard and the launching of the three-masted schooner *Wawona*.

Hans Ditlev Bendixsen (Northwest Seaport)

Hans and Emma Bendixsen walked to the end of Fay Avenue and stepped onto a plank path at the shipyard gate. Hans searched the bay for the tug that would help with the launch, but it was nowhere to be seen. He wanted the ceremony to come off on time with no problems. As he and his wife entered the yard, they may have talked of final details for the ceremony guests, or they may have reflected on their success. The 54-year-old Bendixsen was born on October 14, 1842 in Thisted, Denmark, on the Jutland Peninsula. His father, Frederich Carl Bendixsen, was a consul for the Danish government and a member of a well-to-do family "of high station." His mother, Mariane Emilie Augusta von Mehren, came from the same class.[5] But Hans did not follow his father into public service or enter the family tobacco business.[6] Described as "precocious,"[7] he apprenticed himself in his early teens to Poul Pagh,[8] a shipbuilder in the Danish seaport town of Aalborg. About 1856, he moved to Copenhagen and apprenticed two more years at Poap & Mitchelsen.[9] Around 1858, he shipped as a carpenter on a vessel bound for Brazil.[10]

Within a few years, Bendixsen decided his future was at America's western edge. Rounding Cape Horn, he arrived in San Francisco on June 18, 1863.[11] He worked for shipbuilder Mathew Turner for several years,[12] building the 173-ton brig *Nautilus*, and he collaborated with Charles Murray to construct the 295-ton barkentine *Eureka*.[13] He then moved to the new town of Eureka in Humboldt County to work at Euphronius Cousins' shipyard and others.[14]

Within two or three years of his arrival on Humboldt Bay, Bendixsen laid the keel of his first lumber vessel, the 99-ton river schooner *Fairy Queen*,[15] Taking on a partner named Thomas McDonald, he constructed it on the Eureka waterfront at the foot of L Street[16] near the Dolbeer & Carson mill.[17] Just 27 years old, he launched the vessel on June 26, 1869. Within five years, he built 18 more ships, mostly two-masted lumber schooners and schooners meant for trade with South Pacific islands.

Business boomed for Bendixsen, and in 1873, he shifted operations across Humboldt Bay to Fairhaven, taking over a 14-acre yard run by G.M. Fay & Brother. The yard had a drafting shed, a wood shed, a lodging house, a cook house, 500 feet of bay frontage, and 20 workers.[18] Bendixsen built 12 ships in 1875 (including two at his old Eureka yard), and 11 ships the following year, including his first three-masted schooner, the 348-ton *Excelsior*.[19] In 1877, he launched a similar vessel, the *Compeer*. Local mills couldn't supply lumber in the 80 to 110-foot lengths he needed, so he imported lumber from Puget Sound.[20] Later on, he built his own sawmill, but he may have overextended himself. He fell into financial problems and had to sell

---

Eureka: Timber and Shipbuilding

Eureka was less than two decades old when H.D. Bendixsen arrived to begin his career. While he learned shipbuilding in Denmark, American sailors and gold seekers in the rush of 1849 rediscovered Humboldt Bay, a protected harbor on the northern California coast. Spanish explorers had entered it as early as 1602, but the bay was nearly forgotten until 1849, when the brig *Cameo* explored the area, along with other vessels. The visitors sought the mouth of the Trinity River and a water route to the gold fields in the Coast Ranges. Failing to locate the outlet (the Trinity joins the Klamath River inland), they did find another source of wealth: timber. The *Cameo* carried logs for pilings to San Francisco.

The loggers and sawyers who followed *Cameo* to Humboldt Bay found a rich and dense forest, as verdant as any in the tropics, and as limitless. Pines, firs, and spruces covered the lowlands and hills for 35 or 40 miles east from the beaches to the mountains. The loggers salivated beneath the coast redwood, a species of sequoia that grew up to 350 feet tall. Within a year of white settlement of Eureka in 1850, ships were carrying lumber from primitive sawmills to the Bay Area. But the earliest mills could handle only small logs. In 1852, Capt. James T. Ryan arrived with his steam sidewheeler *Santa Clara.* At a pre-selected point, he ran the vessel aground, turned the steam engine into a power plant for a redwood sawmill, and shipped a load of redwood lumber to San Francisco. By 1854, nine mills cut wood on Humboldt Bay.[21]

everything, including his home, to pay off his debts. Struggling, he leased back his shipyard and took on a partner, Thomas Peterson, for a year. Bendixsen built only eight ships from 1877 to 1879. He hit a low point in the production cycle in 1880, when he built just one vessel, a small 187-ton, three-master called the *Ida McKay.*

But in that year, 1880, on January 20, the entrepreneur married 27-year-old Miss Emma Taegen. Born in 1852 at Emmerich am Rhein, a small town on the German side of the Rhine River, she helped him through seven years of hard times. She "never forgot those bleak years when she rowed across the bay to buy groceries to cook for her husband's crew," one historian wrote. [22] Hans gave his wife "much of the credit for his success."[23] They found a partnership that grew into love, but they never had children.[24]

Starting in 1881, Bendixsen got into a groove, constructing around three ships a year. And the average size of his vessels rose[25] in response to demands for larger ships. The so-called "great schooners" of the period appeared in the 1880s, starting with four masts and later five, six, and more. Bendixsen built his first four-masted lumber schooner in 1887, the 487-ton *Wm. F. Witzemann.* In 1892, he launched the largest wooden vessel on the Pacific Coast at the time, the *Jane L. Stanford,*[26] 970 tons, which could carry 1.5 million board feet of lumber.[27] This four-masted vessel was rigged as a barkentine, a schooner/square-rigger hybrid that took advantage of following winds more efficiently that a standard fore-and-aft schooner. Bendixsen also responded to technological changes, constructing seven steam-powered schooners.[28]

As Bendixsen's reputation grew, most of his competitors on Humboldt Bay got out of the shipbuilding business. As many as a dozen companies built vessels on the bay in the last half of the nineteenth century.[29] By the mid-1890s, two leaders were left: Bendixsen Shipyard and Euphronius Cousins Shipyard, run by Peter Mathews, who later moved his operations to Hoquiam, Wash. In August 1891, the number was almost reduced to one. Disaster struck Bendixsen again when fire destroyed most of his facility. The yard was ripe for a conflagration: A site plan map notes that the buildings were lit by kerosene lanterns and heated by wood refuse. The boilers of donkey engines on site were fired with wood. There were water barrels on the wooden roofs of buildings, a 5,000 gallon water tank on a 124-foot wooden tower, and a steam-powered pump. But there was no watchman and no hoses.[30] Lumber and wood chips covered nearly every foot of the site.[31] But ship construction continued, and Bendixsen rebuilt everything, upgrading the larger buildings with corrugated iron roofs. Operations were back to normal six months later.[32] In 1896, a magazine dubbed Bendixsen Shipyards "the most important wooden ship building yard on the Pacific Coast today."[33]

Bendixsen did more than build ships, he invested in them, adding credibility to his product and regular income to his bank account. Many of his ship contracts came from leading lumber companies, such as Dolbeer & Carson. If the owner offered the opportunity, Bendixsen bought minority interest of anywhere from six to 28 percent in the vessel. He was part-owner of more of his own vessels than any other builder. On a day-to-day basis for *Wawona*, Dolbeer & Carson would charter the vessel from the owners at the prevailing market rates, paying a stipulated freight rate per thousand board feet. "The managing owners collected the freight money from themselves, paid the schooner's expenses, which included a commission on their collections or disbursements, and distributed the profits regularly to the part-owners," wrote maritime historian Harlan Trott.[34] A Bendixsen contemporary said, "[Bendixsen] enjoys today a comfortable income from interest in some vessels which he built on that basis."[35]

Bendixsen also built ships on speculation, and although it's not clear how he financed construction, he may have self-financed the initial construction, building the vessel on a kind of "pay as you go" system. "During the building of a ship, Bendixsen would sell shares of it to local merchants and others who had money to invest," said one source. "By the time the ship was completed, it would be sold."[36] At its launch, *Wawona* cost $29,075 to construct.[37] Bendixsen owned almost 21 percent of the vessel.[38]

*   *   *   *

As the wind at Fairhaven whipped the spotless new pennants on *Wawona*, the clonk of leather soles on wood announced the boss's arrival to the men inside the shipyard office, which was painted bright red with white trim on the windows. *Wawona* was Bendixsen's 92nd vessel. For more than a year, sawyers, shipwrights, carpenters, molders, plankers, dubbers, caulkers, painters, and other craftsmen at H.D. Bendixsen's Shipyard had sculpted wood from North America's most fertile forests into a 165-foot, 468-ton workboat that represented the artistic and engineering height of wooden sailing ship construction.

But unlike today's engineers, who rely on computer modeling, Bendixsen's shipwrights worked from half-hull models that covered two walls of the office. A store room held patterns and paperwork. A typewriter and account books sat on a chest-high table. The yard superintendent stepped off the high stool when Bendixsen opened the door. The owner greeted the super, and he asked about last minute preparations for the launch. As he made ready to send *Wawona* down the ways, he knew that the days of the sailing ship were numbered; his workers were putting together a wooden ship driven by steam.[39]

As a crowd gathered around *Wawona*, Emma went down to the shore to greet the launch ceremony guests. Some checked their watches, an eye out for the expected tugboat. The guest list likely included the owners: John Dolbeer, an innovative industrialist who lived in San Francisco; William Carson, Dolbeer's partner in Dolbeer & Carson Lumber Company and owner of an enormous mansion in Eureka; A. Cavner and J. Lundstrom of Eureka; and Captain Olaf Isaacksen, *Wawona*'s first master. Emma greeted each of these important businessmen with an enthusiastic smile and congratulations. She was naturally outgoing; in her retirement years, she befriended a retired seaman, loved to play cards in a parlor covered with paintings of Bendixsen's ships, drove an electric car, ordered around a cook and a maid, and kept a parrot named Polly, which sat on her shoulder during walks.[40]

The Steam Donkey

In 1882, John Dolbeer patented one of the most important machines of the late nineteenth century, the steam donkey engine, which replaced teams of oxen in timber-cutting. Essentially, Dolbeer adapted a shipboard steam winch for use in the forests. He mounted the winch, with its accompanying boiler, piston and cylinder, crank, and gearing, on a heavy wooden sled. Later models used a vertical capstan to pull manila or wire rope, doing work similar to the bull teams, that is, dragging logs out of the woods, onto skid roads, and down to the rivers or mills. For the next generation, the huffing and puffing of the steam donkey and its variations, along with its shrill whistle, echoed on timberland from California to British Columbia. Bendixsen put a steam donkey on *Wawona's* deck to help seamen raise her heavy fore, main, and mizzen sails.

In the maritime-dependent communities around Humboldt Bay, ship launchings such as *Wawona's* were civic events: Besides the owners, local dignitaries, businessmen, and their spouses and children attended. Some guests made the mile or so crossing from Eureka by rowboat. Everyone was in their Sunday best. The ceremony program may have featured music; the 1891 launching of Bendixsen's three-masted schooner *Roy Somers* was accompanied by "the shrill notes of a Scotch bagpipe."[41]

A new reporter for the *Humboldt Standard* in Eureka found Emma inspecting the pies at the food table and he asked her to explain her husband's contribution to the shipbuilding industry. Hans built his business around a specialized technology. In his early years as a shipwright, he learned that the fast growing timber companies needed a new type of vessel for transporting lumber. The first lumber ships mid-century were general cargo vessels pressed into lumber droghing. But stevedores struggled to get long planks or structural timbers in the ships' small hatches, and storing lumber on deck made the ships top-heavy. Early west coast shipwrights cut hatches in the sterns to ease loading. But these hatches could open in heavy seas and sink a vessel. Gradually, the timber companies demanded their own fleets ships designed exclusively to carry lumber.

The fore-and-aft rigged lumber schooner, including *Wawona*, evolved out of this demand. Schooners, which first appeared in eighteenth-century New England, handled better in the prevailing winds along the Pacific Coast and they could maneuver more easily than square-riggers in the tight quarters of the coast-line's small harbors. The first lumber schooners had two masts, then three.

The lumber schooner hulls had one deck, a broad beam, and they were flat, meaning only a short distance separated the keel and the deck, compared to other vessels. Dockworkers loaded lumber into the hold through outsized deck hatches, or through small hatches in the stern counter. They also stacked lumber on deck twice a man's height and more. Once the load was delivered, the ships would usually return to the mill "in ballast," that is, without cargo, although the owners might offer charters for non-lumber cargoes during slow periods.[42] The ships also required a crew of just five to seven men to operate, which kept labor costs down.[43]

In the shipyard office, Bendixsen conferred with the superintendent and nod-ded without saying a word. "While he was particular about the work that was done, Bendixsen was never known to have ever given credit to anyone, regardless of how good a job was done," remembered Harlan Gow, one of Bendixsen's ship-wrights.[44] Silent, but apparently satisfied, the boss decided to join his guests for *Wawona*'s launching.

Stepping out the front door of the office onto a small porch, Bendixsen saw three ships: *Wawona*, and two others under construction, surrounded by work-men. "One ship would be in 'frame,' one in 'sealing,' and one being planned to completion," Gow said.[45] At its peak, Bendixsen employed 150 people, and his yard was constantly busy. Wood chips from Bendixsen's main raw material, Dou-glass-fir, mixed with the beach sand and dirt at his feet. Bendixsen and the other Humboldt County shipbuilders pioneered the use of Doug fir, which they referred to as "Humboldt pine," "red fir," or "Oregon pine." Eastern shipbuilders scorned the wood, saying it was too soft for ships. But western shipwrights argued for its fine, dense grain and ability to hold iron bolts. And the 300-foot height of the trees meant that lumber could be cut to 125-foot lengths, reducing the needs for joints or "scarfs" that reduced structural integrity.[46]

Some of Bendixsen's logs probably came from Freshwater, just a few miles east of Eureka,[47] in a stand owned by the Excelsior Redwood Company.[48] Tugboats delivered a raft of logs regularly to his yard, mooring them off the beach next to his 20,000 square-foot sawmill. The building was 250 feet long, 80 feet wide, and perhaps as tall.[49] Smoke poured from the stack of the steam donkey engine that powered the saw, the planer, and the machinery that shifted the logs. A worker guided logs from a log raft toward the log way and a chain that dragged it into the head rig, which was a double-circular saw, two single circular saws mounted one above the other. The spinning teeth *chirrrred* as they chewed into the wood.

Sections of clear, knotless wood fell away from the log, and sawyers guided the log into the saws for another swipe. The cuts were transferred to the planer, which ground the flat surfaces smooth. The planer could handle planks up to 10 inches thick.[50] The longest, largest, and heaviest pieces, as much as 20 inches on each side, became the keel, the keelson, the assistant keelson, also called the "sister," the keelson rider, the garboard, the stanchions, the bottom planks, the floor ceiling planks, the bilge ceiling planks, the shelves, the clamps, the main cap rails, and the masts. The samson post, a 20-inch by 20-inch behemoth 20 feet long cut from the heart of the tree, was so huge a grown man could not wrap his arms around it. Men driving mules loaded the cut pieces onto carts and laid them in the area reserved for seasoning, where up to three years of Pacific winds would dry and strengthen the wood.

Away from the sawmill, at the shipwright's building, men worked with a donkey-powered band saw, while others cut with axes, adzes and other hand tools, fashioning pieces for the stem, including the stemson, the apron, the gripe, and deadwood. Other wood was hewn into the stern post, with the accompanying rudder post and counter timbers. The shipwrights also fabricated and assembled parts for the frames, the curved ribs which gave *Wawona*'s hull its shape and volume. Men laid two sets of 10-inch thick timbers called "futtocks" on top of the other. Differing lengths of futtocks overlapped one another and when bolted together formed a single frame. The shipwrights attached approximately 40 frames to *Wawona*'s keel nine inches apart.[51]

On the schooner's single deck, the deck beams lay on the shelves, which themselves sat on clamps, two lengths of wood equal in importance to the frames and the keel. Each clamp was a continuous timber that ran from bow to stern and attached to the inside of each frame. Imagine a series of "U" shaped frames, attached at the bottom to a single piece of milled wood, the keel, and fastened together at the top with continuous timbers on either side of the "U." Most shipbuilders had to join smaller lengths of wood together to create a keel and clamps. But Bendixsen's mill could mill whole 125-foot logs. That meant each of his keels and clamps could be one single timber, making the entire hull assembly stronger and more durable while retaining flexibility.

The knees were the final piece of the structural puzzle. Knees were massive chunks of curved members sculpted from the point where the main roots of the tree buttressed the base of the trunk. Workmen inserted 44 custom-fitted knees into the angle where the deck beam met the shelf, adding the strength to handle hundreds of thousands of board feet of lumber stored on deck for the trip down the Pacific Coast. Iron drifts, headless rods driven by sledgehammers, added more strength, not only to the knees, but throughout the hull. The sledges flattened one end of the rod into a head.[52]

Working on the two vessels next to *Wawona* in framing and in sealing, workmen called "plankers" laid streaks of planking along the outside of the frame, while other men lined the inside of the frame with ceiling. By the time the outer and inner planks were laid, the hull was nearly two feet thick.[53] Working ahead of the plankers was a specialist called a "dubber." He carefully chipped the surface of the frame with an adze to ensure the plank laid flat against the wood. If the dubber worked too slow, or the planks did not lay "fair," the work had to be redone.[54]

Following the dubbers, other plankers bored one-inch holes through the plank into the frame and fastened the plank to the frame with "trunnels," also called treenails, which were usually made of imported Eastern locust.[55] One of Harlan Gow's first jobs at Bendixsen's yard was crawling under the boat, trimming the plugs off the treenails overhead, and planing them down with a hand planer. "This was a tough job," he said. "Ship-building was not meant to be easy."[56] After the planks were trimmed, caulkers pounded loose jute or hemp fibers called "oakum" in the seams between the planks, sealing the seam with boiling tar.

In the spar-making shop and the joiner shop, shipwrights and their apprentices chiseled and scraped long timbers into booms, gaffs, masts, and spars, which would carry sails. The workers carved eastern hardwoods into the gaff and boom jaws, the parts that rubbed against the masts. The cleats, cavails, and pinrails were also fabricated from hardwood. Arizona mesquite made up the corners of the bitts.[57] Much of the fine woodwork, such as the paneling in the cabins or the window frames and the skylights, was done in the joiner shop.[58]

Despite his taciturn manner, and refusal to give credit where credit was due, Bendixsen understood the back-breaking nature of shipbuilding, and he tried to take care of his people. Wages were low: He paid his men from $1.50 to $3.50 a day. But he required just an eight-hour shift, "which was something of a novelty on Humboldt Bay," one source noted. "Bendixsen interpreted this as being: 'as much as you can do in eight hours.'" Many of his workmen lived with their families in the hamlet of Fairhaven next to the yard. Some lived in Eureka and commuted across the bay in rowboats. "For the single men, the boarders, the shipyard ran a good cookhouse."[59]

The shipbuilder also took an interest in his workers' welfare outside the job. Though many of his craftsmen came from New England, many came from his native Denmark. He spoke his native language to his Danish workers. In 1900, a Danish-American fraternity held a convention near Eureka, and Bendixsen declared an open house at Fairhaven. "That night, when Bendixsen workers knocked off late to catch the train" writes Harlan Trott, in *The Schooner That Came Home*, about the preservation of Bendixsen's ship *C.A. Thayer*, "the big-hearted boss chartered a special train to transport them to the Danish fete at Ferndale."[60] Bendixsen kept in close touch with his customers and business contacts by joining two fraternities: the Independent Order of Odd Fellows, which focused on charitable work, and the local lodge of the Scottish Rite Masons, where he rose to the 32nd degree, a top leadership position.[61]

Wawona delivers lumber in 1899. She is carrying a full load in her hold and on her deck, as well as a load of pilings under the foresail boom. (Northwest Seaport)

Bendixsen conferred with the foreman when a cry came up from the beach, "Here comes the tug!" followed by a shrill toot from the tug's whistle. Both men turned to the water and Bendixsen glanced at his watch: Just a few minutes before high tide. He trotted to the ways while the superintendent yelled for everyone to stop work and gather round the *Wawona*. In a moment, all sawing, chopping, and pounding stopped while a team of men in dungarees, flannel shirts, and cloth caps or felt hats gathered by the vessel. Bendixsen circled around *Wawona*, looking for any flaw, crawling underneath to check the keel blocks, the cradle, the ways, and the drag hawser. Satisfied, he stepped over the supports and wood chips to the dignitaries, and shook everyone's hand. He stood by Emma and strained to see *Wawona*'s pennant flapping in the breeze 130 feet above him, surrounded by signal flags and Old Glory. Seamen called *Wawona*'s rig "baldheaded," meaning she lacked the topmasts of a standard schooner. That meant she could carry a larger spread of canvas.[62]

Mounting a small platform at *Wawona*'s bow, a young woman waited under the "fiddlehead," a curved piece of wood in place of a figurehead and scored with graceful shapes that resembled the head of a fiddle. Yellow paint filled the delicate gouges and grooves, and the white petals of a pansy accented the carving at the bowsprit. The woman held a bottle of champagne wrapped in red, white and blue ribbon.

Bendixsen nodded to the superintendent.

"Wedge up!" the super shouted, and the *clock, clock, clock* of sledgehammers on wood filled the silence. The team, working in the shadow of *Wawona*'s 468-ton bulk, knocked out the blocks of fir under the keel, starting at the stern post and inching their way forward. The ship's black hull slowly settled on the cradle, a pair of structures on either side of the keel, about a third of the way to the edge of the hull's curve. An occasional creak escaped the lattice of wood in the cradle. Meanwhile, two men put a fresh mixture of tallow and soap on the launching ways, a pair of parallel skids running to the water. In about 15 minutes, all the keel blocks were knocked away and the sledge team emerged from under *Wawona*.

A set of bolts on the "sliding ways", a skid the carries the cradle on the launching ways, was now the only thing holding *Wawona* from the water. Just behind the bolts, toward *Wawona*, an apprentice carpenter had drawn a line across the wood, and marked intervals of one inch down the timber. Two pairs of carpenters each laid a crosscut saw on the line and waited.

Bendixsen checked his watch: 2:00 p.m. He nodded again to the super.

"Stop at your first mark!" the super barked, and two pairs of carpenters let their saw bite slowly into the wood down to the first inch mark. The two teams worked in tandem, lest one cradle start to slide before the other and bring the vessel down on its side.

"Stop at your second mark!" the super yelled, and the carpenters sawed, then stopped.

"Saw away!!" Now the carpenters worked as fast as they could, taking huge bites out of the timber, with sawdust piling up on each side. A sudden *CRACK!* stopped them, and they dropped the saws and scattered as the remaining wood tore and parted and *Wawona's* slide began. The young woman, told the crack is her signal, and seeing the bow pull away from her, whacked the stem with the champagne, breaking the bottle, and christening the ship. Sticky, fizzy wine splashed on the dignitaries, and everyone raised a cheer as *Wawona* picked up speed, two, four, eight, twelve, fourteen feet per second, the cradle groaning as it carried her full weight over the ways, smoke rising from the hot tallow, and the sea parting with a slowly rising hiss, welcoming her by moving aside, and the tug's whistle screamed, along with the donkeys' whistles on shore, *Wawona's* stern lifting, the rudder locked in place, the cradle letting her go, and the drag hawser pulling on an anchor, slowing her down as if the land did not want her to leave, but she said goodbye to the land and the man who built her when the bow finally settled into the foam kicked up by the black hull, and she floated free. The cheers died down, and the whistles faded, and a deck hand on the tug threw a line aboard to capture her and put her to work.[63] The tug led *Wawona*, the largest vessel of her type built on the west coast, to a mill to load her first cargo, bound for San Diego.[64] A carpenter chiseled into a deck beam *Wawona's* registration number: 81576.

✳　　✳　　✳　　✳

After *Wawona*, Bendixsen built 17 more vessels: seven four-masted schooners, five steam schooners, two barkentines, two three-masted baldheaded schooners, and a four-masted oil-tank barge.[65] Nudged by friends and Emma, he named his 100th ship *H.D. Bendixsen*, a 641-ton, four-masted lumber schooner, after himself in 1898. The last ship he designed was the 772-ton, four-masted lumber schooner *Alvena*, launched in 1901. By the time he sold his shipyard that year, as historian Harriet DeLong put it, "the sturdy Dane [had] built 113 equally sturdy vessels."

The Meaning of "Wawona"

Lore passed down to caretakers of the *Wawona* claims that the word "wawona" is Yosemite Indian onomatopoeia for the hoot of an owl. The author has also seen "wawona" defined as a mountain flower. Words in many languages often have several meanings. But the author is inclined to select an-

> other suggested meaning, "big tree," given *Wawona*'s original purpose as a lumber carrier.[66]

He also netted $250,000 for himself and his wife.[67]

Bendixsen made plans to return to Denmark and retire. In the early 1890s, he and his wife had traveled to Denmark, "where his family welcomed him with parties and much celebration," DeLong writes. "The intense man she married surprised Emma by singing, dancing, and laughing in a way she did not imagine possible."[68] Hans and Emma left Eureka in February, 1902. When they reached San Francisco, Bendixsen heard that the son of a friend had died in Eureka. Bendixsen returned to Eureka for the funeral, while Emma waited in San Francisco. In Eureka, Bendixsen suffered a heart attack. The doctor also diagnosed jaundice.[69] The shipbuilder died on February 12, 1902. He was 60 years old.

The news of Bendixsen's death shocked the shipping and lumber industry. "Shops closed their shutters in Fairhaven and Eureka, and all up and down the coast, the ocean flags of Matson, Spreckels, E.K. Wood, Minor, Nelson and others[70], flew at half mast in honor of the shipbuilding Dane," one chronicler wrote.[71] "He was an honest man who had built honest ships," DeLong said.[72] Emma took her husband's body to Denmark, and buried him in Thisted in May, erecting "a magnificent and expensive monument."[73]

Emma survived Hans by a more than a half-century. Moving to Alameda, Calif., she married a man named Jensen, though she preferred to be called Mrs. Bendixsen-Jensen. She died in October, 1954, aged 102. In their will, Hans and Emma gave $25,000 to Thisted for a children's home, vocational training for young men, support for the poor and fishermen's widows, and a local museum. The town newspaper called the bequest "a golden rain."[74]

The lumber and shipping companies that bought ships from Bendixsen's appreciated them for their craftsmanship, their quality, and their shapeliness. A seaman could pick out a Bendixsen vessel as if it were a thoroughbred horse. But Bendixsen's ships were first and foremost workboats. *Wawona* was a beast of burden; her cargoes of lumber unremarkable. But her first master, Olaf Isaacksen, handed command to a man who would turn heads.

CHAPTER 2

▼

MASTER, MANAGER, AND
INFINITE YANKEE

Monday, July 31, 1899
Port Blakely Mill, Port Blakely, Washington

The letter stung Captain Ralph Erskine Peasley as if he were slashed with a knife. The 33-year-old master of the lumber schooner *Wawona* read the document delivered with his other paperwork and personal letters at the Port Blakely Mill Company office near his berth at Port Blakely on Puget Sound across from Seattle. The typewritten correspondence, and an accompanying statement in the driving hand of someone who pored over account books six days a week, came from the San Francisco office of the Dolbeer & Carson Lumber Company, Peasley's employer for about six months.

"Dear Sir," the company wrote, "We feel that you have an extravagant steward aboard the *Wawona* and thought best to call you attention to his bills." The letter laid out a case for profligacy on the part of the cook (and by implication Peasley), compared to another of Dolbeer & Carson's vessels, the *Maweema*, and *Wawona* under Peasley's predecessor, Captain Olaf Isaacksen. *Maweema* cost just $3.35 a day to supply with food for the crew over the past year, while *Wawona* under Isaacksen cost even less, $3.33 a day. "In the last 182 days, her provision bill has jumped to $4.74 per day, or a raise of 41½ %, so we would wish you would see if your cook is not unduly wasteful."[1]

Capt. Ralph E. "Matt" Peasley with a companion identified as an "actress." The photo was probably taken in the 1920s. The ship behind Peasley is probably his favorite, Vigilant. (Northwest Seaport)

Though Peasley was a good company man, the equivalent of a mid-level executive in a modern corporation, a piece of him chafed, like a line rubbing against a spar. Peasley was first a seaman and second a manager, and he longed to leave port and feel the swell of the Pacific under his feet again. The home office's prickly bean-counting had little to do with coaxing the wind to move hundreds of thousands of board feet of lumber from the mills of Puget Sound and Grays Harbor on Washington State's coast over the open ocean to the company's lumber yards along the coast of California.[2] For the moment, however, Peasley had lumber to load. In rolled sleeves, loosened collar, and duck trousers, the lanky, 6-foot 3-inch, 190-pound Mainer stuffed the papers into his hip pocket and strode back and forth in *Wawona's* hold under her hatches, bellowing at sweat-drenched longshoremen and seaman in the late July heat.

Peasley supervised them for two weeks at the Port Blakely Mill as they loaded more than a half-million board feet of standardized lengths of lumber cut from the fir, spruce, cedar and hemlock forests of western Washington State. Taking the wood through hatches on deck and in the stern, the longshoremen stored twelve-by-twelves for structural support, two-by-fours for walls, and one-by-threes for the trim of houses under construction in the growing cities of the Golden State. Some of the boards and planks were 40 feet long.[3] Peasley left no space unfilled; the lumber was loaded to follow the ship's "sheer" or the curve of the hull as seen from the side, right up to the deck. *Wawona* would not "leave port with a crack of daylight unused," according to historian Harlan Trott.[4] Outside, band saws and circular saws in the world's largest sawmill screamed as they sliced through logs, and other lumber schooners or square-riggers took on their own lumber cargoes at the wharves or waited their turn in the anchorage.

Once *Wawona's* hold was full, the dockworkers and seamen stacked lumber twice a man's height and more on deck under the eye of the mate. More than half of the lumber cargo was stowed on deck, and the mate followed Peasley's lead, pressing the lumber against the shrouds, ensuring that the crew had only just enough room to raise or lower *Wawona's* canvas. "Great chains kept the...deck-load from shifting, set fiddle taut with steel turnbuckles, slobbered with grease and tallow to keep boarding seas from rusting the threads," Trott wrote.

Once loaded, and crew for the voyage hired, Peasley immediately called for a harbor tug, which pulled him out of Port Blakeley into Puget Sound. Another tug hooked up for the day-long tow to Cape Flattery and the open sea. During his stint as *Wawona's* master, starting in 1899, Peasley was second to no one in his knowledge of the sea. His father, Henry C. Peasley, was a farmer in Maine, a Civil War veteran, and listed as a "master mariner" in the 1880 census. He commanded the *Clement* from 1879 to 1883. His first American ancestor on the Peasley side arrived in New England in the early seventeenth century. His mother, Elizabeth Rose, a teacher, gave birth to Ralph on May 30, 1866 in the village of Jonesport, Maine, "down east." Ralph, the eldest, was followed by Evelyne, Lena, Jerome, Margaret, and Annette. All the children were born within twelve years of each other. Elizabeth served as the local president of the Women's Christian Temperance Union. She also taught school and she was the first treasurer for the first public library in Jonesport.[5]

Books did not interest her son. Ralph Peasley went to sea in 1880 at 14, learning the art of seamanship from men who fished for cod on the freezing Grand Banks. One of his first berths was the 97-ton *Nettie B. Dobbins.* At 17, he voyaged to Rio de Janeiro in a square rigger,[6] earning a promotion to third mate.[7]

R.E. Peasley with his wife, Burrows "Burrie" Dalton Peasley. (Northwest Seaport)

Peasley came around Cape Horn to the west coast of the United States as second mate on a clipper ship[8] and made it to Seattle in November 1888. "I was twenty-one, and I'd always been on the Atlantic Coast, when I suddenly decided to come to a coast that didn't have 'hornets' in the water," Peasley said. "Don't you know what I mean by 'hornet'? Didn't you ever have the tips of your fingers frozen? Well!"[9] He commanded his first ship, a brig, at age 22.[10] He may have headed west because he had several relatives in the region. He worked for a cousin on a logging crew in Burlington, Washington, a half-day's ride from Anacortes on Puget Sound. The next year, he moved in with a cousin in Montesano, about a half-day's ride from Aberdeen, a port town on Grays Harbor.[11]

Peasley's maritime career took off. He shipped as first mate in the spring of 1889 aboard the three-masted *Pioneer*[12] under Capt. Charles Hughes, commanded the *J.M. Weatherwax* in 1892, and took a turn as mate on *Gardiner City* under Captain "Coal Tar" Jack McMasters. All the ships were based in Grays Harbor. The Simpson Lumber Company hired him to command its lumber schooners *Melancthon* and *Louis*, the first five-masted "great schooner" on the Pacific Coast.[13]

Peasley earned a reputation for daring and delivering to owners. While master of the *Louis* in the spring of 1896, he reportedly brought it to the mouth of the Yangtze River after a typhoon. He had never seen the river before. But he decided to pilot the ship himself up the river, because he did not trust the Chinese pilot. He brought the *Louis* safely to port, and set a passage record at the same time.[14] By the time he took command of *Wawona*, Peasley had established himself as someone you'd want on your team.

Peasley fit snugly into the transplanted New England culture of the late nineteenth century Pacific Coast; many maritime business in the Pacific Northwest were founded or run by New Englanders.[15] But he felt homesick and lonely from time to time. He took one summer to visit his mother and siblings in Jonesport. His mother may have been ill.[16] Peasley helped his youngest sister Annette, whom he called "Nettie," pay for college.[17]

The captain of *Wawona* was also very eligible; he owned a 6/96th (6.25 percent) share of the ship, which grossed him $25 to $90 of each voyage's profits, in addition to his $100 a month salary.[18] Presenting this package, Peasley asked for the hand of Burrows Dalton, daughter of a fellow sailor, Capt. James Dalton of Aberdeen and his wife, Emily S. Dalton.[19] Burrie Dalton was born on January 19, 1868 at Montague, Michigan,[20] and her family may have been part of a wave of emigrants to Grays Harbor from the timber and lumber communities of the Upper Midwest in the late nineteenth century. She worked as a bookkeeper at the Anderson and Middleton Lumber Company in Aberdeen, where she met Peasley when he loaded lumber for California. The 35-year-old Burrie lived with her mother.[21]

When Ralph and Burrie were married,[22] *Wawona*'s owners gave Peasley $50 as a wedding gift. The couple traveled together on *Wawona* several times, a privilege reserved for ship captains. The pair reportedly logged a quarter million miles together.[23] Only a few photos of the couple survive, mostly from their later years, showing Burrie to be a stout, strong-looking woman. The couple lived together in the same house on East First Street in Aberdeen for 28 years. They never had children.

*   *   *   *

Peasley was most at home when he was at sea. He strode *Wawona*'s poop deck, dressed in a high pressure cap, a black shin-length topcoat, and sea boots. In his coat pocket, he kept a calfskin wallet embossed with a scene from Japan depicting a teahouse, a boat with a full sail, and Mt. Fujiyama.[24] He had clear, blue eyes, a walrus mustache framing a quick smile, and he barked orders with an "effortless roar."[25]

The seamen scrambled to obey, clambering on top of the deck load to get from stem to stern and reverse, firing up a donkey engine to help raise canvas. *Wawona* had a comparatively simple sail plan: Her three largest sails were the foresail, mainsail, and mizzen or "spanker." Going forward from the foremast, she sported a staysail or "jumbo," an inner jib, an outer jib, and a flying jib, most attached to a jib-boom, which was an extension of the bowsprit.[26] While watching the sails rise toward the masthead, Peasley gave orders to the helm: "Pay her off a mite," then "Steady as she goes." In the mornings, he'd check the "morning bank," clouds on the horizon in colors of purple and orange which could signal a storm or calm weather. [27] In the waning days of sail, and rise of steam and diesel, Peasley was a romantic, and he loved his work. "The steamer is great, but give me a ship that sails," Peasley declared. "I want no screech of a whistle nor throb of engines; The sight of straining sails fills me with a never-ending pleasure. There will never be any steam ships for me."[28]

Peasley and his officers ate and slept in the main cabin aft, which featured a "parlor" and a private room with a double bed for the captain. The captain had a private head at the stern, while other men relieved themselves over the side at the forepeak. Peasley was loyal to men of his own station and above.[29] He read his correspondence from company headquarters on a small sofa underneath a kerosene lamp while smoking a cigar.

Most of the letters focus on the commonplace problems of managing a wooden cargo ship. They concerned freight rates, wharf facilities, trip times, damage to *Wawona* in port,[30] and in one exchange, a dispute with an Aberdeen mill over who should pay for a horse to move around lumber.[31] Peasley oversaw *Wawona*'s first haul out for bottom cleaning and painting with worm-killing copper paint. He frequently submitted bills for supplies, such as manila lines, coal oil for cooking, sacked house coal for heating, machine oil for lubrication, and galvanized sheaves for repairing blocks. He also bought canvas, sail twine, sail needles to patch his sails,[32] and new sails after major storms.[33] The earliest surviving letter from Dolbeer & Carson features a long, confusing litany of accounting problems related to Peasley's personal account, hinting at the trouble any new employee has figuring out the company's way of doing things, compounded by his lack of formal education.[34]

He would also read letters from his wife, Burrie.

> My dear old man,
>   No letters yesterday or today. What is the matter? I surely thought I would get a letter today and although very tired, I went to the post office tonight after it but it was not there. I intended to write to your mother today, but was so busy all day that I did not find time and tonight I am too tired to think. I am writing this in bed so as to have it ready to go out in the morning when some of the men go to the P.O. It is raining pitchforks and axe handles tonight and I think I can sleep soundly as a consequence. I must not write very long as it is chilly and I am sneezing. I hope you will receive this before you can sail. I have had no letter to say when you thought when you would be ready for sea again.
>   There is absolutely no news to write. This is the deadest town for news that I ever saw.
>   Was down to Mrs. Campbell's yesterday a little while in the afternoon to play the new game of 500 with her, Eva Long, and Mrs. Stein. Eva and I beat one game of the two we played they beat the other, so we will have to have the rubber another time. Belle wants me to go to Hoquiam next Sunday with her to the ballgame between Hoquiam and Centralia, but I am going to save money by staying home and painting the bedstead white for my room.
>   Well dear, I hope you will have a quick and fine trip and return all safe.
>   Your loving wife,
>   Burrie Dalton Peasley
>   [P.S.] Mother has just called from the next room for me to give you her love so here goes with my own love to Ralph.[35]

Peasley wrote his responding letters to Burrie and his bosses on a writing desk under the cabin skylight.

The captain spun stories over a whiskey after a supper of codfish "tongues and sounds," a Down East delicacy "boiled with some sort of sauce," recalled Ed Van Syckle.[36] One time, another ship he commanded, *Vigilant*, was heading for Honolulu with a load of Australian coal.

> She was barely keeping her tops'ls filled in the faint breeze when a smoke-belching steamer passed close aboard. Peasley wrinkled his nose as coal fumes wafted across his deck—he had no use for steam anyway. He clamped his

cigar, muttered, and reluctantly recognized a greeting from the steamer's bridge. The old tramp showed him a churning wake.

But Peasley's hour was coming. The steamer was barely hull down before a breeze gathered. The sweet-sailing windjammer livened. As the wind strengthened the *Vigilant* began to snore with her scuppers under—Peasley once sailed her 315 miles in 24 hours. Throughout the night the wind blew fresh and strong, and by the time the morning bank lifted the big schooner lay off Honolulu harbor, her sail furled with just enough canvas to keep her position until the tug arrived.

Waiting in this position, Peasley was leisurely leaning on his taffrail watching the steamer coming up, dragging a long plume of smoke—the same ship that had been so insulting the day before. The *Vigilant* had passed her during the night.

The steamer's skipper leaned from the wing of his bridge, and shook a fist playfully.

"Where'nell did you come from?" he bellowed.

"Brisbane!" Peasley roared back with a grin.[37]

The master may have told stories he didn't want repeated. What of a 1920 letter written in Spanish from a woman pleading with Peasley to write to her about a son she hadn't seen in five years? The young man apparently sailed with Peasley after a lumber delivery to South America.[38] And what's the story behind a receipt for a copper still and $360 in fines for "failure to manifest 5 tins of opium?" The documents were accompanied by two receipts for a total of $800 to bail out someone named "James Butt," probably a crewman.[39]

The Changing Nature of Maritime Work

Ralph Peasley captained *Wawona* at the beginning of a major transformation of maritime work. For centuries until the late nineteenth century, seamen at work were hardly more than serfs, in bondage to their master for the duration of the voyage. In medieval times, "desertion," that is, quitting a voyage before its end, could result in execution. Most American seamen in the merchant services had the same legal status as Native Americans: more or less wards of the state. In 1897, the year *Wawona* was launched, the U.S.

Supreme Court declared that the seamen were "deficient in that full and intelligent responsibility for their acts which is accredited to ordinary adults." The court went on to say that the Thirteenth Amendment, which banned slavery, did not apply to seamen.

Peasley probably used "crimps" for at least some of his voyages, although there's no record of it. To find a job at the turn of the twentieth century, seamen relied on a crimp, an agent who worked as a middleman between the ship owner/captain and a prospective crew member. Seamen can be thought of as seagoing "temps" or itinerant workers. Because they could wind up in any of a half dozen ports on the west coast at any time, sailors needed a dependable place on shore to eat and sleep. A crimp typically ran a boarding house for seamen. "The crimp enticed the sailor into his establishment and catered to his appetite for food and drink, until 'Jack' had run up a substantial bill and the crimp could claim a sizable advance on his next wage payment," wrote labor historian Bruce Nelson. Crimps (and through them, the ship owners) used this system to keep mariners in a state of "carefree but enforced dependency."

The crimp system was shot through with graft and favoritism; Seamen sometimes bribed crimps to get the best jobs. With help sometimes from other seamen, the worst crimps "shanghaied" prospective crew members, getting them dead drunk or beating them senseless and depositing them on a ship involuntarily, where they became virtual slaves. Port Townsend, the main port of entry to Puget Sound during *Wawona's* lumber carrying days, was notorious for its crimps.

Once on board and essentially trapped for two or three months, common seamen faced uncertain working conditions. A captain had godlike powers over them, enjoying legal authority to do whatever he pleased. Seamen feared the "bucko," an officer, often a mate, who brutalized underperformers. A pamphlet published in 1895 by a sailors union documented seven deaths of seamen at the hands of superiors. Richard Henry Dana, a maritime lawyer whose memoir *Two Years Before the Mast* is an American classic, said convictions against bucko officers were "hardly worth procuring," because courts did not believe a seaman's testimony.

By 1900, the seeds of a more equitable relationship between ship owners, captains, and crews had been sown. Activists, including Andrew Furuseth of the Sailors Union of the Pacific, led strikes and other labor actions that slowly drew power away from capital. For example, they demanded the right to apportion jobs fairly by forcing ship captains to use a union hiring hall, rather than the hated crimps. But Peasley and *Wawona*'s owners were distrustful of unions, and the flowering of union power on the docks was still decades away.

Even in the 1930s, a generation after Peasley's experience in *Wawona*, some seaman suffered terrible working conditions. Seattleite Jimmy Crooks shipped aboard the steamship *Andrea F. Luckenbach* from San Francisco to Puget Sound ports. Crooks said seamen were quartered in a small room. They were issued a "donkey's breakfast," a thin mattress stuffed with straw, and a blanket. The straw crawled with lice, bedbugs, and fleas. "If you wished to sit down, you sat on the edge of your bunk for there was not a bench or chair in the room," Crooks recalled. "Steel bunks were arranged to accommodate twelve men and some were divided only by a piece of iron pipe and if the ship was rolling heavily, there was nothing to stop you from rolling into the other guy's bunk. In some bunks, your head was right alongside someone else's feet."

The *Luckenbach*'s crew worked as much as sixteen hours a day, seven days a week, for as little as $32.50 a month. Crooks remembers the crew's mess, which sported a heavy steel table and steel benches secured to the deck. Cups, plates, knives, forks, and spoons were all made of tin. "The food served was of the poorest quality obtainable and to ask for a second helping would have been grounds for immediate discharge…No prison cell ever built contained less luxurious accommodations insofar as comfort was concerned." Complaints were dangerous. "If [the seamen] didn't like it, they could get off the ship. There were always plenty of men ready to take their place."[40]

Peasley and most other masters and ship owners were, according to long tradition, paternal, but standoffish in relationships with common seamen. On *Wawona*, common seamen and other crew lived forward on deck in a deckhouse with a six-bunk forecastle and galley. This was above standard for the time. In many vessels, the forecastle was below the deck in the dark and dank forepeak at the bow. "The deckhouse provided more light and ventilation for the forecastle," Trott said, "which made a more comfortable place for men to live, improving their health and morale."[41]

For each voyage, Peasley recruited four seamen, the donkey engine operator/carpenter, and the cook.[42] He often employed the same mates over several voyages. The pay was decent. For a 1900 voyage, Peasley hired a first mate at $55 a month, a second mate at $50 a month, and five sailors at $40 each a month. Their pay was around double that of sailors who made trans-Pacific trips.[43] They ranged in age from late teens to early 60s.[44] He also hired a Chinese cook by the name of Lam Hing and paid him $50 a month, assuming minority cooks were paid the same as whites. (In the shipping industry, minorities were typically relegated to the role of cook or steward.) Lam Hing was the only likely non-Caucasian to sail on *Wawona* during her entire working career.[45]

Working conditions aboard *Wawona* during Peasley's tenure were better than average, due to her unique design, and the need for specialized crews who could handle lumber as well as sails. Some of the seamen on lumber schooners also worked in the forests of northern California, Oregon, and Washington.[46] Trott said the baldheaded schooner was a favorite berth on the west coast. "In the beat to windward on the return trip north, there was no climbing aloft to shift the topsails when tacking," he wrote. "Consequently, there was more of the abundant life on those vessels."[47] But work at sea is always dangerous, and *Wawona* apparently lost her first seaman under Peasley, when a second mate fell out of a small boat and was drowned.[48]

If one of *Wawona*'s crew needed medical treatment at sea, he turned to Peasley, who apparently had no medical training and little more than crude medicines. On a trip to Santa Rosalia, Mexico with a load of lumber, one of Peasley's men, August Tarkelson, suffered a fever. In his log entry, Peasley described his prescription: "Emetic, liquid food, milk, tea, coffee, barley water, rice water, water wine and lemonade. Freshwater baths every day with rough rubbing of limbs and chest. One capsule of quinine at about 5 p.m. every day. One dose of Bicarbonate of soda every day in a pt. of water. Which treatment brought him through all right."[49]

By most accounts, Peasley was tough, principled, but not brutal, unlike other merchant captains and officers, for whom instilling terror was a primary leadership skill. The available records show no violent conflicts between Peasley and any of his crew while he was master of *Wawona* or of any other vessel during his career.[50] "He was not a severe man; he could bend," wrote Ed Van Syckle.[51] Perhaps the small, almost intimate crews aboard lumber schooners made fear an unnecessary tactic. However, one letter from Dolbeer & Carson refers to a man named Gifford, who apparently deserted *Wawona* "and was very annoying" and "is not entitled to any consideration from us."[52]

Most of Peasley's labor headaches came from union activity. In July, 1901, nine unions, including the SUP, struck the San Francisco docks. Thousands of maritime workers walked off the job. Writing to Peasley while the captain was visiting his mother in Maine, his bosses at Dolbeer & Carson complained about the "stagnation of business along the coast owing to the widespread condition of the strike. San Francisco harbor, as you probably know, is glutted with vessels laden with lumber with no immediate prospect of their being discharged and other cities along the coast are to a more or less extent tied up by the sympathetic strike of the sailors and longshoremen." *Wawona*, under Peasley's first mate, Alexander Beattie, was in San Pedro waiting to be unloaded. "We hope the vessel will have fair dispatch, though the uneasy attitude of the sailors at the present time makes it a little doubtful about her getting out as soon as Mr. Beattie anticipates." The strike ended on October 2, when California Governor Henry Gage announced a settlement. *Wawona* was still waiting to be unloaded on October 18, when Peasley arrived in Los Angeles to take over from Beattie.[53]

Union tensions around *Wawona* flared in November. "We note what you say about reports that may come to our ears or knowledge criticizing your loading," Dolbeer & Carson wrote on November 21. "You go ahead and do as your judgment directs. When we want to turn the vessel over to the longshoremen, we shall give you ample notice. Until then, you are in command of the vessel, and we are not afraid to trust you in these matters." An account statement accompanying the letter contains intriguing entries: two referring to Sailors Union of the Pacific organizer Andrew Furuseth ("A. Furuseth") directly, one a telegram, and the other "fare of cook to San Pedro." Two other entries refer to payments, called "subscriptions," to a "fund for facilitating lumber discharge at San Francisco, a/c strike." The entries are dated September 13 and October 5. None of the correspondence explains the payments.[54] They could be reimbursements of some kind, or they could be payoffs to the union in order to get cargo moving and *Wawona* back to work.

Peasley had at least one recorded confrontation with unionists. *Wawona* arrived at Washington State's Willapa Bay in May, 1904 to take on a load of lumber. On May 13, the *Willapa Harbor Pilot* reported that the recently organized longshoremen's union "had their first tilt with a master of a sailing vessel last week. The *Wawona*, Capt. Peasley, was loading at the Siler Mill at Raymond with non-union longshoremen. The union demanded...that its members be employed."

The union also threatened to ask the seamen to walk off the job in sympathy. But Peasley refused to budge. At the critical moment, a steamer arrived and hired all the union men, diffusing the confrontation, and Peasley finished loading with non-union stevedores.[55] Peasley talked to the mill owner shortly after the incident. Responding to Peasley's report, Dolbeer & Carson believed the "visit will result in their taking better care of you hereafter when you load there."[56]

*   *   *   *

In 1906, after more than six years as *Wawona*'s captain, Ralph Peasley quit her for a life ashore, handing command to Capt. Conrad Scheel.[57] Peasley had spent 26 years at sea, and at 40 years old, he was ready for a change. He bought the Grays Harbor Ship Chandlery in Aberdeen, a town equal in importance at the time to Seattle, Tacoma, and Everett, and sold supplies and provisions to fellow sea captains and common seamen. He also took a job as superintendent of the open shop Grays Harbor Stevedoring Company, formed by local shipping and mill men as a lower cost alternative to local longshoremen's unions. [58]

On June 11, 1909, arson destroyed Peasley's chandlery, along with a plumbing company and a rooming-house in the same building. He lost $10,000 in inventory, though he was insured for $4,000. Peasley believed union extremists set the fire, but a connection was never proven.[59] The fire may have been one reason why Peasley probably carried a gun.[60]

After the fire, Peasley returned to what he did best, commanding sailing ships on the open ocean, and he mastered the lumber ships *Mary E. Foster*, *Omega*, *Seminole*, and *E.K. Wood*. But his life took a new tack in 1915, when Peter Kyne, a shipping clerk Peasley knew while captain of *Wawona*, published a best-selling novel *Cappy Ricks, or the Subjugation of Matt Peasley*. Kyne based the cigar-smoking, yarn-spinning, big-fisted character of "Matt Peasley" on Ralph Peasley.

Overnight, the real Peasley became the most famous ship captain in America. Newspaper reporters met the seaman at every port, salivating for a hair-raising tale. People wanted their picture taken with him. A pair of photos shows Peasley and a pretty young woman with luxuriant dark hair. She is identified as an "actress." A stiff breeze blows a light dress away from her bare legs and feet.[61] Strangers hailed him on the street by his fictional name, "Matt." The *Seattle Post-Intelligencer* once ran a feature story with a photo of the captain, calling him "Matt Peasley" in the headline. The story never mentioned his real given name. A seaman once teased Peasley about his nickname. "That's all right, call me Captain Matt," Peasley said. "That's because I don't care anymore. When those stories first began, I used to be mightily embarrassed—yes, and pretty mad about it too. I'd never turn my head an inch when I'd hear someone call me that—even the pretty girls! But a person can get used to anything."[62] For a time, the Down Easter from Jonesport, Maine, the "infinite Yankee," as one writer called him, took his place alongside other literary sailors, including Ahab, Billy Budd, and Richard Henry Dana.

Matt Peasley

My name is Ralph E. Peasley
    The mate of "Cappy Ricks,"
I'm skipper of the *Vigilant*
    With all her five tall sticks;
With all her five gaff-topsails,
    Her flying foresail spread,
The spankerboom abaft, sir,
    The jib-sheets up ahead.

If you would know just where we go,
Well, we both sail down to Callao,
    To Newcastle and old Shanghai,
    We go together, she and I.

I'm a sailorman from Maine, sir,
    The folks were sailors, too.
I started on the banks, sir,
    As other sailors do;
But when I saw the tall ships,
    With royals at the fore,
Well, I took me to the square ships
    And all their ancient lore.
Where weather shroud and cro' jack braces
Crooned in the wind that whipped their faces—
Those deepwater men from Boston town
As they sang their chanties while tarring down.

A dozen ships of sail, sir,
    I've conned upon the sea,
But never a ship of steam, sir,
    Has held a berth for me.
There's more of screeching windlass,

And less of screaming gulls,
Aye, give me a ship that spreads her sails
And rolls in the troughs with sharks and whales,
It's a sailor I am, and a sailor's dream
Is never a ship that goes by steam.

It's nigh to three-score years now
    That mark my graying hair,
Which once did shine like ebony,
    in old New England's airs;
But the windy roaring forties,
    And the bergs that lap the Horn
Will silver tinge the darkest locks
    By any human born.
It's a bleak wind and a bitter boss
When you sail below the southern cross.
It's the west winds that madly whine
When you round the Cape in sixty-nine.

They're losing out, the square ships
    The deep sea men are dying.
The clippers have gone down, sir,
    Where sailors' winds are sighing.
They're building fore-an-aft ships,
    to haul the coasting trade,
Or lumber for the islands
    Where the brown Kanakas wade.
So I'm sailing the schooner *Vigilant*
    From the foot of her five tall sticks,
And I sign the articles Peasley,
    "The mate of 'Cappy Ricks.'"

Published July 4, 1976 in the Aberdeen Daily World. *The author is unknown.*[63]

In 1931, now 65 years old, Peasley settled into the quiet life of a retired sea captain,[64] though he took a job as a state liquor inspector, driving around Grays Harbor in a big Ford with a V-8 engine.[65] He participated in debates that led to the creation of the Washington State Liquor Control Board.[66] He also served as a member of the Grays Harbor Port Commission.[67] He agreed to portray Capt. Robert Gray, the eighteenth-century Yankee merchant mariner who gave his name to Grays Harbor, in Hoquiam's 1939 Paul Bunyan Golden Jubilee celebration.[68] He still had "a hankerin'" to go back to sea,"[69] and when war came in 1941, the 75-year-old said he would renew his master's license. "Something might come up and I want to be ready to go to sea again," he said.[70]

He lost Burrie on December 19, 1941, aged 73. She died of a heart blockage, and she was cremated at Fern Hill Cemetery in Aberdeen. Peasley shipped her ashes to relatives in Whitehall, Michigan.[71] He worked through the war years as a guard patrolling the Aberdeen waterfront, eyes out for saboteurs and Imperial Japanese submarines.

In May, 1945, just as he was planning to visit Jonesport, then travel to Chesapeake Bay to bring home a seventy-seven foot yawl, Peasley suffered a stroke. In the hospital, he "regaled the nurses with seagoing persiflage, and confounded the attendants with shipboard instructions: 'to starboard with this,' or 'come up to loo'ard, and lively does it now.'"[72] The Chesapeake trip was cancelled, but he recovered enough to walk with a cane.[73] Two years later, he was in Aberdeen's St. Joseph Hospital again. On his 81st birthday, the nurses decorated his room with flowers, friends sent him gifts, and a photographer brought in a model of five-masted bark, which brought tears to the old man's eyes.[74] Around this time, his favorite command, *Vigilant*, wrecked off the coast of Chile.[75] Peasley died on December 13, 1948. *The New York Times* ran a one-sentence obituary.[76]

Even though he had not set foot on *Wawona* since 1906, and she had gone on to a new career, he never forgot her. Peasley once visited the ship in Seattle, sat at his old desk, and told stories about storms and 16-foot deck loads.[77] *Wawona* herself, if she could talk, would have returned the favor, speaking of another captain who believed his wife's hats had special powers, and the first mate who buried him.

C H A P T E R   3

▼

CAPTAIN'S LAST BED

Tuesday, April 21, 1914
100 Miles East of Vancouver Island in the North Pacific

Captain Charles Foss wiped his hand across his plump, mustached, uncertain face, wondering what to do. He leaned on the newly painted rail of *Wawona*, staring out at the calm sea, his bowler hat pushed back, looking for any sign of wind. The man at the helm, one of three dozen fishermen aboard the newly refitted schooner, held the ship's wheel only because the master was on the poop deck, not because the ship was going anywhere. For almost two days since the tug had let *Wawona* go off Cape Flattery at the entrance to the Strait of Juan de Fuca, the vessel was becalmed, halted just as she embarked on her first journey to the Bering Sea and the codfish grounds. Even the salt water off Vancouver Island, in the region where the North Equatorial Current divides, some of it heading south to California, some of it heading north to Alaska, seemed unsure how to proceed. On a Tuesday morning in April 1914, Foss needed to make some luck.

The 46-year-old seaman straightened up and darted a look at the idling helmsman. Without a word, he stepped down the steep companionway into his cabin. A small desk, faded from sun and moisture-laden air, held sheaves of papers, an open chart, and a log book with crisp new paper. A spindly chair, uncomfortable for the big Foss, waited at the desk. A small, but more comfortable sofa sat under a window. Tossing his bowler on the sofa, Foss pulled out a drawer underneath his double bed. Rummaging through some clothing and personal items, he found what he sought: his wife's hat. Taking a breath, he put it on his head.

Capt. Charles Foss (Northwest Seaport)

He climbed the companionway, and the helmsman, startled at Foss' reappearance, saw a thick-waisted, short man in sea boots, wool pants, a navy turtleneck sweater and black wool coat wearing a forest green, wide-brimmed Easter straw from Chicago with a large white and lime green plume of ostrich feathers, accented with silken flowers and tiny glass beads. Foss ignored the gape-mouthed helmsman and searched the horizon from the starboard rail. A gull landed on the cabin roof, plunked down, and squawked off key at Foss, as if confused by the odd sight. The helmsman's eye caught Foss', and Foss stared the man down until he turned away in submission. The master of *Wawona* calmly lit a pipe and waited.

An hour or so later, clouds moved in, but the air was still and the water like a mirror. Impatient, Foss walked back and forth along the taffrail, *Wawona*'s wide beam giving him plenty of room to pace. The tiniest whiff of breeze carried away his pipe smoke and ruffled the ostrich feathers. Quietly, he chanted to himself, "Come on, old man, give us a wind."[1] Then he heard a shout. Forward, a fisherman pointed beyond the port quarter, and Foss saw the water riffling, a wave of air stirring the sea, almost like a wall heading straight for his ship. Silently, Foss coaxed the ghostly movement. The curious gull took off, and in a few seconds, the wind enfolded his vessel like a blanket, filling the sails, rising quickly, heeling her over with a groan from the masts and shrouds, and a wake appeared behind *Wawona*. The helmsman held onto the wheel, and Foss held onto his hat, barking an order, smiling under last year's millinery, the silken flowers dancing in the freshening breeze. *Wawona* was finally under way, and Foss silently thanked the wind gods and the owners of downtown Seattle's department stores. Damn those who don't think the Good Lord needs a hand now and then.

No one would argue with an eccentric man who chose fisherman's ways to protect the blessings that came his way, particularly if he believed they would help him bring home good catches. He often wore the same frequently patched blue-serge suit, as well as occasionally donning his wife's headgear. He avoided cameras, and like most seamen, he refused to start a voyage on Fridays, particularly Friday the 13th. "If there were any superstitions at all, Foss had them," said one former crewman.[2] Oddly enough, the number 13, which many people consider unlucky, would figure high in his last days.

Little is known of Foss' childhood and youth.[3] He was born in November 1867, in Norway.[4] He emigrated to the United States in 1895 and a census taker in found him in Skagway, Alaska in 1900. He lived in the tent city that sprang up in the wake of the 1896 gold rush. But he was not after dust and nuggets. Reporting his occupations as "sailor" and "laborer," he crewed and unloaded the steamers that brought miners and their supplies from the lower 48. He listed Seattle as his home town, and though he told the census taker he was head of his household, it's not clear if the seaman was married or had children in 1900.[5] He was married by 1910, but the census takers did not list any children in their Seattle house on Beacon Hill.[6] Despite this, he supported his mother and father-in-law, and possibly others of his wife's relatives.[7]

Cod fishing in the North Pacific

Russian explorers first noticed the Pacific Cod, *Gadus macrocephalus*, as early as 1765 near the Fox Islands, a subgroup of the Aleutian Islands. But fishermen wouldn't bring in commercial quantities of cod until 1863, when the brig *Timandra* landed its first load of salt cod at San Francisco. Businessmen, many of them former ship captains, founded the first processing facilities for further curing and packing around San Francisco Bay a few years later, making it the first center of the west coast salt cod industry. At its peak in 1870, 22 vessels offloaded 1.467 million preserved fish at Bay Area docks. San Francisco ships landed a slightly larger amount in 1906, but with fewer vessels.

A New Englander, Captain J.A. Matheson of Provincetown, Mass., founded the first salt cod company on Puget Sound in 1891. He brought his schooner *Lizzie Colby* around Cape Horn to Anacortes, Wash., starting a trend that moved the center of the salt cod business north. Puget Sound was several sailing days, sometimes weeks, closer to the fishing grounds, which reduced operating expenses and the potential for cargo spoilage. The Scandinavian immigrants around Puget Sound also provided a ready market. By the end of World War I, eight Puget Sound cod companies had sent schooners north to Alaska.

A salt salmon and canned salmon industry developed in parallel with the salt cod industry, though the former got most of the public glory. The lumber carrier *C.A. Thayer*, a sister to *Wawona*, worked in the salt salmon industry before going into salt cod. Unlike the cod boats, the big square-rigged ships of the Alaska Packers Association, such as the *Star of Alaska*, were iron or steel-hulled. (The *Star of Alaska* was privately purchased in 1954 and turned into a museum ship. Renamed the *Balclutha*, she is berthed at the San Francisco National Maritime Historical Park and she is also a National Historic Landmark.)

The cod industry was always dwarfed by the salmon industry. In 1915, salmon boats and shore operations caught and processed 436 million pounds of fish, valued at $8.6 million. The same year, the cod industry landed approximately 57 million pounds of fish. (The author arrived at the figure by multiplying the 1915 cod catch, 3,801, 586 by an estimated average weight of 15 pounds each.) Nine years later, the cod catch was worth just $544,000. The entire cod industry peaked around the same time. In 1916, schooners home-ported in Washington State brought in 1.6 million fish. California fish boats brought in 1.127 million cod that year. The next year, San Francisco and Puget Sound boats landed near-equal amounts, totaling 2.685 million fish.[8]

The cod industry then went into a long decline. Over the next three decades, consumer tastes and habits changed, and refrigeration replaced salting as a preservation technique.

Foss sailed in codfish schooners in the early years of the Puget Sound codfish industry. In 1908, he was master of the schooner *Joseph Russ*,[9] one of a fleet of 15 mostly two and three-masted sailing schooners, based in Puget Sound and the San Francisco Bay area, which caught cod near the Shumagin Islands in the Gulf of Alaska, the Aleutian Islands and the Alaska Peninsula.[10]

Foss escaped disaster in 1912. On April 21, on his way to the Bering Sea cod grounds, a storm drove the *Russ* far to the north of the normal route, dashing it on the rocks at Chirikof Island, a hundred-odd miles southwest of Kodiak Island. The rocks destroyed the ship and killed the first mate, J. Jorgensen. But Foss and 29 sailors and fishermen made it to the beach. They had no food or water.

The second mate, A. E. "Little Scotty" Reeve, and five volunteers put out in two small boats to seek assistance. They battled for eleven days through constant storms to reach Chignik on the Alaska Peninsula, arriving two hours before the steamer *Dora*, which departed immediately to the scene of the *Russ* wreck, reaching it the following evening. Twelve hours later, all the shipwrecked fishermen, including Foss, were safely on the *Dora*.[12]

In 1914, Foss marveled at his new ship, the *Wawona*. Robinson Fisheries of Anacortes, Wash., acquired the vessel the previous year for $8,000, shortly after Conrad Scheel, *Wawona*'s third captain, "laid up" or idled *Wawona* when he returned home from her eighty-sixth voyage delivering lumber from Aberdeen to San Diego.[13] Though commercial sail was fast declining in favor of steam, in the cod fishing trade, good sailing vessels were still in demand, and a rising inventory of laid up lumber schooners signaled an opportunity to snag a bargain. Their broad beams and deep hulls meant lots of room for a large cargo of fish as well as supplies and a fishing crew. The wooden construction was an asset as well: "You can't put codfish into an iron ship," a salt cod industry veteran explained. "The [curing] salt would destroy the ship and the rust from the iron would destroy the fish."[14] And the ships met the time-to-market test. Top speeds were around 14 knots, even with cargo. They often outran steamers in a fair wind.

Robinson Fisheries

William Fears Robinson founded Robinson Fisheries in 1897, moving to Anacortes, Wash. from New England to Anacortes, Wash., which was fast becoming a major cod processing center on the west coast, earning the nickname "Gloucester of the Pacific." Robinson built his facility at the foot of M Avenue, where his first schooner, the two-masted *Alice*, moored at his wharf to unload. After Robinson's death in 1916, the business was taken over his brother-in-law, John E. "Jack" Trafton, who ran it with his son Edward "Ted" Trafton under the name Trafton and Son. The family business included son Ellsworth, who was captain of the Robinson-owned tug, *Challenge*, which sometimes towed Robinson vessels to sea. The Traftons also owned a factory for rendering fish guts into glue, fish meal, and fish oil.[11]

The Trafton Family, left to right, Edward "Ted," John E. "Jack," and Ellsworth, owners of Robinson Fisheries and the last commercial owner of Wawona. (Linda Trafton Haakenson)

Robinson Fisheries modified *Wawona* for its own needs, constructing a forecastle underneath the forepeak for the fishing crew of up to 45 men, enlarging the galley on the deck, and installing bigger water tanks.[15] The fragrance of freshly cut two by fours and six by eights still infused the hold. Foss told the crew, "You are lucky to be on the *Wawona*. She is a fine ship, a $55,000 hotel."[16]

Cod Fishing with Sail

One of the main mysteries of the salt cod industry is why owners continued using wooden sailing vessels well into the age of steam, coal and even diesel. Some of the answer lies in the nature of the fishery. Cod vessels could catch all their fish far offshore in open water, while halibut fishermen, for example, caught fish close to shore as well as in deeper water; propellers gave halibut fishermen more flexibility to go where the fish were. Steam and diesel engines also made for dependable deliveries of fresh fish to the dock, which isn't as important when codfish fish are preserved at sea in salt. The cod boats delivered preserved cod to the dock, where the fish went through additional processing before being shipped to retail markets.

The 1914 trip from Cape Flattery to Unimak Pass, the most easterly deepwater entrance to the Bering Sea, located between Unimak Island and the Krenitzen Islands, a subgroup of the Aleutian Islands, took only seven days, a near record if not one in fact. Fishing was good and the weather kind. But *Wawona* had a brush with war. In late August, the Coast Guard cutter *Manning* told Foss that German, English and French armies were battling in Europe. Foss was already on his way home, but he grew nervous about losing his ship and cargo so close to Canada, which was sympathetic to Great Britain. Around September 1, 19-year-old John F. "Jack" Healey, making his first and only trip aboard a fishing boat, was at the wheel when *Wawona* hit a "dead, flat calm" off Vancouver Island, British Columbia. Foss told him, "Keep her off that Johnny Bull shore, boy, or they'll take everything we've got."

A salmon troller came alongside the next morning and told Foss that German warships cruised off Cape Flattery. But the engine-less *Wawona* was stuck in the calm, defenseless against a potential attack or seizure. Two of *Wawona*'s crew volunteered to row sixty miles to Neah Bay and telephone for a tug. A tug arrived, but failed to hook up to *Wawona*, instead towing two other unidentified sailing ships into the Strait of Juan de Fuca.

Wawona drifted into the Strait, and Foss could not control her fate. At midnight, a freighter with lights doused on account of the war nearly ran *Wawona* down. The mate on watch frantically rang *Wawona's* bell to warn the freighter's crew. "I was alone at the wheel with only the first mate on deck," Healey said, "and we both figured she missed us by about fifty feet." She came close enough "to spit on each plate."[17]

A breeze came up the following morning, and *Wawona* sailed into Anacortes and she warped onto the Robinson Fisheries wharf. She unloaded a record catch of 240,000 Pacific Cod, preserved in salt and weighing 1.1 million pounds. Foss and his fishermen would break that record the next season, landing 258,323 fish weighing 1.15 million pounds.[18]

Foss' and *Wawona's* luck would hold true through World War I, which brought with it a shortage of ships and plenty of charter work. She was contracted to carry cargo from San Francisco to Hilo, Hawaii in 1917. Foss returned to San Francisco, loaded sea salt, and headed to Anacortes. In the fall of 1918, after her normal Bering Sea trip, she went into dry dock, then loaded 440,000 board feet of lumber for the Fiji Islands capital of Suva, *Wawona's* last port of call as a lumber carrier. She carried copra, the raw material for coconut oil, back to Puget Sound, returning just in time for the 1919 cod fishing season.[19] From this point on, *Wawona* stayed a fishing boat, although she fished for Bering Sea salmon instead of cod in 1921.[20]

For a seaman in the days of sail, a good race was one way to charge the spirit. In 1934, Foss and fellow skipper John Grotle were having a drink together the night before *Wawona* and Grotle's ship, the *Azalea* were scheduled to leave Seattle for the Bering Sea. The two vessels were virtually identical in age and design; *Azalea*, like *Wawona*, was built in H.D. Bendixsen's shipyard. The two men struck a bargain (with the approval of the ships' owners), and someone told the Seattle newspapers. A race was on. It would rival "any of the historic Gloucester fishermen competitions...over one of the roughest and most treacherous courses in the world," one reporter wrote.[21]

A Lost *Wawona* Fisherman

Some of Charles Foss' men would not share his good fortune. On April 27, 1917, Russian-born Maikel Maitak fell overboard and drowned. The 34-year-old Russian listed Seattle as his residence. He stood five feet, six inches tall. He had blue eyes, brown hair, a ruddy complexion, and tattoo marks on both hands. The fisherman apparently had no family and no property in the United States. In fact, he owed $36.22 to the ship's owners after purchasing items from the on-board commissary. "His personal effects were of no commercial value, probably wouldn't bring ten dollars altogether," said a Department of Commerce report on the death signed by Foss. The man's belongings were turned over to Robinson Fisheries so it could recover some of the debt. Maitak died two months after becoming an American citizen. [22]

Disaster nearly ended the race before it began. Two tugboats, the *Katahdin* and the *Challenge*, were dispatched to take the *Wawona* and the *Azalea* to the Pacific off Cape Flattery. A gale blew up in the Strait of Juan de Fuca, and the *Challenge's* towline to the *Azalea* snapped. The wind drove the 70-foot tug toward the beach at Dungeness Light near the town of Sequim. But she collided with the bow of the *Katahdin*, which may have saved *Challenge* from destruction. Then the *Katahdin's* engine failed. Meanwhile, both the sailing ships drifted in the Strait at the mercy of the wind.

Challenge collected herself and the captain decided to tow the *Wawona* and the *Azalea* one at a time to the lightship *Swiftsure*, starting place for the race. [23] *Wawona* was first. Then came *Azalea*. All was well until a point 75 miles west of Port Angeles, two-thirds of the way to the open sea. *Challenge's* camshaft cracked. *Challenge* and *Azalea* fell toward the rocks at Cape Flattery, tied together and powerless. Captain Grotle ordered sails set on *Azalea*, and a light west wind puffed her canvas. *Azalea* towed *Challenge* into the protection of Clallam Bay. Another tug arrived, the *Albert*, and it towed *Azalea* to the starting line.

On April 16, the race began. Passing steamers relayed position updates to newspapers back home. Though the captains could see each other only part of the time, the ships were neck and neck most of the way. One ship held the lead. Ninety miles from Unimak Pass, the entrance to the Bering Sea and the finish line, both ships passed the four-masted *Sophie Christensen*, the biggest vessel in the codfish fleet, also on its way to the cod banks. The *Sophie Christensen* had left Seattle three days *before* the racers. On May 5, Foss wired his arrival at Unimak Pass, the finish line, ninety miles ahead of Grotle and *Azalea*. Foss also beat Grotle with his catch that year: 308,000 fish to 247,000 fish.[24]

*   *   *   *

In August 1935, Foss was master of his trade. Despite his strange habits, Foss' reputation as a successful master and fisherman attracted people, including solid officers, such as Thorsten Haugen, nicknamed "Tom." He was born in the fishing village of Hommelvik, Norway, east of the city of Trondheim, on October 12, 1886.[25] Family tradition said he suffered a "serious medical problem" as a baby, enough to threaten his life, and his parents took him to England for transfusions. He was never seriously ill again. At age 19, he sailed in European steamships. Emigrating to the United States, he worked as a logger and railroader in Minnesota, Arizona, and British Columbia.

When he lost his job in Canada, he went back to the sea. He shipped on board the *Tom & Al*, a halibut fishing schooner, and various cargo ships operating out of Anacortes.[26] He then went to work for Robinson Fisheries, sailing in all the company's ships. Foss hired him as second mate on the *Wawona*, later promoting him to first mate, perhaps seeing the same man another crewman saw years later. "Captain Haugen was a quick, fair skipper, and a good guy," a former crewmate said. "He was a hell of a hard worker, and the epitome of what you'd think a skipper to be. He would be right out on deck with us, counting the fish, and helping to load them into the salt."[27] Foss needed strong men like Haugen, because age was catching up to him, and his luck was wearing thin. He was 67 years old, overweight and irritable. (Or as one crewman put it, "roly-poly and rather grump."[28]) If he was like his colleagues, he probably drank and smoked too much. And that spring's voyage wore down everyone. A three-day storm in Unimak Pass ripped *Wawona*'s sails, smashed her windows, broke her water casks, destroyed five fishing dories,[29] and filled the forecastle with four feet of water. Foss limped into Dutch Harbor on Unalaska Island to make repairs. Ready for a new start, Foss headed out into the Bering Sea, but he could not find a breeze. His motorized dories had to tow him to the fishing grounds for more than a day before a wind came up. Mount Shishaldin, the 9,372-foot volcano on Unimak Island, blew her top, "belching out volcanic ash so the sun disappeared for two days and the men had to wear handkerchiefs on their faces," according to one account.[30]

Captain Thorsten "Tom" Haugen. (Northwest Seaport)

Fishing was good through the high latitude spring and summer, despite the troubles. On the morning of August 13, Foss wired Anacortes from the Bering Sea that he was bound for home carrying 307,000 fish.[31] It was the last message he ever sent. He ordered second-in-command Haugen to set a course south through Unimak Pass. A gale had come up, and the wind tore in from the Pacific, blocking their way. Haugen and his helmsman tacked first this way and then the other, barely making headway, the cliffs and mountains of the flanking islands clearly visible to port and starboard. More than one ship had come to her end in the pass. Foss grew impatient, and then exploded. "[He] stomped to the wheel and shouted…, 'Stop easing that fores'l.'"[32] Another witness said Foss screamed,

"I'll get the damned thing through!" Foss grabbed the wheel, slumped forward, and fell to the deck.[33]

Haugen was now in command.

He hesitated, but only for a moment. Kneeling beside the unconscious Foss in the biting wind, he called to his captain, perhaps in Norwegian, but Foss was unresponsive. Lifting him by the shoulders with his strong arms and big hands, he ordered his men to help him move Foss' heavy body onto to the main cabin roof, where he was laid next to the skylight out of the way. Someone covered it with canvas. *Wawona* was out of control, and Haugen fought to put her back on a southern course toward the Pacific Ocean. In the confusion, one of the fishermen stepped on Foss' chest. A loud "woooo!!" came out of the corpse's mouth, and the man yelled "He's alive! He's alive!"[34] But Foss was dead. Haugen called for the radio operator and sent this message:

FM SCHOONER WAWONA (K G N D)
1:20 PM TO (N R U B) CUTTER CHELAN
PLEASE SEND CUTTER IMMEDIATELY TO WAWONA NOW IN PASS AS SKIPPER HAS STROKE AND EITHER DIED OR IS DYING
HOUGEN (sic) MATE [35]

Chelan answered a few minutes later and started for *Wawona*.

MSG FM U S C G C CHELAN
MASTER
SCHOONER WAWONA
CHELAN UNDER WAY AND PROCEEDING YOUR ASSISTANCE WITH MEDICAL OFFICER ON BOARD. KEEP PATIENT WARM AND QUITE (sic) AND INFORM CHELAN PRESENT CONDITION
KIELHORN COMMANDING [36]

Haugen responded.

FM SCHOONER WAWONA
TO COMMANDER
CUTTER CHELAN
TO ALL APPEARANCES CAPTAIN FOSS IS DEAD
TOM HOUGEN MATE [37]

Haugen abandoned the attempt at Unimak Pass and sailed west.

FM SCHOONER WAWONA
TO COMMANDER
CUTTER CHELAN
PLEASE COME AND TAKE MASTER OFF AS WE GOT A DEEP
LOADED VESSEL AND UNABLE TO GO IN ANYWHERE. WE ALSO
GOT ABOUT A MONTHS PASSAGE BEFORE GETTING TO ANA-
CORTES SO UNABLE TO TAKE DEAD SKIPPER. WE ARE N E BY E
ABOUT 12 MILES OFF AKUN HEAD
TOM HOUGEN MATE [38]

The Coast Guard radioed Haugen that Dutch Harbor had no facilities for embalming and transporting Foss' body to Seattle. Captain Kielhorn also told Haugen he had asked his commanding officer at Bering Sea Patrol headquarters whether he could take Foss' body.[39] Haugen didn't wait for the Coast Guard to make up its mind. He sent a wire to J.E. Trafton, owner of Robinson Fisheries, in Anacortes.

FM SCHOONER WAWONA
TO TRAFTON
ROBINSON FISHERIES
ANACORTES (WASHN)
CAPTAIN FOSS EXPIRED 11 AM THIRTEENTH IN PASS STOP
COMMANDER COAST GUARD STATES THAT NO FACILITIES IN
UNALASKA FOR TRANSPORTATION OF BODY HOME STOP WE
PROCEEDING TO LOST HARBOR FOR BURIAL
TOM HOUGEN [40]

Captain Kielhorn on the *Chelan* heard Haugen's message to Anacortes and offered to help Haugen build a coffin for Foss.[41] But Haugen's men had already started making preparations for the burial, including using pine planks on board for the coffin. At Akun Head, the northern headland of Akun Island, *Chelan* took hold of *Wawona* and towed her into Lost Harbor on the protected west side of island. Haugen knew the anchorage well; Foss stopped there every year for water. Haugen dropped anchor at 9:30 p.m. and sent a message to Kielhorn thanking him for his help: "Your kindness and assistance to *Wawona* has been highly appreciated and shall never be forgotten."[42]

Wawona's crew added a headstone to the grave of Capt. Foss in the spring of 1936. Note the toolbox center left. Wawona is anchored in the distance. (Northwest Seaport)

The next morning, Haugen and some of *Wawona's* crew put Foss' body into the coffin and loaded it onto a dory, a small wooden fishing craft similar to the Gloucester dory but modified for Bering Sea work. Other men climbed into two or three other dories. They started the outboard motors, and in a puff of blue smoke, they eased toward the shore. Draping the coffin with a U.S. flag, they carried the Old Man's body to a point a few feet above the high-tide line below a bluff. Five men dug a grave in the black, marshy earth. Six others stood by, mist coating their oilskins.[43] The men fell silent, and a breeze rustled the beach grass at their feet. The sky was clear. Snowfields traced lines on the mountain peaks surrounding the bay. A seaman read a few lines from his Bible,[44] and at 7:30 a.m., the fishermen lowered the coffin into Foss' final resting place. One of the men noticed that Foss, the believer in signs, died on the 13th, was ferried to his grave by No. 13 dory, and was buried by 13 men.[45] A fisherman took photos of the grave to give to Marion Foss. On the back of one photograph someone wrote, "Capt's Last Bed."[46]

When the crew returned to *Wawona*, *Chelan* took hold of her and towed her out to the Bering Sea. Haugen, now master, set sail for home. He had a hold full of fish, an exhausted crew, and he had just lost a friend with whom he had worked for more than a decade. But unlike the aftermath of many deaths and burials at sea, Haugen knew he could decorate the grave properly. The next spring, he would bring Foss a gift.

CHAPTER 4

▼

MAY YOU WET WELL ALL THE SALT

Tuesday, April 14, 1936
The Merchant's Café, 109 Yesler Way, Seattle

On April 14, 1936, in the midst of the Great Depression, Don McInturf needed a job. For weeks, he visited every newly arrived cargo ship and passenger steamer asking for work. He spent days outside the Seattle's dockside union halls and Pioneer Square job brokers and he wandered the central waterfront piers and wharves with hundreds of other men. He was willing to try anything: He quit a job as a shoe salesman after one day when a woman wanted to see all the shoes in the store.[1] He worked at a bakery at one point. Only a tiny fraction of the workforce had his electronics skills. He had ten years of experience since the day he finished his YMCA radio course after high school in Tacoma, and he had shipped aboard ocean-going passenger steamers as a radio operator through the late 1920s and early 1930s.[2] Not that his education and experience mattered. The signs on all the doors said the same to everyone: "No work today."

Slurping soup in a hole-in-the-wall café, he studied the newspapers and hoped the "Arrivals and Departures" column signaled an opportunity. Maybe the marine reporters would hint that a ship might need a radio operator. But the columns said nothing. He'd sailed on passenger liners to Tokyo, Sidney, Manila, as far as the Tasman Sea off the south coast of Australia. But no one bought tickets any more. Out-of-work fishermen, loggers, and longshoremen grumbled beside him, sometimes to others, sometimes to themselves. Cigarette smoke stained the windows. McInturf dropped a quarter and a dime on the table for his soup and beer and left his newspapers behind.

Don McInturf, Wawona's radio operator in 1936 (Northwest Seaport)

The sun blinded him for a second outside the saloon. A few of the Skid Row pawnbrokers and flophouse owners had planted flowers in window boxes, and the blossoms' early spring colors cheered the street people. Lime green shoots decorated a few trees along the sidewalk outside the flophouses. Inside, unemployed men, including seamen like McInturf, held their hands near the wood stove, or slept off the previous night's binge. Some were poor fishermen, forced to live on Skid Row and rent a room with ten or twelve other men, subsisting on hard tack, fish, potatoes, and onions.[3] Laundry hung over the stove to dry.[4] A few of the men faced their next night in a shack in Hooverville, a few blocks away. Six hundred men lived there on a mud flat.[5] The desperately poor crawled over the shantytown's garbage dump, scavenging anything they could sell, eat, or use to repair their hovels.[6]

Dodging a streetcar advertising fur storage at the Bon Marche department store, he wandered toward the city's employment office. Five or six men scanned the listings hanging neatly in the window. The city maintained the office "in cooperation with the U.S. Employment Service."[7] A young woman clipped a new listing to a string with a dozen others. Moving closer, shading his eyes against the sun, he stood on tiptoe to get a better look. His heart skipped a beat: A ship needed a radio operator.

He ran down the hill to the streetcar station near the docks. He nearly tripped over an old Indian woman selling baskets and mats to passersby. She sold a woven sheath for a pint bottle.[8] McInturf bumped into pedestrians, mostly men in dungarees, work shirts, suit coats or jackets, and worn shoes. Some were bareheaded, like him. Some wore cloth caps. Others wore a fedora with a silk ribbon suggesting better luck in the past. A pair of loggers, judging by their extra heavy boots, flannel shirts, and woolen skull caps, stumbled out of a saloon. Commuters elbowed their way toward small passenger steamers that ferried them to Poulsbo, Everett, Tacoma, Vashon Island, and every other small town and growing city on Puget Sound. Steamers, tugs, and fishing boats tied up for more than a mile up and down the shore. The stacks of steam train engines erupted with coal and oil smoke as they moved carloads along Railroad Avenue. A tourist family parked its Model A in front of Ye Olde Curiosity Shop to examine the store's mummy and shrunken heads.

The streetcar to Ballard, a suburb of Seattle at the time, clacked into the station above Fisherman's Terminal. The smoke-spewing waste burner of the Stimson Mill guarded Ballard town. At the Dock, dozens of salmon trollers, halibut schooners, and other vessels waited for crews to take them out into Puget Sound and the Pacific Ocean. McInturf saw two triplets of masts 110-feet tall that dwarfed the masts and booms of nearby craft. *Azalea*, berthed beside *Wawona*, was just twenty feet shorter than her fraternal twin. Fresh forest green paint protected the wood planking of both ships from the waterline to a white line that marked the deck. The bulwarks above the deck line were painted black. Eighteen motorized fishing dories, descendants of the dories used on the Grand Banks in the North Atlantic, hung from port and starboard davits, sat across the deck hatches, or parked on the galley roof. One hung from stern davits.[9]

The End of Commercial Sail

The age of commercial sail was in its death throes in the 1930s. In both the deepwater and coastwise trades, wind-driven ships were victims of rising insurance costs, scarce crews, and competition from steamers with bigger holds and dependable arrivals. A single line of decrepit square riggers based in Finland carried cargoes of Australian wheat around Cape Horn. On the east coast of the United States, schooners were relegated to rum-running during Prohibition. A few two-masted "salt-bankers," sail-powered fishing vessels that caught and processed cod on board with salt, sailed 1,000 miles from Gloucester, Mass. to the North Atlantic cod banks. On the west coast, the number of operating sail-powered general cargo vessels was reduced to three, including the *Vigilant,* the *Commodore* and the steel-hulled bark *Kaiulani.* [10] The *Wawona* and the cod boats based in Puget Sound and the San Francisco Bay Area represented the largest and last fleet of American commercial sailing ships that competed within a single industry.

The radio operator immediately recognized *Wawona* and *Azalea.* Every year, the papers covered their preparations for sea in detail. *The Seattle Times* published a photo of both vessels at Fisherman's Terminal.[11] He had also seen them laid up together in Lake Union during the winter. As the weather warmed, tugs towed the ships to piers, and the captain, cook and men hired at two dollars a day[12] prepared the larder and loaded supplies, including stove coal for heating and cooking, gasoline for the dory outboard motors and a dynamo, and 350 tons of sea salt, the mineral that made the whole venture possible. A newspaper photographer took a picture of a man scraping one of *Wawona*'s masts, removing old beef tallow. He'd shortly slap on new tallow that would lubricate the gaffs, hoops, and booms.[13]

Some of *Wawona*'s complement, besides the captain, received special attention. A reporter from *The Seattle Star* wrote a brief feature story about the *Wawona*'s cook, Jean Bagger, whom he called "jovial and efficient in his chosen work." An accompanying mug shot showed Bagger in hat, coat, tie, and shy smile. "Right now," the reporter wrote, "Jean is concerned about getting that big galley stove aboard *Wawona* in shape for his next season's work."[14] Two other newspaper items appeared in the spring of 1936. One announced that Robinson Fisheries had officially appointed Tom Haugen master of *Wawona,* taking over from the late Capt. Foss.[15] And a photo showed Haugen holding an armful of life jackets.[16]

Wawona's shore crew also broke out the sails from winter storage. They would bend them on the *Wawona's* masts, raising and lowering the canvas to check the fit. The sail raising attracted old hands, who signed on for another season.[17] Some fishermen rotated among the various cod fishing ships over the years. Others stayed with the same ship and captain five or six seasons in a row. Prospective crews including fishermen new to the community, college kids needing money for their education, naïve adventurers, unemployed men with families, and men who had no other place to go.

McInturf noticed a man passing by with a hand truck and a crated object wrapping in burlap. Curious, McInturf asked the man what it was. "A headstone," the man said, and shifted it up *Wawona's* gangplank with the help of another man.

McInturf hailed Captain Haugen, whom he recognized from the lifejacket photo. The cap's bill shaded Haugen's wide-set blue eyes as he directed his hired men with a Norwegian immigrant's meter. A permanent seaman's squint against the sun's glare mirrored the lines of worry on his forehead. Haugen let the young man on board and McInturf, trembling inside but careful not to show it, asked if *Wawona* still needed a radio operator. Haugen studied the 31-year-old, blond-haired native of Colorado, born August 4, 1904 in Longmont,[18] and questioned him about his mechanical skills, saying the radio man on his ship took care of the gasoline engines that ran the windlass and the dynamo. McInturf said he could do the job.

Haugen led McInturf to the radio room, located aft in the main cabin. McInturf sat down and pulled the keypad toward him. He threw a switch on the set's black face plate, waited a moment for the vacuum tubes to warm, and tapped a test pattern. McInturf smiled and nodded at the skipper, who ordered him to be at the dock the next morning.

McInturf exulted as he took two sheets of radio log paper and slipped carbon paper between them. He made his first entry on April 14, 1936 at 04:48 GCT in a clear, open cursive, pressing down with his pencil so that the copy was equally clear: "West & Palmer, testing equipment, finish testing set." He signed his name "M' Inturf."

*   *   *   *

McInturf woke up at 2 a.m. on Wednesday, April 15, 1936, sailing day. His wife, Irene, rose as well. Don and Irene sat in the kitchen of their small house in the working class Seattle neighborhood of Columbia City. They shared a meal of eggs, bacon, toast, and coffee, their last meal together until September. Irene listened to her husband's chatter. He seemed more excited about this trip than past ones. There weren't any commercial sailing ships any more, he said. Irene said little. She didn't talk about her fear that this breakfast would be the last meal they'd ever share. She had the same fear every time he shipped out. He always came back. But he never shipped out on a fishing boat before.

McInturf packed his duffel and lit his pipe. Irene gathered Diane from her bedroom. Diane stayed asleep, even as her mother shifted her over to her father's arms. The family left the house and walked to the streetcar station two blocks away.[19] The stars welcomed them. The streetcar stopped, picked up the family, and trundled downtown. Nothing moved on the docks. A derelict snored in a doorway. The family transferred to another streetcar, which took them to Ballard and Fishermen's Terminal.

The McInturfs found the *Wawona* and *Azalea* crawling with men. Electric lights shone over the scene. White coal smoke drifted from the galley stovepipe near the forecastle and the parlor stovepipe by the mizzen mast. Diane roused, and she chewed on a slice of apple. She and her mother sat on a curb. Diane leaned close to her mother, and watched all the activity. Hunching their shoulders against the chill, men idled on the pier, following the action as well. Irene stared ahead, not really interested in the *Wawona*'s final preparations for sea.

Wawona's last hours at home this season were frantic. Several items were delivered on sailing day, including new navigation charts, writing materials, stamps, invoices for goods on board, a new log book, several old logs for reference, and a farewell note. A car from Northwest Instrument Company delivered one of the most important items: the chronometer. Masters needed it to determine a longitude, or number of degrees west or east of the prime meridian at Greenwich, England. Northwest Instrument had kept the chronometer over the winter, and technicians checked its accuracy before delivering it to Haugen.[20]

The eastern sky over the Cascade Mountains lightened, the new sun blotting all but the brightest stars of the early spring constellations. A waning crescent moon dipped toward the Olympic Mountains to the west. McInturf saw his breath in the morning air. A bakery truck unloaded a supply of fresh bread. Then a butcher's van backed up to within a few feet of *Wawona*'s bow. A man opened the back, and McInturf saw halves of beef hanging from the roof. A couple of men hefted a beef half and carried it up the gangway. They dropped it near the tarred lines of the main mast shrouds. Bagger supervised as the men tied lines around the meat and hoisted it into the rigging, high enough to make theft difficult.[21]

Some of the crew had already shown up, while others were delivered by Seattle cops in a paddy wagon. Some of the fishermen had landed in jail the night before, and Haugen had bailed them out.[22] The captain pushed the men onto the gangway, then looked about, as if something were missing. McInturf took this as a cue. Bending down, he tapped the bowl of his pipe on the curb, dislodging ashes.

"Time to go," he said.

Irene stood and picked up Diane, who lay her head on her mother's shoulder. Don and Irene kissed, and Don kissed his daughter's hair. Irene stared at Mac, and he turned away. He picked up his duffel and followed a seaman in a rumpled coat up the gangway. The man stopped and held on the railing tightly. He started again, took a few steps, and put his hand to his right ear. McInturf couldn't tell if he was in pain or just drunk. One of the mates spoke to the seaman and opened his coat, as if looking for something. Then the mate smiled and said something to the fellow, who nodded and stumbled toward the main hatch, his hand over his ear. When McInturf's time came, the mate stopped him, and asked if he had any liquor in his duffel or his coat. McInturf said no, and the mate let him pass. McInturf noticed a box at the mate's feet with a few half-empty bottles.

Out in the waterway, two tugs, the *Valencia* and the *Challenge*, approached the *Wawona*. Their stacks urped puffs of thin smoke as the captains slowed, waiting for Haugen's word. He glanced at the tugs and along the wharf. He strode down the gangway in big steps to the men waiting on the pier, barked at the group, and one of the men hesitated. Then the man "took a pier-head jump," as seamen called it, bounding up the gangplank with nothing more than the clothes on his back, filling the place of a no-show.

Returning to the ship, Haugen paced the deck, pulling on halyards, shrouds and lashings, and pushing on fuel drums, booms, and dories. He walked past McInturf, ignoring him. The seaman who covered his ear coiled some rope around a belaying pin, winced, and covered his ear with a hand again. Haugen stepped up to the poop and the rail. He peered over the side, studied the graceful sheer of *Wawona*, and flicked a spent cigarette into the oily water. Some of the men watched him. He spoke to the quartermaster, Berger Jensen, the first mate, who nodded.

Haugen waited. Time to go.

"SINGLE UP!" he yelled.

Nick Field, the second mate, repeated the order up and down the deck. Men scurried to the forward and after bitts on the port side, the one next to the pier. The sailors cast away all but two of the mooring lines holding *Wawona* to the pier. Meanwhile, the *Challenge* approached the starboard side. A deck hand tossed a line to men on the *Wawona*'s stern, who secured it to the after bitts.

"LET GO!" Haugen bellowed.[23]

An unidentified woman watches Wawona depart Seattle through the Hiram Chittenden Locks. (Dave Wright Collection)

The men on the port side tossed the last mooring lines to the dock, and the *Challenge* slowly tugged *Wawona*'s stern into the waterway. The tug moved to *Wawona*'s bow and the deck hand passed a line to men at the forward bitts. The tug nudged the ship into the traffic lane in Salmon Bay. *Challenge* pointed *Wawona*'s bow toward Puget Sound, then backed away. The *Valencia* approached, and a hand threw a messenger line to fishermen on *Wawona*'s bow, and they hauled aboard a thick hawser that looped over *Wawona*'s samson post. The *Valencia*'s captain added a few revolutions to his propeller, and the hawser tightened.[24]

Irene followed the *Wawona*'s movement toward the locks and she listened to the captain's orders along with a few other women who'd come to see their men off. *Wawona* caught everyone's eye along the shore. Her masts towered above most of the buildings. Only the stacks at the Simpson Mill were taller. A U.S. flag flew from the mizzen's masthead. A few people called to the fishermen. Some of the women waved, but Irene could not play the game. She neither smiled, nor frowned, nor waved. A woman in her forties introduced herself as Anne, Tom Haugen's wife, and asked if Irene would like to drive over to the locks to watch *Wawona* leave. Irene picked up Diane and got in Anne's car.

Valencia and *Wawona* slid into the lock reserved for large ships at the Hiram M. Chittenden Locks, where the fresh water of Lake Union met the saltwater of Puget Sound. *Wawona* tied up to the bollards in the lock chamber, and for a moment the ship was attached to the land again. Anne, Irene, and the other women stood within a few feet of the lock chamber as the lock master opened the valves. Seamen kept the mooring lines taut as the ship descended 11 feet to sea level. The west gate opened, and *Valencia*'s hawser once again tightened. A fish jumped in the swirling pool beyond the gate. At 7:30 a.m., 90 minutes after leaving Fishermen's Dock, Haugen dropped anchor in Shilshole Bay, just off Ballard, with *Valencia* standing by.[25]

When the ship cleared the locks, the women drove to the Ballard ferry dock. Irene and Diane watched the ship roll gently in the swell for a few minutes, the *Valencia* a hundred yards or so to the north. Irene couldn't tell who was who on *Wawona*'s deck any more. The ship was too far away. Diane started fussing, partly from hunger, partly from her father's goodbye. Giving her more apple slices, Irene brushed away tears, first her own, and then her daughter's. Anne gave Irene her phone number, and she dropped Irene and her daughter at the streetcar stop. All the women went home to wait.

*   *   *   *

Bagger served lunch as soon as *Wawona* dropped anchor. The men elbowed their way into the galley near the forecastle hatch. The galley table offered beef steak, pork chops, mashed potatoes, viscous and lumpy gravy, boiled peas and beans, bread slices, a bowl of butter, apple pie, peach pie, and coffee. Steel knives and forks clanked on the ceramic plates so loudly Haugen could hear the din on the poop deck aft. The men devoured the meal as if they hadn't eaten in days. Some had not eaten in truth for more than 24 hours. McInturf smelled wine on the crew, and he smelled beer in the galley, along with the food. Bagger can cook, he thought, even if he's a drunk. And the drunken crew ate like horses.

Nicknames

Aberdeen journalist Ed Van Syckle, poking fun at the maritime sobriquets of Grays Harbor, Washington ship captains, said nicknames were one way for sailing Scandinavians to distinguish "innumerable Johnsons" from each other: "Perhaps he was 'Single Reef' Johnson or 'Rough Pile' Johnson, 'Glassy Eye,' 'Baby,' 'Cordwood,' 'Slabwood,' 'Scantling Bill,' 'Swell Head,' 'Hungry,' 'Watchtackle,' 'Coffee,' 'Doughnut,' and 'Scarface' Johnson." [26]

The mates put some men to work moving gear, splicing cord, and clearing trash. McInturf organized the radio room, which doubled as his berth. McInturf's bantam height of five-four gave him some room to spare on his bunk for storage. Pushed into a corner of his cotton mattress, his duffel bulged with supplies he bought at the Sunde and d'Evers chandlery down on Seattle's central waterfront. He packed six pairs of socks, a pair of rubber pants, a pair of sea boots, two suits of light underwear, six packages of razor blades, two pounds of Edgeworth tobacco in tins, a carton of Bull Durham cigarettes, and a pair of nippers. Two spools of white dreadnaught cord would help him while away his down time with a knot-tying project. Photos of his family hung on a wall, and a copy of *David Copperfield* took up a niche. He carefully hid a .38 Colt revolver. A rag rug decorated the deck.[27]

Other men organized their bunks in the forecastle. Twenty-seven squeezed into a space the size of an average bedroom.[28] McInturf stuck in his head to say hello, the air already dank with human sweat. He and the others shook hands, renewed acquaintances, or introduced themselves by their nicknames. Men on *Wawona* went by "Pike," "Denver," "King Ole," and "Big Carl." Haugen went by "Tom," perhaps because owners with New England roots couldn't pronounce his Christian name, "Thorsten." McInturf introduced himself to the rest of the crew as "Mac," though some called him "Sparks." Whatever they called him, he made friends quickly. He and four or five men struck a bargain to let their beards grow until they returned to Seattle. The first man who shaved would buy a case of beer for the rest.[29] (He doesn't say who eventually wins.)

The first mate called everyone out on deck, lined them up and told them to sign the articles, the contract to work the cod season on *Wawona*. One by one, the men put their names on the two-page paper. The line slowed for a moment while a younger fisherman read some of the words to an older man: "Agreement for Codfishing [sic] Voyage, 1936, Schooner *Wawona*. In lieu of monthly wages, each fisherman, fish dresser, or seaman, shall receive as compensation such sums as are set opposite his name..."[30]

McInturf had a separate contract with the company paying $90 a month.[31] But he wanted to fish as well for the extra money. The document set the minimum length of fish brought on board: 26 inches. Once caught, the fish "shall have their throats cut as soon as possible." Each man would be paid based on the weight of the fish when the catch was unloaded at Anacortes in September, pro-rated according to the number of fish caught and dressed. The crew would elect a "delegate" from among their ranks to tally the weight of the fish when they were unloaded. The delegate would compare his tally with a company tally done at the same time "to avoid mistakes." The company also agreed to pay an advance of $50 per thousand fish caught upon arrival at the dock and the balance once the fish load's total weight was determined.

"No extra pay shall be due to the fishermen or monthly men for heaving anchor, or doing any other necessary work for the success of the trip or the safety of the vessel," the articles said. "No overtime pay shall be paid to any man signing these articles."

The contract also laid out two penalties:

- A "willful or fraudulent miscount" of fish would be fined one thousand fish for each offence, with the thousand fish distributed among the crew.

- Any fisherman refusing to take out his dory and fish in "suitable" weather would be fined one hundred fish for each refusal.

Here was the pay schedule for 1936:

First Mate	$.020625/lb
Second Mate	$.020625/lb
Fisherman	$.0175/lb
Splitter	$1.475/ton
2nd Splitter	$1.375/ton

Salter	$1.475/ton
2nd Salter	$1.375/ton
Header	$.325/ton
Dresser	$.30/ton
Watchman	$.325/ton

Bagger was paid $150 a month, and his helper, called the "flunkey," got $50 a month. Haugen's share was four dollars a ton of dressed and salted fish.[32]

Taking the paper from the last signer, Haugen ordered the second mate, Nick Field, to open the slop chest, the onboard commissary. The men filed back to the wheel at the stern. Field opened the companionway door, and he handed out the same kind of gear McInturf found at Sunde and d'Evers. The inventory included pocket knives, flashlights, batteries, packages of pinochle cards, Copenhagen chewing tobacco, union suits, pairs of thigh-high boots, blue and white shirts, pants, gloves, socks, hats, soap, razor blades, and tobacco pipes.[33] Cartons of cigarettes sealed by U.S. Customs lacked federal tax stamps; they would be consumed when the ship passed the three-mile territorial limit off the coast.

Haugen noted all the sales in an account book. One of the fishermen already owed the company $296.80, though most of it was for a new outboard dory motor bought on shore.[34] McInturf felt lucky. He'd be paid more than $400, no matter how many fish he caught. There was a chance some of these men might take home much less after they paid their debts.

Haugen glanced at his watch: 2:00 p.m. He called for McInturf and told him to start the gas engine and ordered Jensen to weigh anchor. The anchor chain clattered through the hawse pipe under the strain of the windlass. Field secured the anchor to the cathead and Jensen signaled the *Valencia*. Nick Field took the wheel while Haugen went below to enter his departure into the log.

Overnight, *Wawona* turned northwest into the Strait of Juan de Fuca between Canada and the U.S. The next day, after a bit of excitement when the towline parted, *Wawona* passed Cape Flattery and entered the open sea. McInturf tore off a sheet of tablet paper and rolled it into the manual typewriter. Normally, he used the typewriter for his radio log entries. But now, he wanted to make the first entry in his personal log, writing single-spaced sentences all in capital letters. "Towed to sea by tug *Valencia*, arriving off Tatoosh at noon the 16th and cast off at 3 p.m. Dead calm and heavy ground swell, not even steerage way. Most of crew drunk or rum dumb and the first-trippers are getting a workout," that is, suffering seasickness.[35] He would make dozens more entries on another 35 pages between now and the Anacortes homecoming in September. He'd comment on fishing, food, drink, friends, enemies, homemade wine, Capt. Haugen, nearly getting lost, storms, and the living creatures of the sea. He eased the paper off the roller, and he stored the sheet carefully for shipment home via the Coast Guard's Bering Sea Patrol.

Haugen interrupted and pointed to the radio set. He told McInturf to call the Coast Guard station at Neah Bay and tell them Herman Maser had a swelling behind the ear and was in severe pain.[36] The Coast Guard relayed the message to the Marine Hospital on Beacon Hill in Seattle, which asked Haugen to give Maser aspirin, a quarter grain of morphine, and put cold compresses behind the ear.[37] Just as the Coast Guard repeated the message, Maser came into the main cabin's saloon, and McInturf recognized him as the sailor who was holding his ear in pain. Haugen treated Maser with the compresses and at 6:05 p.m., the Neah Bay station called *Wawona* again.[38]

NOW VIA NPD MC
COAST GUARD POWER BOAT FROM NEAH BAY IS STANDING OUT TO YOU REPORTED POSITION FIVE MILES SOUTH SWIFT-SURE LIGHTSHIP POWER BOAT WILL TAKE MAN TO NEAH BAY WHERE HE WILL BE TRANSFERRED TO COAST GUARD AMBU-LANCE PLANE FOR FLIGHT TO PORT ANGELES HOSPITAL
NPD

The Coast Guard surf boat came alongside *Wawona* at 11:00 p.m. Nineteen miles off Cape Flattery, Maser climbed down a Jacob's ladder to the small craft's pitching deck. Haugen watched the boat's lights disappear in the west. He was now a fisherman short.[39]

Two days later, McInturf sat in front of his typewriter and he banged an entry into his journal. The cook was "in terrible shape" and his supper was cold. "Most of the crew still drunk."[40] Haugen set seven watches, with two two-hour "dog" watches in the afternoon to allow the crew to share the burden of watches throughout the 24-hour day. First Mate Berger Jensen, a fisherman, was on first watch, Second Mate Nick Field, a fisherman, on second watch; Third Mate Jim McNeary, a fish dresser, on third watch, and Fourth Mate Hugo Nelson, also a fish dresser, on fourth watch. Every crew member took a one-hour turn at the wheel, except the mate on watch, who kept the schedule.[41]

Wawona crept against the swell. The wind, first from the east-southeast, swung over to the east. Raising his sextant, Haugen took a noon sight, his first as official master of *Wawona*, and the first of many over the next five months. Checking the reading against his nautical almanac, and making some calculations with a pencil, he marked his position in his log at latitude 48° 29' North, longitude 125° 42' West.[42] He set his course according to the time-tested "great circle," following a 2,200 mile curve over the Earth's sphere to the northwest. Clouds moved in from the southeast, bringing a misty rain. *Wawona* was bound for the Bering Sea. J.E. Trafton, *Wawona's* owner, wrote to him, wishing good weather "so that you may wet all the salt and bring back a good trip of codfish."[43]

*   *   *   *

The passage outbound from Cape Flattery was uneventful, "steady as a liner[;] the sails hold her so,"[44] McInturf remarked, but mother nature got fidgety as *Wawona* approached the codfish banks. Albatross predicted severe weather for days. "We knew a gale and nasty weather was coming up some time ago as the gooneys pulled in their necks," McInturf wrote on May 1. "That is, while resting on the water, they held their heads close to their bodies and that's a sure sign."[45]

Haugen noted a change in the weather in his log. "Light breeze," he wrote at 10 a.m. The wind speed was about four or five knots. "Fresh breeze, rough sea," he noted ten hours later. Waves were six to eight feet. The wind, blowing from 17 to 21 knots, broke the crests of the waves into white horses. The helmsman held to a course almost due west.[46] Haugen climbed into his bunk and slept.

McInturf got excited. "No landlubber can realize what it means to run into a gale after several days of smooth sailing," he typed. "With the first roll, you hold your breath, wondering how much of your gear is unsecured and what is going to break. With me it's wondering if anything is near my transmitter or will something carry away and smash my receiver…We are rolling enough now to tip over a chair, driving rain and spray makes the deck a miserable place to be."[47]

The elements offered little new to Haugen the next morning, from his point of view. At 9:00 a.m. on May 2, he repeated his entry of the previous evening, adding only the word "cloudy."[48] McInturf, the rookie wind sailor, watched the sea grow unfriendly. "Every once in a while a big wave comes over the side. One almost got me this morning while standing outside the galley door, but I made it inside just in time, much to the disgust of the watch on deck. [Bob] Snow got caught amidships earlier and even had his boots full." The ship's roll to the left and the right passed 45 degrees, preventing sleep. "If you were to fill your coffee cup half full and then tip it enough to spill some, you would have an idea of how much we roll."[49]

Haugen checked his course, southwest a half west, written on the slate by the last mate on watch along with the wind direction, sea conditions, and distanced traveled as measured by the taffrail log. Deducing his position from these figures, he calculated that the course took him too far south. He decided at 1:00 p.m. to tack. Haugen stood by the helm and told first mate Berger Jensen he will "jibe ship." The mate ran down the deck telling everyone to stand by and watch for swinging booms. Haugen yelled "Ready about?"

The mate said, "Ready!"

"Helm, hard-a-lee!" Haugen shouted.

The helmsman turned the wheel to the left and the rudder answered. *Wawona* swung first into then away from the wind in a slow U-turn. It was actually more like half a figure eight. Seeing her wake about three-quarters of the way into the circle, the helm straightened *Wawona* out by bringing the wheel amidships. At the same moment, the booms and the gaffs swung across the center of the ship; Haugen ducked as the spanker boom flew over his head. The sails went "pop" as they lost the wind and gained it again. The ship heeled over, and the fishermen on watch sheeted home the sails, trimming them so that *Wawona* was in a broad reach. Haugen ordered a new course: west by north a half north. He wrote "jibed ship" in the log.[50] It would be the first of several similar maneuvers over the next days.

Geography rewarded Haugen's instinct three hours later. "Land ho!" shouted the lookout. Nick Field responded "Where away?" and the lookout pointed to starboard. "The deck looked like a madhouse," McInturf wrote. The forecastle and the galley and the main cabin emptied of fishermen and sailors. They all crammed the rail, looking to the right of the bowsprit, straining to see what the lookout had spotted through rain, sleet, snow, and the pitching of *Wawona* in the heavy swell. McInturf drew on his freshly lit pipe. "We have just raised Ugly Mug Rock and can just make out the loom of Scotch Cap."[51] The gray headland guarding the entrance to the Bering Sea was the first solid ground McInturf had seen since April 16.

Scotch Cap, so-called because the rock formation reminded explorers of a Scottish glengarry cap, marked the southernmost tip of Unimak Island, the first large island in the Aleutian Island chain. Many of the fishermen doffed their caps in respect to Mt. Shishaldin, the active volcano at the center of the island. Tradition said failure to show obeisance to "Old Moses" was bad luck. They couldn't see its 9,372-foot peak through the clouds. But they knew smoke was probably puffing from its caldera. And they knew it could erupt at any time, choking the air with ash and cinders. It had erupted more than a dozen times since 1775, most recently from February to May in 1932.[52]

The light on the cliff below Scotch Cap may have caught the lookout's eye. Every ship headed into the Bering Sea passed under Scotch Cap Light. It blinked from a wood tower on top of an octagonal building built in 1903.[53] The lighthouse keeper on duty on the evening of May 2, 1936 may have seen *Wawona* as she approached Unimak Pass. Her three masts echoed the peaks of "Ugly Mug," or Ugamak Island, five miles away or so due south of the light. Ugamak is the easternmost of the Krenitzen Islands, a subgroup of the Aleutians that includes Akun Island and Lost Harbor, Haugen's objective on this day.

Ugamak Island and Scotch Cap stood like gateposts on this approach to the Bering Sea. McInturf saw how they acted like the walls of a funnel, constricting the passage of the winds. When the winds came from the north, they drew energy from the eastern tip of Eurasia, the East Siberian Sea, the Chukchi Sea, the Bering Sea itself, the Arctic Ocean and ultimately the coriolis effect of the earth's spin.

The sun and the moon got into the act too, playing tug of war with the water as it sloshed back and forth between the abyssal North Pacific Ocean and the shallow Bering Sea. The water accelerated in a Bernoulli effect as its flowed through Unimak Pass, rising over and falling down a submerged saddle shown on navigation charts between the two landmarks. The charts warned of rip tides on either side of the saddle where the currents tear at each other. At maximum flood tide, the current flows at 3.4 knots; at maximum ebb, 3.0 knots.[54] Either way, it's "like a river," McInturf noted.[55] A sailing schooner on its way to lucrative schools of cod bucked a tide that for six hours helped and six hours hindered. That's in addition to a fight with winds that drove rain sideways.

Haugen's task was to take *Wawona* thirty or so nautical miles due west with a gale out of the northwest, almost directly in his face. All or most of his canvas was up, including the four sails over the bow, the foresail, mainsail, and the spanker over his stern.[56]

He turned in about 1:00 a.m. He bounced around in his bunk in the private bedroom in the main cabin, three steps and a six-foot companionway from the wheel. McInturf dozed in his bunk a few feet away. The off-watch mates slept nearby. Bagger snored in his bunk, also in the main cabin. Most of the rest of the crew tried to rest in the forecastle.

The helmsman kept to a tacking course of west by south. The lookout at the bow studied the sea for the lights of another ship or kelp that indicated shallows. He also listened for the crash of surf against rock. The mate on watch hoped other ships saw *Wawona's* running lights, red on the port bow and green on the starboard. A white light hung on the stern. The night watchman prowled the ship, looking for unsecured gear or unauthorized pilfering of galley stores by sleepless fishermen.

Haugen got up before four the next morning. He jibed ship, heading north, and two hours later jibed ship again, heading west northwest. McInturf rose at seven. "We've been beating through the Pass all night and haven't made much headway; bucking head swells and head wind…[we] have made four tacks in the last five hours. The Old Man figures on making Lost Harbor some time this afternoon."[57]

The wind rising, Haugen logged "gale" when he saw streaks of foam blow off the top of the 20-foot waves. At 11:00 a.m., the flying jib ripped and carried away.[58] "All hands are now on the forecastle head now trying to make it fast," McInturf reports. "But they saw it too late to save it; nothing left but shreds."[59] Edging out to the end of the jib boom in black oilskins, a fisherman tied down the remains of the jib. He braced his feet on a martingale as salt spray barely above the freezing point cut into his exposed fingers and face. Others reefed the mainsail and the spanker, showing less canvas to the wind and easing the strain on the masts and the rigging that held the masts solid to the keel.

McInturf, most of the fishermen, and even Haugen escaped the gale by huddling in the main cabin or the galley. "As I sit here in my cabin the wind just shrieks, spray sounds like small gravel, and every now and then we took a big [wave] clear over the house." The rolls were so deep, chairs sometimes fell over. The men on watch know nothing but misery. "They have to stand their watch on deck right out in the open. The quartermaster is tied to the wheel to keep from being washed over the side. They remind me of a bunch of chickens out in a rainstorm, huddled up near the after deckhouse against the pouring down rain or snow and them standing in water up to their ankles. But we ride it all like a duck and it's just a question of time until this norwester dies down and gives us a chance to get into Lost Harbor."[60]

Not yet. Bagger served a lunch of roast beef, mashed spuds, carrots and butter, hot rolls, brown gravy and mince pie. It's an uncomfortable meal for McInturf. "There are eight of us to a side on a long bench, and every man has to brace the bench, else all hands would go over backwards." At 1:30 p.m., the mate, on Haugen's orders, shouted "All hands on deck to shorten sail!"[61]

McInturf scrambled with his crewmates. "Swells getting bigger, never saw them so big. They look like mountains that will surely roll over us. But they don't. We rise up on the crest, tremble for a second, and then down again."[62] As the fishermen took in the foresail, it ripped in two from top to bottom. The torn canvas flogged the men's faces. Ordering his men to bend on a new foresail, Haugen hove to, turning *Wawona* into the wind. Some men cut away the sail's remnants. Others hurried to the sail locker underneath the wheel for the new foresail.

They walked smartly up the deck to the foremast, their heavy load spread among them, and they quickly bent the sail to the gaff and its boom. At the midship house, McInturf started the gas engine for the sail winch. Seamen wrapped a gaff's manila halyards five or six times around drums on a gypsy winch, throat halyard on the port side, peak halyard on the starboard, and they took up the halyard slack. The mate yelled at McInturf to engage the clutch. The crewmen kept the halyard taut as the engine pulled on the thick manila line. The engine strained; Haugen heard it running down. Slowly, the gaff lifted, and the sail filled, anchored by the boom. "And is the Old Man doing a sword dance on the cabin roof, yelling like a mad man, 'Haul 'er in. Haul 'er in. Slack the gaff.'" The crew made the lines fast on pin rails, coiling the ends out of the way.[63]

Lost Harbor came in sight. But the wind turned, pushing *Wawona* back into the Bering Sea and toward the North Pacific. Rather than resume the game, Haugen decided to wait, heave to in the Pass, double-reef his sails, put his bow into the wind, and drift with the current. Haugen bided his time, waiting for a fair breeze so he can make another try for Lost Harbor.

Tacking again and again, *Wawona* passed Scotch Cap a second time on May 4, and McInturf saw two wrecked ships, a steamer and a sailing ship, both unidentified. At 6:00 p.m., McInturf spotted North Head on Akutan Island, only a mile or so from Lost Harbor. But again the winds changed and pushed *Wawona* back. McInturf sent a telegram to his wife and daughter: "Entering Bering Sea tonight. Love you and Diane. Regards all. Donald."[64] It was the only telegram in which he sent his love explicitly.

The next day, Haugen brought *Wawona* close to North Head one more time, swung her around and headed southeast into Akutan Bay. The bay split Akutan Island from its eastern neighbor, Akun Island. Haugen was in the home stretch, and at 5:00 p.m. on May 5, he dropped anchor in Lost Harbor, on the western shore of Akun Island.[65] *Wawona* was three weeks out of Seattle.

"Lost Harbor is a good name for this place," McInturf wrote in his journal. "Have never seen a more desolate looking place. All the mountains are covered with snow, and the wind is just like ice. Sun is shining brightly and it is warm if you are in the lee some place and out of the wind."[66] During the stopover, the crew topped off the water tanks.

Haugen and some of the crew needed to talk to loved ones. McInturf tapped out messages on his radio, asking Dutch Harbor to send a telegram from Haugen to his wife in Seattle telling her he had safely arrived at Lost Harbor.[67] One man reported his arrival to his girlfriend in Seattle,[68] another to his wife.[69] Haugen telegrammed in Anacortes and reported "All well."[70]

The next morning, Haugen wrote a letter to J.E. Trafton, his boss. He reported his struggle through the "awful storm." "The deck engine don't seems to have any power. She can't take the sails up." He lamented the loss of Herman Maser, "but he was an awfully sick man; his head swelled up like a balloon. But I am putting one of the dress gang boys in the dory; we can always get along on deck."[71] Despite the problems, he said everyone was healthy. Hope was high for a good season of fishing, but he had a special task to complete.

On May 7, Haugen prepared to pay respects to his former captain, Charles Foss. "Some of the boys was up to Captain Foss grave last night and it was all fixed up fine," Haugen wrote to Trafton, adding that the local people had cared for the dead man's resting place. "Will probably take the stone ashore tonight."[72] Haugen was not a man to share grief or sadness with his men or his superiors, but he may have shared them with his wife, Anne, home in a Seattle apartment.[73]

As evening neared, Haugen ordered some men to load a brass name plate, a piece of wood carved into a cursive "*Wawona*," and a bag of concrete into a dory. Other men brought up the headstone, uncrating it and removing the burlap. Most of the crew loaded into dories for the trip ashore. At the grave, one of the fishermen mixed the concrete with water from a nearby trout stream. He poured a slab over the grave six feet long and four feet wide, embedding the brass plate and the carved wood into the concrete. The stone read, "Charles Foss, 1867— 1935."[74] Marion Foss had sent along seeds of pansies, forget-me-nots, and a maple tree, which the seamen planted around the slab.[75]

Some of the fishermen gathered up their tools and headed for the dories. Others, such as McInturf, gathered to make plans. They had a snack in mind.

C H A P T E R   5

▼

SNAFFLING THE CODFISH

May-June, 1936
Bristol Bay, The Bering Sea

After the burial service on May 7, Don McInturf, Orville Paxton, Albert Van
Arsdale and about twenty others of *Wawona*'s crew carried burlap sacks and lead
weights to a stream a few dozen yards from the grave. Haugen gave them leave to
make the first catch of the season. But their quarry was trout, not cod, and hundreds of fish lolled in a pool. "We had two sacks sewed together and weighted
down with leads to net them with." McInturf wrote in his journal. "Well, the
gang would walk up the stream to drive them all ahead of us, then we would set
the net and drive them back down the stream, dollys, cut throats, brooks, and
salmon trout, and did we get a mess, hundreds of them and big ones, too."

About eight in the evening, after gutting the fish and loading them into the
dories, the expedition clambered aboard *Wawona*. Most of the crew secured the
dories in *Wawona*'s davits or on deck, while McInturf and Paxton sought out
Jean Bagger in the galley. The radio man asked the cook permission to set the
table and fry up the trout, and Bagger said fine, as long as they cleaned up. "And
so I started in to cook trout, cooked them in big baking pans, Van cooked the
fried spuds and Paxton made the java and the rest stood around and passed advise
[sic], well when the fish were done and the potatoes we rang the bell and Paxton
and I went down and invited the skipper and Jean[1] up for a mug up of trout and

did they come or did they, well, if Pak hadnt [sic] filled my plate and his we wouldn't have got a thing, everyone had a lot of fun anyway…We had a batter of eggs and cracker crumbs for them and boy were they done to a turn, for cooking them I got out of washing the dishes or helping with them."

A fishermen with two of his cod. (Northwest Seaport)

McInturf clacked his notes about the burial, the trout, and the snack. "Here is a bunch of commercial fishermen," McInturf wrote, "fishing for a living, wading around among them, spending their leisure hours fishing and mugging up on them for fun." The revelry would soon end and the real work of the trip, the dangerous work, would begin the next day.[2]

From the time *Wawona* departed Cape Flattery through the first day of fishing on May 8, McInturf had apprenticed himself to the experienced men. He started with making handline gear. "The Old Man passed out fish hooks, line for snoot lines, bait knives, files and stones today," he wrote. "And I finally learned how to fasten a line onto a hook that has no eye and also how to run an eye splice in a cotton line that looks half ways neat."[3] The fishermen preferred "J"-shaped hooks with the shank flattened at the top instead of looped into an eye. Made in Norway, these hooks and their barbs were sharpened needle keen with a stone so that bait slipped on quickly and easily. Each hook required a special splice for the snoot line or gangion. Fishermen unraveled the three threads, slipped in the shank, and rewove the line with a sail needle. The splices prevented large jellyfish from getting entangled in the hook. Each fisherman went through two dozen sets of hooks and gangions as the cod fish's needle teeth sliced through the cotton.

With hooks, line, and tools in hand, the fishermen gathered in knots of two or three, sitting on *Wawona*'s deck in the sun against a bulwark or the outside wall of the galley, offering each other advice or mocking someone's skill An experienced fisherman took great care with his rig; some fishermen believed cod only struck gear crafted in a specific way, ignoring poorly made rigs. Others thought crappy equipment caught as many fish as a first-class setup.[4] The state of the gear was more a reflection of pride in craftsmanship than outwitting the brain of a fish.

The fishermen manufactured their own spreaders, for example, which held the snoot lines and hooks. Taking a six to eight-inch length of 1/2-inch copper or brass bar, they drilled holes in the center and each end. A specially made swivel was riveted to each hole, and the entire assembling bent into an arc. The snoot lines were attached to the swivels with eye splices. McInturf tied his cotton tarred line to the center swivel, and he wound the line onto a reel made from hardwood slats. He made his reel from scratch materials onboard *Wawona*.

The center hole in the spreader also held the homemade lead sinker. Haugen ordered the small portable forge brought out on deck, and he handed out five pound chunks of lead. A man loaded coal into the forge and blew air on the fire with an attached, hand-cranked bellows.[5] The chunks of lead were melted in a ladle, and someone checked the heat by thrusting a folded piece of paper into the liquid. If the paper burned smartly, but not rapidly, the heat was correct.

Meanwhile, another man carved a piece of wood into a form, wrapping the form with another sheet of paper. Holding it in a bucket at rim height, a man poured salt around the form, packing down the salt tightly. The wood was removed, and molten lead poured into the empty space. A swivel was embedded at the top. When cool enough to handle, the new sinker was removed, and another one poured. McInturf attached his sinker to the center hole, and his handline rig was complete.

Three Wawona fishermen. (Northwest Seaport)

"Never saw such a bunch to help one another out," McInturf wrote. "Ole Berg spends all his time working on someone else's dory, if I ask a fisherman about something I have to argue in order to have him show me, he will want to do it himself for me. I mentioned that I'd have to get busy on my brass spreaders soon and two hours later Carl [Pearson] came in with two for me. Jimmy [McNeary] carved my fish handle out, and the wood is hard as iron[,] and so it is all over the ship, everyone helps the other one out and there is never a word of discord."[6]

The dress gang made its own tools as well. These men gut and salted the fish. The 14-member group was divided into two teams, each with a splitter, a header, two idlers to move fish around, a spare man to help where needed, and two salters who worked in the hold.[7] The splitters were designated "first" and "second"; they each led one of the teams, with the first splitter as chief of all. The splitters and headers whittled handles from straight-grained pine for pre-manufactured blades supplied by Haugen. Placing the blade's stem in a groove cut into the handle, the men wrapped the handle in magazine-weight paper, letting the paper extend toward the blade about a half-inch. The splitters and headers then went to the forge and the bucket of salt. Like the fishermen, they created a form in the salt with the wood and the paper, inserting the blade into a small potato to keep it cool. The form with the blade was removed, the paper unwrapped, and the lead filed down to a custom fit. They also needed several knives, each with a slightly different grip to rest the hand while working.

*   *   *   *

Wawona kept to a northeast course after Lost Harbor, creeping along the northern shore of Unimak Island, the almost perfect cone of snow-covered Mount Shishaldin dominating the southern horizon. Haugen slipped toward Bristol Bay, following the cold shallows or "banks" near shore, where the fish schooled, taking soundings by casting a lead. The crew daubed the bottom of the heavy metal cylinder with butter, and when it touched bottom, material would stick. Haugen prospected like a gold miner, examining the bottom sample after the lead was raised: fine sand was good, mud meant no fish.[8] If a good spot was found, Haugen would drop anchor until the fish ran out, hoist the anchor, and find another spot. He sometimes dropped and weighed anchor twice a day, making early berths at Slime Bank, Amak Island, Black Hill, and Nelson's Lagoon.

McInturf lowered his line from *Wawona*'s rail, along with the other monthly men and the dress gang when they weren't dressing fish. He caught four cod his first day. He held *Gadus macrocephalus*, a large, big-eyed, big-mouthed, ugly fish with a tapered mottled-gray body measuring anywhere from two to three feet long. The gas in the fish's sound or gas bladder, which helped it hold position just above the sea bottom like a submarine, expanded as McInturf pulled the fish from the depths, making the animal appear larger than normal. Really big ones weighed 60 pounds. Two fleshy whiskers protruded from the lower jaw, which alerted the cod to shrimp and eulachon (smelt) as it rummaged in the sand.[9] The fish ranges from Cape Flattery to St. Lawrence Island near the Bering Strait, but most hang around the Aleutian Islands and the Alaska Peninsula. In the eastern

Pacific, they collect primarily in the Okhotsk Sea, where nineteenth century fisherman from California first made significant catches.

On his second day of fishing, McInturf caught nineteen cod the before running out of bait. The fishermen would sometimes haul up other fish ("bycatch" in modern parlance), including halibut, and cut it up for bait. "If some of the shoppers in the public markets could see what we use for bait, they would break out in tears, halibut, weighing from ten lb to fifty lb. We fillet them and then cut strips about five inches long and an inch wide…The black or halibut back is considered best….[10] We also got several spider crabs, three feet across and good to eat, several skates and silver heads, the latter are no good, neither are the skates." Some fishermen liked crab eggs: One scooped up a handful from a female and ate them. [11]

Foolish Fish

Some individual cod fish are particularly stupid. School teacher Edgar O. Campbell lived on St. Lawrence Island in the northern Bering Sea. Despite the local Inuit's practice of staying within a half-mile from shore in their traditional boats, Campbell said, the natives brought in huge numbers of cod in winter.

> How do you suppose this happens? I have supposed that, as the top of the sea coats over with slushy, soft ice, the cod, for some reason or other, it may be for air [for their bladders], jump through the ice and fall on the surface, their weight not being sufficient to carry them below into water again. At any rate they soon freeze and as soon as the ice is solid enough to walk on, the Eskimo bring them home in great piles, like cordwood. This happened twice since we came in 1901. In such years the fox catch is sure to be light, for the fox are so well fed they are wary of prepared bait. [12]

A fisherman with extra bait shared with others—most of the time. "Every now and then, one of the boys will start to haul in, get his line to the top of the water, make it fast and roll a smoke, then when things get busy, and the boys are pulling them in, he will ease the halibut on deck, hold him high, and knock him in the head with a furtive air and ditch it away. I do it, all of us do it. But of course dont admit it unless we have to."[13]

McInturf quickly got the hang of the standard jigging technique, letting down the line and jerking it up and down every few seconds. He also mastered the nippers he bought in Seattle. The large rubber bracelets, grooved in the center, fit around the palm and back of the hand. The tarred cotton line lay in the groove, and McInturf stopped and started the line by opening and closing his hand like a caliper on a disc brake. The nippers protected the hands as well as gloves, although McInturf turned to gloves when the combination of seawater and the normal nicks and cuts became too much.

Since each line had two hooks, McInturf often pulled up a pair of cod averaging twelve to fifteen pounds each. It wore him out. Imagine lifting a box of books from the top of a twenty story building with the added drag of water and current. Do it at least 100 times in three or four hours to bring in a good catch of 200 fish.[14] Don't forget to remove the hook, make sure the fish meets the 26-inch minimum, and if so, cut its throat, re-bait the hook if needed, and drop the line over the side again. Keep an eye out for marauding sea lions and shitting sea gulls. Do everything twice a day for a week or ten days at a stretch. Fortunately, cod aren't much for fighting, usually. "I might mention in passing that when you've pulled in two fifteen or twenty pounders and your lead from a depth of 40 fathoms [240 feet] your arms feel like a couple of things some one has loaned to you, they couldn't be your own and feel that way."[15] McInturf found out the true meaning of physical labor: "Woke up with both shoulders aching, used Sloans linement [sic] and it burns worse than my arms ached." A few days later: "My hands and shoulder are sore as boils, OK after pulling a few fish in but the minute I stop I have a heck of a time getting started again, cant sleep nights either."[16] The constant exposure of skin to seawater left hands cracked and bleeding. Hooks and fish teeth cut them up as well. "I never had an idea anyone could work the way we do with hands the shape that some of them are."[17]

McInturf's enthusiasm for fishing and the experience aboard a sailing vessel waxed and waned. Some days, he was eager. Some days, he could barely take it anymore. "Checkers," a number of pine planks laid on ends patterned after a checkerboard, prevented the fish from sliding around on the deck. Stepping over the checkers into a slippery mess of fish risked a broken bone. "We have to do a Scottish sword dance over piles of fish in order to get from one end of the ship to the other." And the fish themselves wore on the radio man. "Fish, fish in the water, on the deck, on the table, and in your stomachs," he complained. "I might add at this time that in my estimation, there is nothing deader than a dead fish and to see a checker full of them with their bug eyes kind of kills ones enthusiasm for seafood. I wouldn't eat a cod if I were starving to death now, thousands of em on deck right now, cods with sores on their back, cods with worms yards long, cods with sores inside of them, boy what tasty dishes they'll make for someone this winter."[18]

*   *   *   *

The spring sunrise on the morning of June 2, 1936 dazzled McInturf as Haugen sipped a hot cup of coffee. At about 3:00 a.m., McInturf leaned on *Wawona's* rail, holding his line, which pierced the surface of the Bering Sea next to the schooner's hull. Besides albatross and gulls, McInturf observed sea pigeons, whale birds, "and a small black bird with a curved beak, but I cannot remember its name...The dawn is beautiful up here. Air is fresh, and the sun comes up in a blaze of color, it turns the water lavender and pink and a pretty shade of green." [19] Haugen laconically offered his impression of the atmosphere: "Fine weather."[20]

The mates roused the fishermen in the forecastle, and they crawled out of their bunks. In the month of May, they caught 32,000 cod over 16 days of fishing. On the first day of June, they landed 7,342 more.[21] Of the 90 days or so of a typical season, they'd catch fish on about half, maybe a few more. In their bunks, some slept with their clothes on, others pulled on dungarees, slipping suspenders over flannel shirts or the shoulders of union suits. Pairs of boots waited for some fishermen, plain leather shoes for others. Most wore a cloth cap or an old felt hat. Everything stank of slime, salt and sweat, or as one fisherman put it, "money."[22] They stumbled up the forecastle steps and into the galley where Jean Bagger and his flunkey poured java as hot as the steam in Old Moses' caldera. The galley team had been at work for an hour.

While the fishermen devoured their morning meal, highlighted by homemade donuts, second mate Nick Field chatted with the Old Man at the galley table. Field was a big, energetic, husky man with a clear, loud voice you could hear over the howl of gale, a good attribute in an officer.[23] His brother Ed had a fisherman's berth on *Wawona*. Nick and the captain, best friends as well as workmates, discussed the barometer, the sky, the water, and the men; they had fished for six days without a break. Well, that's why we're here, the fishing, Haugen said. Getting the message, Field went to the forecastle hatch and barked, "Throw them out!"[24] The fishermen who had managed to crawl back into their bunks for a few minutes crawled out again, gathered their gear, lowered their dories into the water, and chugged off to find a berth. A good crew could lower all eighteen dories in as little as seven minutes. In the evening, they could lift and stow the boats in 11 minutes.[25] The dress gang followed the fishermen out of the forecastle, taking the second shift at the galley table.

At his chosen spot on the rail, McInturf felt a tug on his line and pulled it up. An intruder peered at him once it cleared the water. "I was face to face with a skate, with his little beady eyes, set close together and a tail like a rat, only thicker. Well, it was too early to indulge in an oral protest, so I cut his throat and consigned him back to the deep."

Haugen had some good news for McInturf that would turn his mood. He considered the radio man as he gaffed and hoisted a codfish; the rookie angler had snagged his share along with the rest of the boatbound crew. He'd learned good practice, like keeping his bait a fathom or two off the bottom to keep from catching too many halibut. Mac could even tell the difference between a cod and a halibut on deck without seeing it. A halibut sounds like someone is slapping the deck with the palm of his hand: *flop, flop, flop.*[26] The loss of Herman Maser reduced Haugen's chances of matching Charles Foss' average annual catch of 300,000 fish. And the fish were smallish this year so far, though he believed fishing would get better as the season progressed. "Things has been going fairly good so far," he wrote to his boss in Anacortes, "and everybody is in the best of health."[27]

The Dory

Commercial fishermen brought the dory to the Pacific Coast in the last quarter of the nineteenth century. Cod fishing companies set up shore stations on the Alaska Peninsula or in the Aleutian Islands chain and processed fish brought in by dorymen. Other companies sent vessels such as *Wawona* that acted as mother ships for a litter of 15-foot dories. The boats measured about 20 feet overall.

The basic design of the dory went back to the Middle Ages. The earliest depiction of a keel-less, flat-bottomed boat with sides and bottom planked lengthwise appeared in a watercolor called Little House on a Fish Pond by 15th century German artist Albrecht Durer. His illustration signaled a dramatic advance in boatbuilding, spurred by changes in forest products technology that allowed sawyers to cut long, wide, and relatively thin planks, instead of thicker, smaller rough-hewn boards. Boat builders attached the planks to a half-dozen U-shaped, hardwood frames and the dory was born.

European colonists brought the dory to the New World in the seventeenth century and adapted it to the frontier. The French developed a hefty river-going design called "batteau" that carried cargo and nine or ten men, including soldiers to solidify the French government's hold on eastern Canada up and down the St. Lawrence River and the eastern Great Lakes. After the French and Indian Wars of the early eighteenth century, in which the British advanced their hegemony over North America, colonial American boat builders brought the design to New England, and modified it for use in the Grand Banks cod fishery. They liked the design's simplicity, ease of construction, stability in rough water, and its ability to hold hundreds of pounds of fish. The craft could be nested inside one another for storage on a ship's deck. In the nineteenth century, boat builders mass produced dory parts, assembling them into craft of differing lengths. The dory became so ubiquitous that the U.S. government identified a number of standard sizes, as measured by the length of the flat bottom, including 13, 14, 14 1/2, 15, and 15 1/2 feet. A 16-foot dory was used for halibut fishing.[28]

This was Haugen's first trip as captain of any ship, not just the *Wawona*, and he felt the pressure to perform. How could he boost his productive capacity and take better advantage of the current run of luck? He had a spare dory. Who could he send out? There's Hugo Nelson, the first salter, but he didn't want to rob Peter to pay Paul, that is, reduce the dress gang's manpower to catch more fish. He needed everyone in the dress gang where they were. What about Mac?

"The Old Man is going to give me a dory, a spare dory and an engine and let me go out and snaffle the elusive codfish," McInturf wrote. "Hugo the head salter is mad as a hornet. He hates to see anyone get ahead of him and especially a green horn, tried to talk the Old Man out of it, but no soap. I'm going to get it."[29]

"Boy, wait until I get my dory," McInturf added, noting that he had some work to do to get it prepared. The small boat was probably the single most important tool on *Wawona*; it ferried fishermen to and from the spots where the fish lived, it served as a lighter to carry small amounts of supplies to and from shore or other ships, and it transported crew from ship to ship on quick visits. It was versatile, difficult to swamp, and ancient. The *Wawona*'s eighteen dories were virtually identical to the Grand Banks dories used by Gloucester fishermen on the Atlantic Coast, with their crescent sheer, straight sides flaring outward, a narrow stern, and a flat, narrow bottom. The mother ship/small boat combination used in the North Atlantic cod fishery since the 1700s worked just as well in the North Pacific.

The Bering Sea cod fishing dory returns from a berth. (Dave Wright Collection)

The most important advance in dory technology for the Pacific Coast cod fishery arrived with the development of reliable air-cooled outboard motors. In the days before gasoline engines, a fisherman rowed the boat, or he raised a small triangular sail referred to as a "leg-of-mutton." Just before World War I, cod fishermen started experimenting with motors.[30] But it wasn't until 1927 when they made the first major modification to the dory design in perhaps a century. They added an engine well near the stern, and installed a one-cylinder, gasoline-fueled, outboard motor. Early motors put out one to three horsepower; later two-cylinder, alternate-firing models generated nearly 10 horsepower.[31] (Two oars were left in the boat as backup propulsion.)

The added speed and power of an outboard engine created new problems. When the boat was under way, the bows shipped seawater as they dipped into the swells, and so the fishermen added a canvas and wood spray cover, which they called "foc's'le heads." Painted yellow-brown or buff with identifying numbers in white, the covers offered a bit of shelter to passengers and cargo when the dory was used as a transport. Water also tended to come in over the sides, so carpenters raised the gunwales 10 inches with two-by-twelves, which also increased capacity for fish.[32] Because the engine wells and the covers prevented crews from stacking the dories one on top of the other on deck, as they did in pre-motor years, mother ship owners added davits to the rails for some dories, while storing others on decks and hatches. Motors were removed every night to keep them out of the weather. The first wells were open, and later covered to keep water spray off the engine.[33]

In the end, the power dories could carry 50 percent more fish than the older models.[34] The extra capacity, and the practice of paying fishermen by weight, encouraged them to fill the boat. Some boats would come in with only one or two inches of freeboard.[35]

Multi-Modal Motor

In a pinch, a motor could perform double duty as a spare anchor. Fisherman Walter Stockwell, lost in evening fog and missing his anchor, removed the ignition plate, tied on his remaining anchor line, and pitched the motor over the side. The next morning, he pulled up the motor, reinstalled the plate, and sputtered to the *Wawona*.[36]

McInturf's main problem with *Wawona*'s spare dory was the 20-pound stock anchor and the windlass. If the anchor showed cracks or other wear, the crew would break out the forge, heat the metal, and pound out a repair with a heavy hammer. McInturf attached ten feet of twist length chain to the anchor, then 600 feet of nine-thread hard twist line about 3/8-inch in diameter. Turning his attention to the windlass, which the fishermen called a "gurdy," he gathered the line around a spindle with four cleats mounted on a shaft, placing one end of the shaft in a hole in the forward thwart, which was fitted with a ball-bearing assembly salvaged from a wrecking yard and lubricated with tallow from the cook. McInturf hoisted the anchor by turning a handle on the gurdy.[37]

The next morning, McInturf was up around 2:30 a.m. with the rest of the fishermen. He gathered his fishing gear, and stowed it in his dory. His craft was stored on deck, and so he and one or two other men used a boom with a bridle. Hanging down from each end of the bridle was a line with a metal hook, which grabbed a rope strap on the bow and stern of the dory. The men pulled on a line looped through a block and tackle, raised the dory, eased it over *Wawona*'s rail, and lowered it to the water. McInturf climbed down a Jacob's ladder to his dory and put the motor in the well. One of the fishermen had extended the shaft an extra five inches for a better bite in the water. McInturf pulled hard, fast, but steady on the starting cord, and the motor sputtered into life. He turned the boat to windward of *Wawona*, and chugged off to find his first berth.

Passing on the Lore

Don McInturf probably suffered some of the good-natured teasing experienced fishermen inflicted on first trippers. Dave Wright, a fisherman on *Wawona* in the 1940s, recalled a time just after he started using a dory. He followed first mate Berger Jensen to a berth about a half-mile from *Wawona*. Wright let down his line, and started bringing in fish. Anchored a few dozen yards away, Jensen's dory quickly settled into the water, signaling a good catch. Jensen then raised his anchor, started his motor and moved to another spot. Figuring Jensen might have left some fish behind, Wright weighed anchor, despite his good luck at his current spot. Wright moved to Jensen's old berth, and let out his line again. No bites. Meanwhile, Berger took over Wright's previous spot and caught fish. Berger had tricked Wright by putting water in his dory to simulate a good catch. Berger later told Wright he did it to teach him a lesson: "When you're catching fish, don't leave a good spot." It was Berger's way of passing lore to a young man.[38]

Three days later, he found time to update his journal. "The 3rd, 4th, 5th, and 6th will have to be lumped together. We struck fish and have been going night and day. My day has been from two thirty a.m. until ten p.m. Fall in my bunk for a few hours and up at em again. Hands cut, swollen and so sore I have to punch this out on two fingers."[39] He later broke or dislocated the ring finger on his left hand.[40] Sleep came as a wonderful blessing, even in a gale, when the ship's roll would rock the fishermen to sleep. "One noise we all like to hear at night is the crash and snap of the anchor chain, makes quite a lot of noise and shakes the ship quite a lot but as long as we can hear it and feel it we wont drift in some ones back yard anyway."[41]

McInturf went out in his dory as often as he could, when he wasn't required to work the radio or care for the gasoline engines that powered the ship's windlass or the dynamo that charged the ship's batteries. He fell into the routine of picking a spot, dropping anchor, and lowering his line. His take ranged from just a couple of dozen fish to two hundred or so.

The dress gang gutted and split the fish in preparation for salting. The bins in the foreground are called "checkers." (Dave Wright Collection)

McInturf's experienced compatriots kept an eye on the radio man *cum* fisherman. "When I go out it's kind of tough on the gang aboard as they figure they all have to gather on the fan tail [sic] and keep track of me through glasses," he noted. "The other day, when I came in, they told me every move I had made, even told me when I pulled in a bait-sized halibut. The Old Man told Hugo the head salter that I handled the dory like an old timer, he had been watching me through the glasses, too."[42]

Now the dress gang came into play. One team worked on *Wawona's* starboard side, one on the port side. When McInturf returned to the ship with his fish, he threw his bow painter up over the rail. The idler caught the line and secured it to the ship. McInturf grabbed a pugh (pronounced "pew"), which resembled a pitchfork with a single prong. Standing in his dory, he stuck the prong into the fish and flipped it through an opening in the bulwark planking between the cap rail and the deck, timing his throw with the rise and fall of the swell. The spare man counted the fish as they dropped to the deck.[43] The spare man's job was critical; accurate pay for the fisherman depended on an accurate count. An idler, standing in fish up to his knees, pughed fish to the next man. (McInturf had a definite opinion of the task: "[Pugh] is right…Phooey would be more like it."[44]) Fisheries biologist John Cobb offered a precise description of the dress gang's next steps.

> The "throater" seizes the fish by the head with his left hand, places the back on the edge of a table or tub, and by means of a short knife with pointed end makes a cut in each side of the throat just behind the gills (the front of the throat has previously been cut by the fisherman in order to bleed the fish), and a slit is made from the belly to the vent. The "header" then receives the fish and presses it backward across the edge of the table or tub, which results in breaking off the head at the first vertebra. With his left hand he then opens the belly and tears out the viscera. The fish is then passed on to the "splitter," the most important member of the gang, who places the back of the fish against a cleat on a board, and by means of short, heavy knife, rounded at the end and with the blade slightly curved flatwise, continues the split down the belly to near the end of the tail, taking care to keep near the backbone. At about three-fifths of the distance from the neck to the tail the backbone is cut across and is loosened, to that the operator can catch the end in his fingers. Grasping this with his left hand, he cuts under it toward the head of the fish and separates the upper part of the backbone from the fish….[45]

Splitting fish required skill, arm strength, and endurance. A properly split fish had a triangle shape and was nearly flat. A first class splitter was expected to split at least 6,000 fish per day several days in a row.[46] He would split 600 fish an hour, about one every six seconds.[47] Nova Scotian Jim McNeary was third mate and first splitter on *Wawona* in 1936. "Jimmy was real good at [splitting]," a fisherman recalled. "There was no one to relieve him either if he got tired. He could keep his corn cob pipe in one corner of his mouth, talk, and work all at the same time better than any man I have ever known."[48]

Sometimes a man was assigned a special job: "tongue cutter." The header threw the fish head into a box, and the tongue cutter removed the flesh inside the lower jaw, called the "tongue," and tossed the remains over the rail. (Cod tongues were a delicacy, especially fresh. The cook occasionally rolled tongues in bread or cracker crumbs and fried them like oysters.) The tongues went in a 30-gallon barrel. The cutter was paid $6.00 a barrel.[49]

Salter Hugo Nelson salting cod in Wawona's hold. (Northwest Seaport)

Once the fish was headed, gutted and split, idlers plunged the carcass into a tub of seawater, and dropped it on a chute. The fish slid down into the hold to the salters. The entrails, or "gurry," were thrown overboard, creating a feast for crabs and other scavengers. Hundreds of crying seagulls surrounded the *Wawona*, snatching floating fish livers and other parts from the sea surface and filling the air with a constant racket. Fishermen thought gurry drove codfish away, and they tried to keep their dories a good distance from the ship.

The final processing step involved coarse sea salt. Here's Cobb's description:

> The salters lay the fish on their backs, with napes and tails alternating, with the exception of the top layer, which is turned back up. A liberal sprinkling of salt is thrown over each layer, an especially heavy portion being put on where the fish come in contact with partitions or the side of the vessel. The kenches are about 4 feet deep and extend from side to side of the vessel and the full height of the hold. The first kench is usually started in forward part of the

hold, and the salter works toward the after part. As the kenches settle additional fish are placed on top to keep the compartment full.[50]

Two salters worked in the hold, one to lay down salt, sifting it through his palm-up, gloved hand, and another to keep his partner's half-bushel salt bucket full of the precious mineral. Like splitting, salting took skill. If too little salt was applied, the fish might spoil, which would force the crew to resalt the entire kench. Experienced salters could pick out a spoiled fish by its smell, which resembled sauerkraut.[51] Brine dripped down into the bilge, which was pumped out regularly and the brine dumped over the side.

Dress gangs faced their share of occupational hazards. In addition to the usual cuts from razor-sharp knives and sore muscles from 12 hours of dressing fish, dressers often suffered from "gurry boils." The mixture of seawater, blood, jellyfish slime, and fish gore on the dressing tables caused infections on the wrists and the backs of hands. Some were bad enough to keep a man from dressing fish, though he might move to a fisherman's job.[52]

The chief medical officer aboard *Wawona*, Capt. Haugen, had few options in his medicine chest to treat gurry boils or anything else beyond minor injuries. Before leaving Seattle, he stocked needles and sterile cat gut for lacerations, along with tweezers, forceps, antiseptic, aspirin, and vials of morphine.[53] Antibiotic creams for boils and puncture wounds from hooks were years in the future. McInturf dressed a cut on the hand of a fisherman: "...ran a hook into it and has gury [sic] boils all over his wrist."[54]

Home remedies were common. McInturf treated an ordinary boil on the inside of his left knee with hot towels and a plaster of brown sugar and "yellow soap." Two days later, the boil broke: "Wouldn't mind having another, it feels so good when they go away."[55] One fishing captain had a special home remedy for piles. His "fisherman's salve" was a wax-like substance which he heated over a candle and dripped red-hot onto the hemorrhoid. "The treatment was so painful, although surprisingly effective," a crewman said, "that most of the guys did not go in the [captain's] cabin for treatment."[56]

If someone were badly hurt, mentally ill, or violent, *Wawona* called a Coast Guard cutter to take the man to Dutch Harbor. One of *Wawona*'s 1935 crew had a case of gonorrhea so bad Captain Foss had to call a cutter. "We tried to cure patient with our medicine but unsuccessful," he wired.[57] Foss himself came down with food poisoning one year, which forced him to Dutch Harbor for treatment.[58] In 1936, the doctor aboard the cutter *Cyane* visited *Wawona* and pulled two of Nick Field's teeth.[59] Men hallucinated from alcohol withdrawal.[60]

Out-of-control drunks were occasionally hoisted above deck with a block and tackle until they sobered up.[61] One man was imprisoned in his bunk for fighting. The crew nailed boards over the bunk, but he freed his ankles and kicked the boards out.[62] And some days, the paradox of isolation while sharing a tiny vessel with three dozen others was too much for a man. McInturf heard over the radio that the night watchman of another cod vessel "walked out of the galley one noon, tied a dory anchor to his leg, and stepped over the side."[63]

*   *   *   *

On June 20, McInturf woke up at seven a.m. to cold and fog. So far, the pace of fishing was average. *Wawona*'s crew had caught and dressed 100,000 fish, a third of the way to Haugen's goal of 300,000 fish. McInturf skipped fishing from the rail, because of the previous day's gurry. He probably didn't miss it. "Boy but there are certainly lots of things to do that are more congenial to do than stand at the rail of a cod fish schooner at three a.m. and [jig]," he wrote. "Fog drifts around and the rain drizzles down and everything is wet and slippery, slimy and cold and everything is wet and clammy."[64]

At noon, perhaps out of boredom, McInturf lowered his dory into the Bering Sea, and dropped astern of *Wawona* for about 30 minutes and stayed out about two hours. He caught few cod. Then fog began to "thicken up in earnest, so I came on back home."[65] Other *Wawona* fishermen stayed out too long.

Most people in the twenty-first century, even modern professional mariners, can hardly imagine going out alone in a 15-foot boat on the open sea without radio, radar, sonar, several kinds of emergency beacons, or survival suit, not even a life vest, out of sight of the mother ship, except for the mastheads, sometimes, and nothing more than a half-gallon of water in a glass bottle, a bait knife, compass, instinct, and experience as guide. Once a dory was launched, the fisherman was on his own. In the days before outboard motors (and even after), he always headed up wind, so that if he had to quickly return to the mother ship, he could drift back on the tide or she could catch up. If the wind shifted while he was out, and he couldn't row back to the ship, the captain on the mother ship might attach a small line or "painter" to a dory and let it drift astern with the wind, sometimes a half mile or more. The fisherman would grab hold of the empty dory, attach the painter to his dory's bow, and the mother ship crew would haul him home.[66]

A U.S. Coast Guard cutter on patrol in the early 1940s. Note the dories center right.
(Dave Wright Collection)

Gus Dagg, a cod fishing veteran of pre-outboard days, recalled a "terrible southwester" on the *Fanny Dutard*, a three-masted schooner commanded by Captain J.A. Matheson, who opened the first salt cod operation in Anacortes. Matheson was nicknamed "The Squealer" because of his high-pitched voice.[67] "We all made it back to the vessel," Dagg said, "except for one guy who was too far to leeward to buck it back. Everybody was on the stern watching the poor devil struggling to make it, but when he finally disappeared in the fog, the old Squealer was plainly overheard exclaiming, 'Oh my god, he had a brand-new dory, too.' But that was typical of the attitude then; a dory probably cost $40 or $50, a man nothing. I am glad to say, though, that we picked the guy up 30 hours later, in fair condition."[68]

The shifting wind could go from a relative calm to a gale in a few hours. At one point, Haugen hadn't fished for three days due to rough seas, but the weather may have eased just enough for him. He lowered the dories at 4:30 a.m. At about 10:00 a.m., "it breezed up," McInturf said, and a couple of dories returned. Haugen may have changed his mind and signaled the dories to return by raising a jib halfway. In any case, an hour later, a gale was blowing and all but two dories were back. Everyone was at the rail watching for them. They quickly spotted two men struggling to catch *Wawona* in the swells. "First[,] all you could see was a spot of buff for a second and you would wonder if you hadn't seen a gull or just imagined it, but in another minute, off to one side, one would come up again, heeled over on her beam ends and dive down again with spray flying over her, took them about a half an hour to get in and both were half full of water."[69]

McInturf added that gales could come up in minutes. "Last year, one dory was out in a gale. At noon, when the gang went into the mess room, he was sighted about a quarter mile off the port bow. He was never seen again, but his dory was picked up by the *Wm. H. Smith* about two weeks later."[70] McInturf had a brush with danger when he went out in a fog and on his way back, he miscalculated *Wawona*'s position, losing her for about ten minutes.

Sea creatures posed a hazard to men and dories as well as weather. Charles Laakso caught a halibut, and as he was bringing it aboard his dory, he tumbled overboard, "and so they both started for the bottom, but Charley let go, I understand they parted company about three feet down, anyway Charley came in with his oil [skins] hanging on an oar to dry, the oar wasn't really needed, his language would've scorched anything."[71]

Worst Cod fishing Disaster

The worst disaster in the Pacific Coast cod fishing industry occurred in 1909. Matheson Fisheries sent the wooden brig *Harriet G* to the Bering Sea with Captain Robert Firth at the helm. One day, Firth dropped anchor in Dublin Bay, off the north shore of Unimak Island southwest of Slime Bank. Firth launched nine dories with a light southeast wind blowing off the beach. The wind swung around to the west, leaving all the dories between the ship and the beach. The sail-only dories were in the ship's lee, making return difficult. Firth sailed inshore, attempting to rescue the dories, almost grounding his vessel. But he was too late. All the dories were destroyed in

the breakers, killing six men. The three survivors walked to the Cape Sarichef lighthouse to await rescue.[72]

A poisonous brown jellyfish, which measured six to 18 inches across the disk
with tentacles several feet long, concentrated at Slime Bank.[73] Fishermen liked
the location because the cod liked jellyfish eggs and larvae. Nick Field said if a
fisherman caught 1,000 fish there, "he was doing real good."[74] But there was a
price. One veteran called the pain of the jellyfish stings "unbearable." "If you had
a cut or sore on your hands, it would burn like a torch," he said. "If you touched
any other part of your body with this slime on your hands, it would get into your
pores and make life miserable for hours."[75] Jellyfish were a mess for the mother
ship as well. While hoisting anchor, ball of accumulated jellies 10 feet in diameter
would slide down the chain at the water's surface.[76]

Sea mammals were the real trouble. One *Wawona* man lost both his hand
lines when a whale passed under his dory. "He was thankful it didn't foul his
anchor line," McInturf said. "Last year[,] one did foul John Berg's anchor line
and he had to cut it to keep from being towed from Hades to breakfast…Ole
Wick was rammed by one years ago, his dory smashed to splinters and as luck
would have it, the 2nd mate of the vessel he was on happened to see him. They
were the only two fishing that day as it was blowing pretty hard, he had been in
the water for three hours when the mate got to him; all he had to hang on to was
a board from the bottom."[77]

"Day before yesterday when I was out in my dory, I could have tossed a pebble
on one that came up and blowed and circled around, they see the dory and get
curious about it I guess but [they] don't bother one as a rule, the only time they
are dangerous is during the breeding season and thats next month."

Dorymen feared sea lions, which competed directly for fish. Adult males
weighed up to 800 pounds, and they sometimes capsized a loaded dory by hook-
ing a flipper over the side in search of an easy meal. McInturf said some would lay
their head on the engine cover, soaking up the warmth, while others kept away
from the dory, barking and snorting at the occupant. One of the most experienced fishermen aboard *Wawona* kept troublemakers at bay by tossing them fish
heads or whole fish, which the seals tossed around like toys.

One day, a sea lion and a crewman named John Eida went at it. A herd worried *Wawona* that day; one animal grabbed the side of Eida's dory in its teeth and
stole a fish. Angry and alarmed, the fisherman couldn't drive it off. He hove up

his anchor and went over to Olaf Wick's berth, and as McInturf put it, "tried to will it to him."

"What will I do with him?" Eida asked.

"I don't know but get the hell away from here with him," Wick said.

Eida puttered close to six or seven other dories trying to shake the sea lion off, but the creature "was after John and no else," McInturf wrote.

"Well, we were all on the starboard side talking when we heard a dory coming, pretty soon we could hear a funny roar. I climbed up in the rigging and could make out John with something right behind." The crew thought Berg had accidentally hooked a sea lion. "But when he came alongside the ship, we could easily see that there was no line on that lion. And was he mad and was John Eida mad."

Eida stood up in his dory cursing the animal and waving an oar. The creature returned the curses and threats equally. "John cruised around the ship for almost half an hour, turning, twisting, hitting him with one of his oars and everyone aboard ship was yelling but the sea lion would come up within a foot of the ship, stick his head and shoulders out of the water and roar just like a lion, and show his teeth."

"Finally, Pike [Anderson] got his twelve gauge shotgun and shot him in the face, blinding him and he moved off a little ways, so John took me out with my .38 Colt. When we got close to him we could see that he was blind and was rearing up out of the water to hear better so as to get our bearings. Well, we got up to about twenty feet and I shot him in the head, in the ear, I think, and he turned over slowly and sank…I hated to kill him worse than poison, but they sure are a menace to fishermen."

In quieter moments, fishermen would pull baby seals aboard their dories or the mother ship, give them bait, and let them play. "The babys [sic] are about as cute as anything could be, great big eyes and naturally tame and they love to be petted. If only the killer whales would come in, they'd run them from her to the Jap coast."[78]

Assuming you survived a sea lion or whale attack, just getting your dory aboard could break a bone or worse. The task of moving a boat weighing several hundred pounds up and over the rail of a pitching and rolling vessel was awkward and dangerous. One of the dress gang got caught between Number 4 dory and the rail, and he may have broken a rib.[79] Nick Field once hurt himself bad enough taking dories aboard that he could not fish the rest of the season.[80] A fisherman on another ship smashed the dory against his vessel's hull, throwing him overboard. His heavy oil skins and boots dragged him down. "He stayed on top for half the length of the ship, but they couldn't save him on account of the tide

and the heavy seas," McInturf wrote. "He had a bad heart anyway, which probably accounts for his not trying to swim more, probably died right after he hit the
icy water."[81]

The eeriest, most unsettling perils came with fog. "Boy, but it's quiet, out
there in the fog, can't hear a thing, not a sound but the gulls," McInturf wrote.[82]
The white mist covered everything, hiding the ship from fishermen and shipmates from each other. A man had to be comfortable with solitude and the
chance he might not find home in the grey-out. On June 20, fog surprised
Wawona's dory men, and all returned, but three. McInturf's account of the wait
is the most lucid entry in his journal.

> Well, it's ten p.m. and what an evening, three men lost for hours in the
> fog, Ole Wick, Bob Snow, and [Arthur] Paulson. We started blowing the fog
> horn when it first began to thicken up and about six, Ole Wick came in, said
> he had seen Snow and had told him that the vessel lay NE 20 minutes run but
> Snow had said no that his course was WSW 15 minutes run and he had kept
> on his course.
>
> The mate had seen Paulson and waved to him but couldn't be sure if
> Paulson had seen him. I got in touch with *Louise* and she had three men lost.
> About eight p.m. got in touch with her again and her op[erator] said Snow
> had been there and left for home with the proper course. Most of us went aft
> to the after deck then and listened for him, or for Paulson. Pretty soon we
> could hear an engine and so blowed the horn at longer intervals, our fog horn
> is a bellows affair cased in an oblong box that is operated with a lever.
>
> To realize what its like in a case like this, one must draw a picture in his
> minds eye of the after deck of a ship that is crowded with men, the mist swirls
> around and drips from everything that it touches, the deck is wet and slippery
> and the ship heaves in a moderate sea. A man stands at the rail with the fog
> horn and others either pace the deck, stopping every now and then to listen or
> stand in groups telling of others who been lost, or anchored out all night, tell-
> ing about Herman, the man who was lost in his dory for eight days and came
> back crazed from starvation and exposure and the wind sort of whistles and
> moans through the rigging and the sea slapping the side of the ship sounds
> lonesome and colder tha[n] usual, for we know that somewhere out there our
> shipmates are either anchored up and miserable or are running lost.
>
> Then the horn stops and we all listen and theres an engine, its off our
> starboard bow about two points and coming nearer, it stops and we blow the
> horn again, then we stop and listen again and we can tell that he has around a
> hundred and fifty fish by the sound of his exhaust. Then the horn starts again,
> then listen again, and he's running, but he's running past us and in a minute
> it's all quiet again, but for the wind and the sea.
>
> Then in about fifteen minutes we hear an engine again abeam of us,
> blow the horn and listen, listen till it hurts, he's running up to us but he stops

and we blow our horn again and when we stop he's running again, but with a different sound and then we realize that who ever is out there cant locate us, has stopped, probably figured he has over ran and has turned around and is now running away from us, we shout and blow the horn and Pike brings his shot gun and fires it several times and when we stop, the engine is running again, but he grows fainter an[d] fainter and finally dies out.

Lord, but we're helpless here, we could probably have hit him with a piece of coal twice, but the wind has carried the sound of our horn away from him and now his only hope is to get in our lee where it will reach him.

And so the horn starts again. Long blasts and in about an hour we hear an engine again, this time coming up to us from leeward and soon a dory comes out of the mist, cant make out who is in it until its almost alongside. It is Snow.

Snow explained that he was too much to windward of *Wawona* and once he got downwind of the ship, he heard the horn. Paulson eventually came up on *Wawona* in the same way. McInturf checked in with *Louise*, who said at midnight that three of her fishermen are still out.[83] McInturf does not record whether they turned up.

Nature would spare the crew of *Wawona* serious trouble in 1936, despite gales, fog, and sea lions. All would return safe to their homes and many would board the ship again. But one year was different. Nick and Ed Field, the second mate and his brother, sailed together in 1936 and again in the spring of 1941. Storms made the fishing poor, and two crewmen fell seriously ill. On May 27, 1941 Ed returned to his ship after fishing, but Nick did not. Ed waited to hear his brother's booming voice, but the next day, all the crew of a Coast Guard cutter found was a strip of Nick's flannel shirt hanging off his capsized dory. Nick's body was not recovered. No one knows what happened. He was 58 years old.[84]

Fisherman Dave Wright was on the ship with Ed Field that day. How did Ed take his loss? "Well," Wright said, "it's pretty hard to know what a man is thinking."[85] But Orvia Parker, a member of the 1936 crew, was less taciturn. "I feel lucky that I made it back to the ship every time…, but [it] sure hurts to think of the ones that didn't." [86]

CHAPTER 6

▼

THE WAWONA BREWING
SOCIETY

Saturday, July 4, 1936
Ugashik Bay, Alaska Peninsula, The Bering Sea

Throughout the late spring and early summer of 1936, Tom Haugen and the crew of *Wawona* crept up the north shore of the Alaska Peninsula, following the land's gentle slope to the east northeast, passing Port Moller, Cape Seniavan light and Port Heiden. In all, they would traverse 250 miles of shoreline. On Wednesday, June 24, at latitude 57° 35' North, longitude 158° 21' West in 114 feet of water, Haugen struck the mother lode. His fishermen brought in 11,802 fish, more than double the next best day of the season up to that point, and 70 percent better than the next best day of the entire trip. Over the next nine days, the crew caught and dressed 69,996 fish, a quarter of the production for the whole season.[1] On the busiest day of the run, the dress gang worked until 1:30 a.m. to process the catch. One man ate half a lemon cream pie at the end of his shift.[2]

Food and drink of all kinds were central to the physical and mental health of *Wawona*'s crew. Jean Bagger, the cook, understood his role in keeping *Wawona* productive. Good food kept the crew content, even happy, while bad food was cause for mutiny. The 68-year-old cook had a well-stocked larder, enough for five months with no refrigeration and little opportunity to go into port to re-supply.[3]

He stocked canned and dried fruits and vegetables, such as split and whole peas, white and brown beans, apples, apricots, peaches, prunes, and raisins. Fresh oranges, lemons, and seven tons of potatoes kept well in the musty and naturally frigid hold.[4] *Wawona* carried 30 barrels of flour, [5] along with corn meal and rolled oats. Bagger flavored his meals with pepper, sage, savory, cinnamon, ginger, mustard, cloves, allspice, nutmeg, celery salt, chili pepper, caraway seed, and bay leaf.[6]

His food locker under the main cabin held several hundred pounds of eggs, dairy products, and meats. Suppliers sealed each egg with a film of paraffin and they packed the eggs in 15 wooden crates[7] holding 36-dozen each. Bagger turned the cases every week to prevent the yolk from settling to one end of the shell. The egg spoiled if the yolk touched the shell. Bagger stored cheeses, canned milk, and six 112-pound kegs of one-pound butter sticks preserved in brine.[8] Preserved meats included salt beef, also called "salt horse," and salt pork in 250-pound barrels. The list of meats went on: "sweet pickled picnic" (pork shoulder), smoked ham, smoked bacon, summer sausage, garlic sausage, pork sausage, corn mutton, hog jowls, pig's feet, and tripe. Alaska supply companies used special cures for these meats that added shelf life. The items were hung from nails in the overhead deck beams in *Wawona's* store room. Fresh cod and halibut fleshed out the protein diet.

Meat Preservation

Before sailing, butchers brought sides of fresh beef or pork every day for canning. Jean Bagger cut up several hundred pounds into chunks, each chunk weighing about two pounds. The pork was sliced into steaks or chops. Bagger baked all the meat and placed it in metal buckets or tubs holding about 50 pounds, sealing the cans with melted lard or shortening, and storing them in a cool place. The cooks preserved the cooking juice in quart Mason jars for gravy. In Poulsbo, the home of the Pacific Coast Codfish Company, women often prepared the canned meat. [9]

The cook spent much of his time during the trip baking breads, pies and cakes. Bagger stored cases of table salt, baking powder, baking soda, and sugar. Before sailing, he broke fresh blocks of yeast into grain-sized bits and he packed them in glass jars filled with boiled water.

He stowed 6,000 pounds of coffee, the single most important food item on board.[10] An empty coffee pot would cause a near riot. And don't forget the toothpicks.

While *Wawona* was under way, Bagger got up a 2 a.m., and prepared the galley, first brewing coffee in a five-gallon pot with a wide base and a narrow top. Pea soup made before bed simmered in a large pot. The flunkey brought out a sack of potatoes, a case of eggs, a slab of bacon, slat meat, flour, and canned goods. Bagger prepared bread dough, sliced bacon, and fried eggs.[11] He used 3 ½-inch steel frying pans, just right for two eggs. The size and shape worked well on a stove that pitched, yawed, and rolled with the ship.[12] Steel railings kept the coffee and soup pots from flying away.

Bagger served breakfast on fishing days at 4:00 a.m., a little later on the way to and from the fishing grounds. The flunkey stepped outside the galley door with a hand bell, and gave it a "good single ring."[13] The fragrance of 38 loaves of fresh bread greeted the men. The breakfast menu included large portions of canned milk and cereal, hotcakes, butter, syrup, and coffee. Sunday featured ham and eggs. Friday meant donuts and fish, perhaps in deference to some men's religious observances. More than one fisherman marked the days by noting the menu.

Twenty men sat cheek-by-jowl at the galley table. A dampened red-and-white checked tablecloth kept platters and plates from sliding. Captain Haugen sat at the forward end of the table, nearest the door.[14] Table manners were minimal; speed and agility were rewarded. McInturf survived battles of arms and elbows "with a hundred and ninety pound Swede on one side of you and a hundred and ten pound Finn on the other." When reaching across the table, he advised, "sort of stand up, reach for [the dish], at the same time saying 'I'm crossing your bow, brother.' Keep your elbows close to your sides for protection and keep them close to the table. For if you're ever edged away, you'll never get close again."

*   *   *   *

Every morning after breakfast, the crew hooked up a hose to the ship's pumps, with the mates supervising. Two or three men would start at the forepeak with the hose and a broom, working their way aft, first on one side of the galley and then on the other, until they reached the poop and the taffrail. They turned the stream of seawater on the galley floor, removing spilled food and grease. If a bad spill occurred during the day, Bagger scattered salt on the deck to improve traction and reduce the chance of a slippery fall. The hose men then pumped out the bilge.

A fisherman swept the floor of the main cabin and the forecastle, shook down the grates in the stoves, and added more coal from a compartment below the forecastle floor. Inexperienced hands tried to dump ashes on the windward side of *Wawona*, only to have them blown back into their faces[15] McInturf boasted of *Wawona*'s grace when she was cleaned up. "This ship looks just like a yacht alongside the others, clean and trim looking, and we have better lines, too."[16]

As the seamen scrubbed *Wawona* down, the mates adjusted the halyards and other lines, tightening here and loosening there. A mate sent another crewman aloft on a bosun's chair with a pot of beef tallow rendered by the cook. A little lubricating oil kept the tallow soft. Grabbing a swab of rags, he applied the greasy mixture to the jaws of each gaff and boom, along with the sets of mast hoops, which held the sails next to the masts. The crewman also swabbed tallow on any gear that chafed against other gear. Scabrous lines, heavy canvas, and wooden parts constantly rubbed against each other, and the lubricant cut their chance of failure.[17]

To bathe, a fellow crewman hosed you down with seawater. (Northwest Seaport)

Wawona's crew took up another kind of scrubbing if the day was too stormy for fishing. After several weeks of hard work, with time only to eat and sleep, the men in the forecastle were ripe. Sometimes, a crewman literally hosed down his stripped shipmates with seawater. Only the cook received fresh water to wash his clothes, table cloths, and dish towels.[18] Members of a fishing crew usually packed just one or two changes of clothing, and laundered when they had the time. Underwear sometimes darkened from white to a dirty brown.[19] Some fishermen washed their clothes by hanging them over the jib boom on lines. Dungarees, flannel shirts, and union suits plunged into the water as *Wawona* rode the swells. "The constant lifting and dipping of the schooner acted like a washing machine and the clothes came out cleaner and whiter than in any Maytag ad you ever saw," a seaman reported.[20] As the wind filled *Wawona*'s sails, it also dried the garments. The crew called it "blowing the stink out."[21] A salty rime collected on the shirttails and around the ankles of pant legs.

The crew hung newly laundered clothes from a boom, which they called "blowing out the stink." (Northwest Seaport)

Skin and hair had a salty rime, too. Each man had his own porcelain wash basin in the forecastle. He set the basin on a bench, dipped out a pint or so of hot water from a tub, poured in the water, and washed his hands and face. He dumped the dirty water into an empty five-gallon paint bucket and returned the wash basin to a nail on the forecastle bulkhead. He hung a towel on another nail next to the basin. Once full, the bucket of dirty water was dumped overboard.[22] His personal business went overboard as well as he sat on the rail. *Wawona* had no toilet. To make water, you simply aimed over the side. To do a number two, you climbed to the forecastle head at the bow, and hung your derriere over the rail "It is a testament to the wonderful seaworthiness of those old ships that I can never remember getting my behind wet, even in the most raging storm," said one seaman. "A little spray, of course, but no more."[23]

The men shaved in front of a mirror on deck or under a light in the forecastle. (McInturf was proud of his ruddy beard and let it grow. He thought it made him look nautical.) A man earned a few extra dollars by giving haircuts and trimming beards or mustaches. Head lice, as well as body and pubic lice, were endemic on *Wawona*, but elderly fishermen knew what to do in the case of head lice: shave your scalp and wash it with kerosene.[24] Men who chose not to go temporarily bald lived with the vermin. "By selective breeding," remembered one fisherman wryly, "we even developed some pretty fair racing stock."[25]

If the crew bet on the races, the records don't say, but they had few options for recreation on a blowy day. You could rest in your bunk; the forecastle was usually quiet. You could curl up in the fold of a sail for a long nap, especially on sunny days. You could walk with a companion on *Wawona's* long deck, telling stories, with no engine noise to interrupt, only the creaking of rigging and sails. You could play cribbage or poker, usually for matches, cigarettes, cigars, or a pair of canvas gloves.[26] Pinochle was the favorite game in the main cabin, hours upon hours of it. Haugen, Bagger, Joe Johansen, the night watchman, Berger Jensen, and Nick Field played in the "parlor" next to McInturf's room. The radio man transcribed the action: "Jean the cook has his usual luck 'Dammit, I cant even get a melt' etc etc and Joe, or as they call him 'Gas Pipe,' just overlooked three hundred pinochle. And of course, he takes an awful razzing…Even in my sleep I can hear, 'That makes me forty pigs knuckles, that makes me forty peanuts,' or I've got an around the horn, sixty queens, a hundred aces etc etc all day long when we don't fish and some of the profanity is classic."[27]

The fishermen found ways to compete other than fishing and card games. They held rope slicing, knot tying, and beard growing contests. They also raced dories. "Tough luck for the guy who came in last. Everybody made fun of him," one fisherman recalled. "But the guy who came in first was in his glory."[28]

McInturf used up extra hours writing in his journal, though the pitching and rolling of *Wawona* complicated matters. The roll was sometimes so deep that McInturf rigged a rubber band to help his manual typewriter's carriage advance uphill when he hit a key.[29] McInturf also wove a belt with the white dreadnought cord he purchased back in Seattle. He took care of paperwork, applying to the Federal Communications Commission to renew his radio operator's license.[30] He worked crossword puzzles, paged through *David Copperfield*, and scrounged other reading material. "Picked up a 'Vogue' magazine, dated Dec. 1933, read an article on Russia, looked at all the pictures, then started from the back and looked at all the underwear ads, found a dandy one for Carters Foundations in the front by the way...Read a fine story this a.m., by Viki Baum, entitled 'No Man Knows', about a man who was as hot as a fox and twice as shifty, and ov [sic] course, after she had given 'her all,' she had to get killed in an airplane crash."[31]

*   *   *   *

"Dinner" was on the table at 10:00 a.m., and McInturf described a typical mid-day meal early in the voyage: Roast beef, mashed spuds, carrots and butter, hot rolls, brown gravy, and mince pie. The fishermen washed everything down with coffee, boiling hot, with "a *whoosh* to cool it and a *wheep* to drink her down." Leftovers and snacks were available all day at the "mug up" table. And every crew member scraped his own food scraps into the garbage and put his dishes in the sink. Coffee mugs hung on hangers. Bagger cleaned the coffee pot by scrubbing it with salt water, then rinsing it with a cup of fresh water.

Bagger's evening meal, served mid-afternoon, resembled lunch, but with a twist. The crew was mostly Scandinavian, so Bagger often served salted cod with boiled potatoes and a cream sauce. Other days, he'd prepare codfish tongues. Bagger had a specialty: chicken-fried halibut. He'd cut the flesh in strips an inch wide and four inches long, roll them in corn meal or mashed up crackers, and fry them in butter. On Sundays, Bagger handed out two apples or oranges. He added a treat on many days, such as plum duff or cream puffs.

Bagger was generous with portions, but parsimonious with ingredients. Late in the season, he loosened up, however, serving fried eggs at every meal with mashed potatoes at dinner and supper. He also offered pies, puddings, canned vegetables, and hot corn meal muffins. Bagger's frugality paid off with the owner. In a letter to Robinson Fisheries after the voyage, Bagger complained that the bookkeeper had shorted him for two days' work, and he wanted his wages. Maybe the bookkeeper thought he stopped feeding the crew on those days. "Nay, nay," he protests. "I feed the boys. Just ask them. There's always plenty on the tables. They could never understand how I could set such a table. I always make something out of what's left over. That's why I always bring...provisions back."[32] That meant the owners could sell the surplus food and supplies, sometimes to the fishermen's families. J. E. Trafton returned Bagger's favor. He told a newspaper, "Jean can sail on our boats any time he wants to do so."[33]

Coffee, a la Bering

Coffee, the elixir of life aboard a working ship, was always hot in the pot. One year aboard the cod ship *Sophie Christensen*, a seaman by the name of Harry Oosterhais discovered a one-pound unopened can of vacuum-packed premium coffee hidden in a corner. Not one to hoard a pleasure, Oosterhais brewed a pot and shared it with friends. It was much superior to the bulk coffee supplied in 20-pound cans by Seattle grocers. "Boy, it was good to have the evening cup from this small pot!" remembered Ed Shields, a crewman aboard the *Sophie*. "I think the brand was Hills Brothers." Oosterhais doled out his limited stash, often two and three pots worth a night...for three weeks straight. The crew wondered how he did it, but no one questioned him for fear of jinxing a good thing. Sometime later, he revealed his secret: He filled the Hills Brothers' can half-full with ship's bulk coffee, blending the good stuff with the mediocre. No one apparently noticed.[34]

---

*   *   *   *

The long hours of daylight in the high latitudes during late spring and summer meant time to kill, and *Wawona*'s galley morphed into a social center. Crew wandered in to mug up on coffee and shoot the breeze. One man had a talent for fudge-making.[35] Another heated up mince meat spread on a slice of bread.[36] McInturf often fixed himself and others a snack on the galley stove, though he tried as hard as possible to avoid doing the dishes. Much of the galley gossip, in heavily accented English, was about work, and McInturf found it tedious. "Boy, I sure get tired of listening to the same old thing all the time, a bunch of fishermen in the galley—'Well, I ran 30 minutes soueast by east and made berth, nothing doing so I heaved up and went way outside and all I could get was snappers [undersized cod], so I went to the nord and made another berth and picked fifty gurry suckers, if I had went norwest inshore I'd have got a swamper,' etc etc etc."[37]

Some of the talk turned to women ("I'll have to listen to Marino tell about all the women he has made...") and labor relations ("[I'll] argue about unions with Van [Arsdale]").[38] It's the only time McInturf mentions labor issues during the voyage; he rarely complains about pay or working conditions, at least in the sense of a grievance against Robinson Fisheries, *Wawona*'s officers, or the maritime industry in general.

Some fishermen found time to play music during the long trip from home. (Northwest Seaport)

Some of the fishermen brought along musical instruments. "Spent the evening in the galley, Walt [Stockwell] with his mandolin, Pike [Anderson] with his mouth organ, and Marin[o] beating time on a tin pan with two knives," he wrote.[39] "Between Stockwell's mandolin, and Pikes mouth organ and the violin, we had some orchestra, sang everything we knew and some that I may have known but failed to recognize from the way they were rendered, but the spirit was there anyway. Van [Arsdale] cant sing at all but he held the book and led, Marino hi de ho'd every two minutes and Paxton would suggest some song, and while they were starting [I] would think of another one and start right out in a loud voice, Rubinoff [Van Arsdale] was very patient tho [sic], all thru [sic] it and stayed with us till midnight."[40] McInturf sometimes brought up an old wind-up phonograph and played a few scratchy records, if the ship wasn't pitching too much.[41]

Not All Fun Aboard a Cod Ship

It's likely there was some grumbling about *Wawona*. Fisherman Jimmy Crooks sailed on the cod schooner *Fanny Dutard* to the Bering Sea with the rest of the codfish fleet in 1926. During a southeast gale, he was separated from his ship, and he was hauled aboard the *Wawona* to wait out the storm. Capt. Charles Foss confiscated his fish to pay for room and board. It was perfectly legal, but Crooks was angry nonetheless. "The operators of the cod fishing fleet were strictly mercenary," Crooks wrote. "It was hard to have to give your fish away for nothing, but you had the choice to either seek refuge on board any vessel of the fleet or perhaps be drowned if you attempted to land on the rock bound coast of Alaska fifty miles away…I have never encountered conditions so bad, neither have I worked so hard for so little money…" [42]

Unions on Cod Ships

Unions managed to organize workers in many fishing industries, namely cannery workers and halibut fishermen. But the turmoil on the docks in the early twentieth century, including the pivotal years of the 1930s, seemed to have had little immediate impact on the cod fishermen. The Sailors Union of the Pacific, one of the most powerful of the west coast maritime unions, failed to organize the fishermen and dress gangs aboard the codfish boats. The better-than-average conditions aboard the cod boats may have staved off union organizers. Robinson Fisheries, *Wawona*'s owner, started drawing union dues out of its workers' wages by the early 1940s. But it's not clear for which union or unions. [43] Ed Shields in his memoir *Salt of the Sea* that "the codfish men formed their own local in the Codfish Union and were able to negotiate for the summer's pay themselves. This proved very satisfactory for both company and crew." However, there's no mention of this union in 1936 Robinson Fisheries records.

McInturf's job as radio operator let him listen to music from San Francisco. He relayed radio news reports about the Spanish Civil War, a deadly heat wave in

the Midwest ("And we have to run around in our coats and heavy underwear."),
and a typhoid outbreak in Bristol Bay salmon cannery communities that killed
13.[44] He also alerted *Wawona's* crew to the impending arrival of Coast Guard
cutters, which rendered medical help and technical assistance, and delivered
all-important mail. "Everyone is excited, just like Xmas Eve," McInturf wrote.
"Every time I step out on deck some[one] asks, 'Whens the cutter coming Sparks'
or 'Have you heard any more from the cutter'".[45] A visit by the Coast Guard cutter *Cyane* brought letters, "all fine letters and [I feel] like a million." He was
intensely jealous of his wife Irene, a five-foot-two, green-eyed brunette, a
baby-faced woman who resembled a kewpie doll, and he craved letters from
her.[46] His sister Dolores wrote to him, and his daughter Diane sent him a
Father's Day card. Other fishermen received letters, newspapers, and packages of
nuts and candy.

McInturf monitored sports reports, and June 19, 1936 was a historic day.
Up-and-coming African-American Joe Louis and a former heavyweight champion Max Schmeling, a German, would go 15 rounds. In many ways, the
Louis-Schmeling fight highlighted an almost intractable racial and ethnic divide
in America, a divide that McInturf expressed by calling Carmine Marino a
"wop," Scandinavians "squareheads," Japanese "Japs," and the use of a racial slur
aimed at Joe Louis. The words and attitudes were common, almost accepted in
public before the civil rights movement of the next generation. The
Louis-Schmeling fight also highlighted the re-emergence of Germany as a world
power and champion of a twisted belief in the racial superiority of a white "race."
McInturf copied press reports of the fight for his shipmates. "About eight of the
gang crowded in the radio room that should hold about two, and we waited for
the fight results, Louis or Schmeling," McInturf wrote in his journal. "When
Schmeling ko'd the coon we all dashed forward and mugged up again and called
it a day."[47] Schmeling was welcomed back to Germany as a hero of Hitler's Third
Reich. Two years later, Louis fought Schmeling again, knocked him down three
times, and won the rematch.

The long days also presented opportunities for visiting among ships. During
the stop by the *Cyane,* McInturf invited the cutter's radio operator to help him
with a problem. The cod ship *Sophie Christensen* needed radio help as well, and
the impatient commander of *Cyane* wanted to proceed to the *Sophie* and the *Wm.
H. Smith,* a cod boat from San Francisco. Would *Wawona* let him bring his radio
operator over to *Sophie?* Haugen said fine, and he sent off McInturf, Stockwell,
Bob Snow and the "gob" in a dory. Rough seas nearly ended their jaunt. "Boy,
what a run, what a run, had to run by compass as we could only see the *Sophie* a

small part of the time and then just her top masts for an instant as we rode over the top of a big one. Stockwell crawled into the [f]o'castlehead. The sailor crouched just behind it and Snow and [I] stood by the engine. Taking turns navigating and trying to get our hands warm and was it cold. As the knuckle of the third finger of my hand is smashed pretty bad it hurt some when it got cold."[48]

Gay on a Cod Ship

The culture of racism, prevalent throughout American society, probably extended into what modern Americans call sexual orientation. How this played out aboard *Wawona* is unclear. Given general estimates that three to five percent of the entire population of men is homosexual, at least one of *Wawona*'s 36 crew was probably gay. And the crew probably knew it. In a 2004 conversation with the author, former *Wawona* fisherman Dave Wright said a veteran fisherman on one of Wright's trips in the early 1940s "made a pass" at Wright. Uninterested in the man's attentions, Wright told him never to touch him again unless he wanted a beating. The fisherman did not bother Wright again. Wright said the fisherman was also well-known for bringing "his boy" up from Seattle to flophouses in Anacortes.

An hour and fifty minutes later, McInturf arrived at the *Sophie*, only to find that the four-master's radio was fixed, and *Cyane* moving off, leaving her man behind. The dory took off after the cutter, the occupants "waving our hats, yelling and cursing her skipper in English with a spattering of Norse, she stayed under way for about fifteen minutes too, the gob was wig wagging something with his hat and finally she hove to, it sure is a helpless feeling to have a ship leave you that way, to see the white water boil under her stern."

The *Cyane*'s sailor safely aboard, McInturf and the other *Wawona* crew found themselves in the middle of the codfish fleet. They decided a round of their own visiting was in order. "Went back to the *Sophie* again and lied to all hands about the fish we have and took off for the *Louise*." McInturf chewed the fat with the *Louise*'s radio man and enjoyed a meal of baked beans, salt horse, baked potatoes, cabbage, and a "poisonous colored pudding. While we were eating and the Jap cook was making some bread, Capt. Dan Hanson, [*Louise*'s] skipper[,] went into the galley and grabbed some of the dough to fry in a pan, called the cook a little oriental _$&'# [sic] and the Jap answered right back 'To hell with you get out of the galley'. Hanson thinks there's no one like the Jap and they argue all the time."[49]

Visits to communities on land were rare. McInturf and two fishermen took a dory to the hamlet of Akutan, a fur trading post and a former whaling station, across a narrow channel from Akun Island on Akutan Island. The men from *Wawona* met Hugh McGlashan, a Scottish fur trader married to a native woman who had, McInturf records, eighteen children. McInturf visited McGlashan's store and bought a fox fur for his wife, Irene, as well as a fox fur for Captain Haugen, paying $29 on account.[50] The radio operator may have posted letters for Haugen and other crew. The shopping trip expanded into a social event when the entire village turned out to meet the visitors from the lower 48. "They have a dance hall and an orchestra, composed of four pieces, two guitars and mouth organs, and can they play, taught themselves, and so when we were all done with all the furs and bought a little candy they started the music, Paxton and I couldn't dance, having rubber boots on, so just watched, Charlie had his accordion along and he played a few square dances and some Scandinavian music, in between times we made dashes up to the traders house and sampled his home brew, not bad either."

The dancing broke up at midnight, and the three *Wawona* men retired to McGlashan's house and drank beer until two a.m. "Got under way about three a.m., moon shining brightly and sea smooth, one of the most beautiful trips I've ever made, as you go through the channel, there is the Pacific Ocean on one side and the Bering Sea on the other, and hundreds of islands all around and large rocks, saw plenty of sea lions and whales."[51]

Wawona made only one other landfall the entire trip, a stop for water at Bear River, near Cape Seniavan on the north shore of the Alaska Peninsula. Haugen ordered three dozen 32-gallon wooden water barrels broken out of storage. The barrels had a two-inch diameter hole in the side stoppered with a rubber plug. The fishermen tightened the steel hoops, loaded the empty barrels into dories, and sent the boats off to the river's mouth and filled the barrels. At first, the barrels leaked until the water swelled the staves. But soon the barrels tightened up and the dories ferried the water back to the ship. With a boom and block and tackle, the crew lifted the 500-pound barrel over *Wawona*'s rail. [52] Inexplicably, they crew dumped the fresh water into a larger tub used for cleaning fish, and then pumped the water into *Wawona*'s tanks. [53] "Yesterday, we found fish and all kinds of things in it," McInturf wrote.[54]

After two days and several water runs, *Wawona*'s water tanks were full again, but McInturf missed all the action. His job managing the gas motors aboard

Wawona kept him aboard. The returning fishermen reported "brown bear and caribou and when I got my glass I could see two bears and herd of caribou [p]lain as could be," he wrote. "The bears are bad, too. Many a fisherman has been mauled by them. They are the Kodiak bear."[55] And the extra water did not mean extra luxuries. "There will be no more washing clothes unless we get some rain water," McInturf wrote. "I haven't had a bath since sometime in April, around the fifteenth, I guess, we're allowed to dunk ourselves in a bucket now and then, it was once every two weeks for a while but think that will be cut out now."[56]

✳   ✳   ✳   ✳

Alcohol provided an important distraction aboard *Wawona*. Back in April, McInturf made friends with Orville Paxton, the second salter. Along with Pike Anderson, they formed an informal association of like-minded…artisans, you might call them, called the *Wawona* Brewing Society. "Brewing" was technically incorrect, because the group planned to ferment, not brew. In any case, they surveyed the galley and the food lockers and noted the contents. Under cover of *Wawona's* nine-day run of luck, McInturf liberated a three-gallon wooden keg, brown sugar, dried fruit, raisins, six lemons, sourdough starter (for the yeast), and fresh water from the hold and the galley. He scurried about as fishermen heaved 20-pound Bering Sea codfish over the cap rail to the deck. "I felt like a chipmonk [sic], going back and forth from the galley to my room; shirt full, pockets full." McInturf mixed the ingredients in his keg, concocting a liquid that went by many names: firewater, hootch, moonshine, red-eye, rotgut, sauce, smoke, tipple, toddy. McInturf preferred a refined noun: wine. In short order, assisted by *Wawona's* rolling, it was "going to town, fizzing and working fine."[57]

"After I stir it, you could cut the air with a knife but no one has noticed it so far and boy does it taste good or does it," McInturf wrote. But the wine had not yet reached perfection. Later that evening, McInturf visited the galley, just as some men sampled an early vintage alloyed by Anderson, the first unveiling of the Society's work. "It wasn't bad, but kind of sweet and not much kick,"[58] McInturf commented. He planned to unveil his work on the Fourth of July.[59]

Independence Day, 1936 featured plenty of social fireworks on *Wawona*. Haugen noted a gale in his log and 180,246 fish so far. McInturf called the weather cold, foggy, and the seas too choppy for fishing. But Old Glory flapped smartly at the top of the 110-foot mizzen mast, and the men enjoyed Bagger's roast chicken lunch as an old-timer played fiddle. Eight or nine fishermen gathered near McInturf's cabin, which stank of yeast farts and alcohol vapor. "The keg is beside the head of my bunk, I'll have to move it if it gets much worse, must be plenty of alky in it by the smell, and my room doesn't smell exactly like a radio room, either."[60] They opened the keg. "I sat on the deck and scooped it up in a bowl, kind of thick and sweetish," he wrote. He wiped some off his red beard. "We had the window open and pretty soon there were four or five more [fishermen] squatted outside on deck tossing bowls off." Two-thirds of his keg was gone in a few hours. And so were the fishermen, so to speak. One fell down a ladder, but he didn't hurt himself. Another passed out at the galley door.

McInturf and his fellows then discovered the wine's medicinal qualities. "Now it so happens that, just as the drinks had been large in their proportions, so were they laxative in their propensities," McInturf wrote. "[The] head was lined with bare fannies exposed to the elements...They didn't dare leave either, for some time, it just meant a wild dash back."

"Oh yes," McInturf added, "the skipper broke out a bottle of whiskey just before dinner and we sat around and discussed that...And so that was the 4th"[61] The next day, the radio man visited the forecastle and tried to give away his remaining product, "but was greeted with jeers and boos."[62]

But McInturf's buddies were gluttons for punishment. Three days later, Paxton ambled back to McInturf's room and discovered that the radio operator was about to pitch the remaining wine overboard. "So he said, 'Well, drag it out here and let's have a look at it,' and by golly, it was pretty good by this time, so we just locked the door, sat on the deck by the keg with two bowls and drank wine and chewed the fat." The evening wore long, and just as McInturf took his pants off to get ready for bed, Snow joined the group, and things got strange. "Had my pants off when Pax suggested we take the keg and adjourn to the galley, well, in the excitement of avoiding others in the [main] cabin and trying to carry the dam [sic] keg, I went without my pants and so to even it up, Pax and Snow took theirs off too just to be in line, in the galley were Marino, Gress, Parker and several others. We killed the keg, but thank the Lord I took it easy and so did Gress, just ran enough temperature to have a little fun."

McInturf finally went to bed, but "we turned out again. I had forgotten about the other powers of that wine, but as luck would have it, I have the privilege of the capt's bathroom (without a tub) and so just spent the few spare moments sitting on a towing bit[t][63] and watching the others make the mad dash, got to bed about five."[64]

McInturf later enjoyed the fruits of two or three members of the *Wawona* Brewing Society. And there's at least one fisherman not a member of his clique who made wine. One day, Bagger told McInturf he smelled something leaking in a next-door room sheltering a small gas engine used for charging batteries that power shipboard lights. The radio operator investigated, and discovered that a keg stashed by "some low person" had spilt half its contents, some of it running into the galley. "[I] came back and told [Jean] my distilled water had turned over," he wrote. "Left a note on the keg for an interest in the contents."[65] Later, McInturf found another keg in the same room, "way back under the bench," moved it to his berth, strained it, and shared the drink with two friends. "Ah, but it's rare old stuff, too, all of two weeks," he wrote. "And I believe one would call it a fruity port inasmuch as I saw some raisins and a couple of dried peaches, among other things, floating around, when I strained if off."

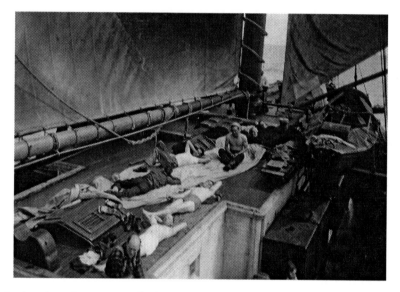

In the relatively warm month of August, some fishermen found time for a sun bath.
(Northwest Seaport)

Haugen, of course, wasn't fooled by McInturf's sneaking around. But there's no hint in McInturf's journal that Haugen clamped down or even discouraged alcohol use.[66] The captain didn't "give a dam [sic] what we do as long as there is no damage done," McInturf wrote.[67] Haugen worried more about catching fish, and the season was already more than half over.

CHAPTER 7

▼

THE SMALLEST MAN ON BOARD

Monday, July 20, 1936
Latitude 57° 46' North, longitude 159° 10' West, The Bering Sea

Fishing steadied into a rhythm throughout July. For weeks, Capt. Haugen kept *Wawona* in a tight area of eastern Bristol Bay often out of sight of land. He berthed in 20 to 30 fathoms of water, from 25 to 90 miles off shore, moving a few miles at a time. Over July's 20 fishing days, the most fishing days of any of the four months when lines were in the water, his fishermen brought in around 4,300 cod a day. But as the end of the month approached, the production curve declined, and so did the crew's patience, with a rising peevishness in proportion.

Haugen hired McInturf as the radio operator, but he assigned the man several other tasks as well. The wireless operator nursed *Wawona*'s three gasoline engines: one to power the anchor windlass, one to raise the sails, and one for the electrical system. McInturf spent much of his time struggling with the last of the trio, which ran two generators, one for the wireless and one for a bank of lead acid batteries similar to car batteries.

Located just forward of the galley, the 32-volt system supplied direct current to lights in the main cabin, galley, and forecastle. The battery engine gave him trouble almost from sailing day. In his journal's third entry, he grumbles of dirty gas and an oily generator belt.[1] He cleaned the gas line and the carburetor and fixed the coil contacts a few days later, but he had "no faith" in the motor: "As fast as I fix one end of the thing, the other goes out." Then the piston "started to pound" and he had to make new parts of iron washers.[2] A few days later, the engine lost compression. With much cursing, he pulled the head, ground a burned exhaust valve, ground the intake value seat as well, installed a new plug and points, "and she is purring fine now."[3] Haugen noticed his work. "The skipper says the gas engines run better now than they ever have and he's been aboard for seventeen years."[4]

Weighing Anchor

Wawona's crew raised the cast-iron anchor with a large, single cylinder, high-compression, 21-horsepower horizontal engine with heavy flywheels. The crew spent more time starting the engine than actually weighing anchor. A crew member manned a clutch lever that stopped and started the winch. The mate, standing on the bow watching the anchor rise, signaled the man at the clutch. A series of teeth in the windlass, much like the teeth on a bicycle's chain wheels, grabbed the hundreds of links of chain. Each iron link, about four inches wide, weighed five pounds. Members of the dress gang guided the fast-moving chain into the chain locker, laying it down in rows so that it would pay out smoothly when the anchor was dropped again. The windlass was halted when the anchor stock entered the hawse pipe. Some seamen avoided the windlass, saying the speed and noise of the chain clattering into the locker was frightening.[5]

Haugen cringed every time he heard the battery engine start. Charging the batteries for lights used up gasoline, and *Wawona* couldn't just pull into the nearest gas pump when fuel ran low. Large steel tanks on deck stored thousands of gallons of gasoline, and Haugen needed every drop of it to run the dory outboards, arguably the most important productivity tool in his arsenal. The dory engines, especially the 9.8 horsepower Johnsons, sucked gas like air. "I'm afraid [that] we will be short of gas this year," he wrote Anacortes. "Thos[e] 10 Horse Power engine Sure is heavy on the gas."[6] Haugen had to buy hundreds of gallons of gas from another vessel in the fleet to keep his dories running.

Other than the dory engines, Haugen needed the windlass engine and the deck engine, but he could get by without the battery engine, even if it meant losing wireless communication. After all, he'd sailed without electricity and radio for half his career. The light globes were safer than the old kerosene lamps, but he saw them more as a luxury. Of the three areas with bulbs, the forecastle had lowest priority. He gave McInturf the job of policing the batteries so that he didn't waste precious gas charging them. Haugen's attitude set up McInturf for on-going conflicts with the fishermen and dress gang.

"Read the riot act to the crew in focastle [sic] about burning more lights than necessary," he wrote. "Either cut it out or no more press," meaning he wouldn't pass along radio news reports; he had a penchant for controlling people by withholding information.[7] But the crew ignored him. Later in the trip, in a bad mood because of "shoulders, hands and arms sore as boils" due to raising cod from 30 fathoms, he accused the forecastle of burning "every light in the place all day long." He unscrewed some of the dozen light bulbs, stashed them in his room, and cut the wiring to the forecastle. "So the gang spent about an hour running from the engine room to the top of the ladder trying to get lights, they tried every switch in the place, then after they had thrown one they would run to the top of the ladder and see what kind of luck they had had."

The fishermen sent a delegate negotiate with McInturf for lights, and McInturf issued another warning to the forecastle about draining the batteries. "One of them spoke up and said that I was apt to lose some friends that way and after I had explained that the dam batteries cant be run on friendship we got along pretty good." McInturf thought it would blow over. "This isn't the first time I have jumped them and I notice my bait bucket is always full of halibut or flounder that they give me."[8]

Old forecastle habits reasserted themselves. This time, McInturf removed globes from individual bunks and elsewhere in the forecastle, prompting Alex Gress, a header, to complain to the Old Man. According to McInturf, Gress "was told that if they didn't cut out the monkey business, all the bunk lights would be jerked out. Alec [sic] and Parker got hot and we had words during which time I told either one of them to step out on deck, they wouldn't so I told them to shut up or I would clean them or at least try right in the forecastle…So that puts me in the dog house with the forecastle."[9]

The dress gang, unmoved, continued to burn power, and McInturf removed two shaving lights. "The Old Man won't give them any more globes either," McInturf wrote. "I have orders to turn them out all together if they get tough about it…. The lights are serious, for if the batteries are allowed to sulphate, I'll never get them up again."[10] Besides conserving gas, McInturf was trying to prevent a problem inherent in lead acid batteries. Lead plates or grids and sulphuric acid in these devices convert electrical energy into chemical energy and back again. If all the energy is discharged, leaving a dead battery, lead sulphate builds up on the plates, and the battery can't be recharged. In other words, McInturf tried to keep most of the lights *on* by getting the fishermen and dress gang to keep some of them *off*. He said they couldn't see his side of the dilemma. But he could've used lessons in tact.

"Dress gang still sore as boils over the lights and they burn all they can all the time now, wont speak [to me]," he wrote,[11] pouting in the engine room by himself. "Dress gang acting like a bunch of little boys, they sweep past, wont speak, do everything they do in 'high dudgeon,' whatever that is." McInturf contemplates retaliation by refusing to relay the radio reports of the Louis-Schmeling fight to the crew. "The Old Man told me today to go ahead and tear out the bunk lights, but am holding off for a while, give em some more rope."[12]

Later: "I peered into the forecastle this afternoon and it looked like Times Square as far as lights were concerned, if I cant get em over it by letting it wear off I have another idea, I'll run the gas engine as long or longer but cut down the charging rate to almost nothing the let the lights go out entirely and then the Old Man will probably charge foward [sic] like an angry god, he hates the bunk lights anyway and I talked him into letting them stay in the first place, and so it goes."[13]

McInturf made good on his threat to withhold news of the outside world, including news of the arrival of the cutter *Cyane* and her precious load of mail. "The fishermen and the dress gang are at loggerheads, too, so we go around and around," he added. But the gods of electricity exacted a price on Mac: the battery engine broke down again with cascading consequences. "I charged forward, found the engine froze, the generator froze, and the charging panel burned out," he wrote. "I had a good notion to break out bawling, but didn't. Took all day to fix it." But the arrival of mail and the excitement over the Louis-Schmeling match raised everyone's spirits: "Friendly relations are once more established," he wrote at the end of episode.

*   *   *   *

Judging by his journal, McInturf generally got along with almost everyone in the crew, despite the spats over lights. He was a generous man who would give you lunch if you were down on your luck. A featherweight boxer with powerful forearms, he had a strong sense of duty, but he was also picky and prickly. "Never trust anybody that doesn't look you straight in the eye," he said.[14] He was reluctant to accept help from others, though some of his pride eased as the trip progressed.[15]

McInturf fancied himself a cook (He liked to make Welsh rarebit at home.[16]), and he ingratiated himself to Jean Bagger by doing little favors, such as soldering holes in water pots and repairing kitchen tools. Bagger wouldn't always reciprocate in the proper way, as far as the radio operator was concerned. One day, he sharpened a knife for the cook, grinding the blade back and giving it a keen edge. Bagger reciprocated poorly in Mac's eyes. "He says it cuts like a razor...and Jean gave me my reward for the knife, a cream puff...He thought I would be tickled to death," McInturf wrote sarcastically.[17]

Bagger never earned McInturf's respect; the radio operator judged Bagger's table with a thumbs down. "Grub getting kind of lousy," he wrote. "Bread pudding, gravy is haywire, too much fish, get it for all three meals and not many vegetables."[18] Later on: "Meat not so good and not many vegetables, lots of fish and salt horse, beans and spuds and canned fruit...16 to 1 milk...I get a kick out of the cold hot cakes on the mug up table, the hot cakes that are left over from breakfast go there and how the fishermen go for em, make sandwiches out of em and just eat em with butter, and cold, too." [19]

"Boy, am I hungry for a lot of things," McInturf pined. "Steak, S T E A K, steak grilled on a quick fire and with plenty of fat and tomatoes and lettuce and onions, anything green and it wouldn't even have to have any dressing either. Fresh eggs, vegetables of any kind, raw or cooked and I could eat beef fat almost raw. And before it, I'd like a nice 'Old Fashioned' with a slice of orange floating around on top."[20]

As the trip wore on, Bagger became irritated with McInturf, and on July 7, the radio operator crossed the line after the *Wawona* Brewing Society finished off Mac's keg of wine. In the galley, late at night, someone suggested eggs and toast. One of the fishermen sliced three loaves of bread and put them in the oven, while another toasted his bread on top of the stove. After scrambled eggs, toast, jelly, and fresh coffee, the Society members hit their bunks. They forgot about the toast in the oven.

The next morning, after suffering again from the wine's "laxative propensities," McInturf and the others filed into the galley. By virtue of his proximity to the officers in the main cabin, Bagger and the forecastle considered McInturf a nominal leader in the hierarchical world of *Wawona*. "When we were all seated, Jean the cook came up to the table with a platter of burned toast, the toast wasn't half as burned as Jean, of course. Being the radio operator I came in for most of the blame, not by name, but most of his remarks were directed at me and he made plenty too so he had his say and we guilty ones thought ours and that was that." The flap ended a couple of days later when Bagger gave McInturf an orange.

Two unidentified fishermen on one of Wawona's last voyages in the 1940s. (Dave Wright Collection)

*   *   *   *

As the sub-Arctic midsummer approached, the tone of McInturf's entries begins to show the strain of four months at sea. "No one aboard this ship can tell anything new anymore by now, so [life] all depends on ones state of mind how the trip goes." Days of rough weather didn't help his mood. "The rolling has been terrible, rails dipping under and decks awash all the time, or nights like those, when the seas are running high, wind is howling through thru the rigging and the clouds race against a leaden sky, I always feel sorry for the sea gulls out there, some sit on the water and ride 'er' out and others wheel around the vessel and they look sort of lonely somehow, I always think of them when I lay warm in bed."[21]

The battery engine conked out again. "If the engines had been overhauled before we left I wouldn't be having so much trouble with them and so if or when they do pip out all together I'll just figure 'to hell with them.'" The bellowing fog horn wears him down further. "It's parked on the cabin right over my room and by the seven virgins of Ballard if I don't run amuck before the day is out it'll be because I go up, and sit by the gas engines, where I cant hear the dam thing…The only thing I'd really like to do right now is tear this typewriter apart with my hands and then go up and pluck that gas engine cylinder from cylinder and chew on the pieces…"[22]

"This has been a very trying week for me," he wrote in mid-July. "Feuds have broken out all over the ship and I've been trying to stay in the middle. I've had one with Big Carl Pearson, a fisherman, because he steals my tools, he's just like a pack rat and because he ran to Jean the cook about our party in the galley and told on me and also with Van Arsdale, but everyone hates him like poison." Little requests chafe on Mac. "I cant walk ten feet on deck without hearing the same old thing, 'When's the cutter coming, Sparks.' My answer is always the same and it stops em, too[:] 'Next week at two o'clock.'" McInturf lists his friends as Orville Paxton, Alex Gress, Haugen, and the mates. He hangs out and plays cards with Paxton and Gress and they listen to music from Japan on the wireless. "I have my days and when I do, I stay aft in my room so as to not hurt anyone's feelings."

On July 24, Alex Gress and John Berg almost came to blows over a piece of equipment. "Things getting worse and worse, that is between each other and we all realize it too, the thing that makes it bad is that, Big Carl (Lard But[t]) Pearson, runs to Jean or the Old Man with everything that he hears as does Stockwell and a few others, but we have them spotted and so know what not to say, little petty things seem to affect them. Many of them have never been to sea and dont know how to live a monotonous life. I do."[23]

"Jean the cook is getting cranky," McInturf added. "He's sort of petty anyway." Perhaps tired of cleaning up after the crew's midnight mug-ups, Bagger decided to douse the galley fire before going to bed to discourage the partying. But Berger Jensen restarted the fire, sparking a set to between the mate and the cook. "[Jean] even told the captain he would have to do something about it, but he cant do much about it as the fishermen and the dress gang would refuse to work if they didn't get their coffee at nights." Bagger kept the fire going in the evening from then on.[24]

McInturf accuses Bagger of favoritism when he sees the cook give pie to Orvia Parker and Walter Stockwell, who flaunt (in McInturf's view) their good connection by eating the pie on deck in view of everyone. "Jean asked me to mend one of his pots today at noon, so I told it was too technical a job for me but that Parker or Stockwell might be able to fix him up ok, he answered 'What the hell's the matter with you, you always used to fix them for me', so I told him, 'Lay some pie on the line first, then I'll fix the pot, 'Oh, that's it,' he said, so I got two pieces of pineapple pie and then soldered a patch on the pot." McInturf was careful to protect his advantage with the cook. "I have all the solder, there is none aboard but mine, and a fine time these politicians would have trying to get any."[25]

The radio man's mood corroded further. On July 27, he lost his dory to another fisherman whose dory engine failed. "I'm salting down a barrel of cod, what for I don't know, never want to see a fish again after this trip." With ten days of fishing left, McInturf said, everyone is ready to go home. But not Haugen. He calculated more than double McInturf's wishful estimate of time until he signaled homeward bound.

✳   ✳   ✳   ✳

McInturf and his clique looked for any diversion, from changing the hiding place of a keg of rotgut to repairing the frequency control on the colicky radio. Nature sometimes broke the tedium. Juvenile and adult whales played around *Wawona*; killer whales were a sign of salmon. One day, shortly after noon, with a bright sun shining into smooth water on *Wawona*'s port side as she glided along, one of the crew looked over the portside rail and said, "There is a whale here." Another man farther aft said, "There is one here, too." They looked up and down the rail and remarked, "Gee, it is all the same one." A member of the dress gang thought of a way to measure its length. He asked one man to mark the rail at the whale's nose when he called out. Then he ran down the deck to the end of the whale's flukes. He yelled to the point man, marked his own place, and measured the distance with a tape, 105 feet, just twenty feet shorter than the deck length of *Wawona*.[26]

The night watchman woke McInturf early one morning to watch a young, six-foot sea lion sleeping on the starboard rail. The perch, about 18 inches wide and eight feet above the water, was a perfect resting spot. The men startled the animal awake and it jumped off, though it tried to retake its spot as the ship rolled toward it. "There were times when he was trying to jump back that his whole body would be out of the water," McInturf recorded.[27]

Occasionally, because of malice, spite, or boredom, the crew's curiosity about the natural world turned murderous. On the last day of July, with only a few fishermen out in dories, McInturf and two men got Haugen's permission to go on what the radio man called "The Great Sealing Expedition." They spotted what appeared to be a black log floating in the water off *Wawona*'s port bow, but when the object moved and showed flippers, they decided to investigate. Bringing his pistol, McInturf and the others rowed out in a dory within six feet of the "log," it raised up, rolled over and dived. It was a nine-foot fur seal bull, dark brown with light brown patches on "the prettiest head I've seen on an animal," a mane several inches long, and it was pissed off. The dory men gave chase. A fisherman launched a homemade harpoon at the seal and missed. "[The seal] would come up, shake his mane, rear half out of the water, and dive straight for the dory. Sure gave a thrill, especially when you thought of what would happen if he came up underneath." The trio chased the seal for two hours, and after failing to harpoon the animal, McInturf fired at him twice with his Colt, hitting him once. Although the seal was big enough to pose a danger, it did not threaten anyone at the time, so the "expedition" can only be described as gratuitous.

*   *   *   *

The first of August brought calm water and poor fishing. Haugen counted around 210,000 fish in his hold, 90,000 short of his goal. His fishermen caught 2,500 to 3,500 fish a day. At that rate, he'd need nearly a month to reach his goal of 300,000 fish. He had water and supplies, but would his men stand the strain?

"Pax hates Stockwell, Gress hates Mike, Jake hates Gress, and Parker hates everyone," Don McInturf wrote in his journal. "Each has his own little group of friends and they hate the other group and so it goes. They speak now and then, but don't ask each other for bait anymore, this'll last till we start home, I guess, when the tension will break."

McInturf fell into a contemplative mood. "The moon came up at eight o'clock and I believe that last night was one of the most beautiful I've ever seen, the sky dark blue, with lacy white clouds drifting across it and the moon full and bright, and its path across the sea like something out of a fairy book. I leaned over the rails for hours and watched it, wondered if Irene could see it." The words of a popular song played in his head as he thought of his wife: "Starry sky, gleaming high, won't you please keep her path aglow."[28]

The sun rose the next day, a Sunday, and it heated the air into something resembling a summer temperature. "The whole crew is topside, half of their clothes off as this is the first day this summer we had had a real chance for sun bath, so spent the day just lying around." Men from the dress gang dived from *Wawona*'s rigging into the pond-like water while McInturf took pictures. (The fishermen were out in the dories.) McInturf dipped into the engine room keg. "Its good wine, kind of dry, not much kick to it but it is refreshing, so we refreshed ourselves most of the afternoon."

McInturf also found pleasure in the little things. "Now tonight I had my first real bath in months, and Berger [Jensen] gave me a bar of Lux soap, all afternoon I've been looking forward to it, have been saving water for over a week, had it ditched in the engine room, so got a tub out of the galley, shut the door and boy oh boy, spent about an hour and then I broke out a suit of underwear that I haven't worn this trip so far and of course it was snow white and the contrast was astonishing. Everyone aboard had to comment on my underwear, haven't seen any white clothes for months, and then I put on a pair of white uniform pants that I had brought, and a white shirt and did I feel dressed up, and with my beard, looked something like the sequel to Jesus."[29]

McInturf's glory lasted only as long as a summer day in the Bering Sea. On August 4, his 32nd birthday, he noted two signs: a rising barometer, and floating backbones. The fishermen believed that when the backbones of newly cleaned cod floated, instead of sinking, bad weather was ahead.[30] But the forecasted storm never arrived, although the sun disappeared behind a veil of clouds and mist.

Perhaps the bones forecast a storm aboard *Wawona*. Other ships in the cod fleet were having trouble: fishermen were coming home to their mother ships almost empty handed. Two dories of men from *Azalea*, Robinson Fisheries' other vessel, visited *Wawona*. "[They] haven't struck fish yet so none of them feel too good. We ready to go home anytime now." *Azalea*'s bad luck spilled over into a "mutiny" there over the food. McInturf predicted another week of fishing.[31]

Bagger's galley fare declined further. "Fresh meat is no more. We have it on the table but it stinks so bad one can eat it."[32] Fish and oysters in a soup is the main meal, enhanced with potatoes and onions, topped off with cream pie. "God am I hungry for some food, food that tastes right, boy will I 'grocery up' when I get home…Never liked lemons plan before, now I love them, crave anything like that, cut a lemon in two and eat everything but the skin, will keep us from getting scurvy too." The typhoid epidemic in Ugashik meant no more stops for water. McInturf fell sick, ate little for days, but he recovered.

Haugen worked his way back to the Alaska Peninsula shore, as did the rest of the fleet, and he dropped his hook at Port Heiden to catch 2,278 fish. On August 14, he sent out the dories in the morning, caught 1,353 fish, then upped anchor at noon for Nelson's Lagoon.[33] McInturf said *Wawona* needed 15,000 more cod to make Haugen's goal, but a gale interfered. A jib carried away and water shipped over the forecastle and the rail. "As I write this, the wind just howls through the rigging…The spray just splashes against my window, one caved in the radio room window the other day. We're making close to ten knots under reefed sails." Haugen had one bit of comfort: *Wawona* was the highliner among the fleet.[34]

On August 15, Bagger woke up McInturf at 2:30 a.m. to carp about dim lights, and McInturf rolled out of bed resentfully, rain pouring down on the cabin roof, and the battery engine wouldn't start. The batteries didn't have enough juice for the coil to work properly. In a foul mood, he borrowed a small battery from his wireless and an hour later got the engine started. Bagger, in the galley next door, gave him no end of grief.

"We fought back and fourth [sic], and this isnt an exaggeration, I was kind of afraid to go into the galley for breakfast, so took a machinist hammer with me. He had said something about working me over with a cleaver and I had told him, 'Go ahead mister and try it and I'll beat your head off with a wrench.' Well, I took a seat at the back of the table and got an empty cup and kept it handy, he would come down and we had it out. I told him to go ahead and get the cleaver and a French knife too and he did. So I ducked under the table and came up at the head and a cup in each hand and he kept the cleaver at this side and so I had him bluffed so followed it up by taking the cleaver away and finishing breakfast. And afterwards I told him I'd kill him if he ever grabbed anything and failed to use it. Think I've got the Indian sign on him, and then at dinner he had a cream pie with moldy coconut in it and he knew it was lousy. Every time I'd take a bite, I'd look and make a face, threw most of it in the garbage can. He couldn't even talk he was so mad but he didn't make a pass at a knife or a cleaver, I've got a knife in my shirt and he knows it and so we get along just dandy."

"Everyone is getting jittery, close to the time we're going home, as I'm the smallest man on board, everyone picks on me, horse around, kids, anyone that's big wouldn't understand. Tonight, Gress started in, I usually let them go ahead cause they don't hurt me anyway. But tonight I slapped an armbar on him and brother did he hit the deck and did he stay there, they know they can get over but forget that I can get under em when I want to..."

"Paxton had to start in on deck too and I let him get his pet head lock, hold it and fool around, but when he let go I had a crotch and cradle and I put it on, so I told him 'Let's play around, you wanted to, you must have. You started in!' and after his head had been bumped and his legs stretched out of shape he was glad to 'quit playing.'"

"I wanna go home, and I wanna go now."

The feud between McInturf and Bagger frightens the rest of the crew; they wait until one or the other is out of the galley before entering. McInturf is desperate for relief from the tension. "Oh God, if you have one fair wind, a spare nor'easter, left over, please send it down in [the] Bering Sea and let us take the lutefisken down to the starving squareheads in Ballard..."[35]

The Good Lord answered his prayer the next day, Sunday, for a wind which would take them southwest toward Unimak Pass. "About three p.m., we felt several puffs...and so help me it was noreaster," he wrote. "Well, I was fishing at the time, and started hauling in both lines and Snow dashed forward and heaved up the anchor and I didn't stop to reel the lines but went after and started the engine and started for home. Snow stood in the bow, waving my blazer and yelling like a mad man, and I was yelling at every dory we could see. We both were acting like a couple of nuts, but man this was a 'fair' wind and we were 'homeward' bound."

McInturf doesn't say whether Haugen authorized Snow's call to the dories, which began returning to *Wawona*, but Haugen later asks the crew at dinner what they thought about going home. Haugen was still short of his catch goal, but he authorizes McInturf to start the anchor winch engine, and the fishermen take this as a sign they were heading for the Pass. "The fo'castle sounded like a girls dormitory, laughing and squealing and general hell-raising. Marino, Gress and I took three long pulls at the jug of wine apiece in celebration." McInturf went to bed "with a good stiff nor'easter blowing."[36]

God's grace was good for only one day. The wind hauled around to the southeast on the seventeenth, blowing gale force, taking out the flying jib,[37] driving *Wawona* in the wrong direction. The water was too deep for her to drop to anchor and at least hold position. Fishing was impossible. "So if this keeps up we'll raise the Pribloff [sic] Islands before so very long. Man, how the wind does blow, can hardly stand on deck and its awash all the time...If this isn't a mess, cant reef down and we're sailing norwest, by the four remaining virgins on King Street, and it's liable to blow this way for several days. Oh well, I have three cans of peaches in my bunk and a couple of gallons of sourdough wine."[38]

On Tuesday, August 18, the weather calmed down a bit and Haugen weighed the value of more fishing. But the fishermen were done. After breakfast, Haugen spoke with the officers. He "asked Berger, the mate, what we should do, fish some more or go home. Berger said to do what he thot [sic] best, well the Old Man thot [sic] it over for a while and said the hell with it, tear up the checkers and we'll start for home and so up they came." The crew worked all day to prepare *Wawona* for the trip home. The wireless transmitter had given up the ghost, but a cutter was close by, ready to deliver mail. With a blinker light, McInturf asked the cutter to relay a message to Robinson Fisheries in Anacortes. J.E. Trafton read it the next day.

SCHOONER WAWONA—DUTCH HARBOR ALASKA
0400 GCT AUG 19 1936
ROFICO
ANACORTES-WASH
ONEFOURFIVE ONESIXZERO HOMEWARD BOUND
HAUGAN [sic][39]

By prior agreement, Haugen sent Trafton a number half the size of his actual haul to confuse competitors. Haugen actually departed the fishing grounds with 290,320 cod in his hold. But he missed his goal by 9,680 fish. He noted the weight of his catch, 423 tons, in his log.[40] Although Haugen's feelings at that moment are unknown, McInturf was subdued. The wind was from the west, not the northeast. "Anyway, this is start."[41]

*   *   *   *

Now that *Wawona* was homeward bound, the wind again chose not to cooperate. She was becalmed the day after Haugen's decision. Or light winds barely pushed her along. She looked good, however: "Fishermen have all their engines cleaned up and stowed away now and the deck looks like a yacht." *Wawona* edged her way southwest and sighted Unimak Pass. Haugen crawled through the Pass for three days, finally reaching the Pacific on August 25.

Soon after *Wawona* entered the North Pacific, McInturf lost his pipe of ten years. "[I'd] rather lose my transmitter and all the gas engines." He spent the passage south tying knots, tending his gas engines, and listening "to the eternal pinochle game in the cabin…"[42] Just before *Wawona* reached Cape Flattery, McInturf gave up on Bagger. "I stole the cooks keys from the head of his bunk while he was asleep and we took a layer of eggs out of a case in his locker in galley. Pa[x]ton, Marino, Van, Snow, Pike and I had seventeen pieces of toast, made omlettes [sic], ham and onion and some plain, plenty of em too."[43]

When The Pass Beat Haugen and *Wawona*

On *Wawona*'s last cod trip, Haugen couldn't get through Unimak Pass without help. On August 25, 1947, he gave up an 11-day battle with wave upon wave of gales that churned powerful tides. He ran low on food and water as he tried to transit the pass, and he finally radioed for a tug. The Navy sent *ATA 196*, which found *Wawona* at anchor north of the pass, unable to move south. But once the tug let go *Wawona* after pulling her through the gap, she sped the 2,200 miles from the pass to Cape Flattery in only 11 days. [44]

Channel fever infected the radio man. "Everyone is getting jittery, nervous, cant eat, cranky. I'm terrible and I know it and cant help it, dam the ship, dam the gang aboard and [in] fact dam everything but land and home. I just feel mean." Then Big Carl Pearson got in his way. "Boy oh boy, I'd take about two weeks to kill him with a dull knife, everyone hates him." Pearson built a shelf in McInturf's engine room for his dory outboard motor, and in a fit of pique, McInturf threw the engine on deck, tore the shelf down, and heaved the shelf over the side. Pearson complained to Haugen, but the captain did nothing. "It was a mean trick, a narrow minded thing to do, but dammit I felt better afterwards," McInturf wrote. It's the last entry in his journal.[45]

On September 7, Haugen sent a message to Robinson Fisheries: "10 miles off Cape Flattery."[46] *Wawona* was home, a week short of five months since departure on April 15. Haugen also wired his wife Anne in Seattle, telling her, "Off Cape Flattery."[47] J.E. Trafton dispatched his tug, *Challenge*, and wired Haugen the next morning saying that the tug would reach *Wawona* that afternoon.[48] The tug brought supplies to *Wawona*, including fresh vegetables.[49] Trafton also wired Anne Haugen, telling her *Wawona* would soon be home.[50] He sent three more telegrams, including one to Mrs. D. McInturf, 7232 Seward Park Ave., Seattle, "Expect *Wawona* to arrive late Wednesday."[51]

Irene and Diane traveled to Anacortes to meet husband and father.[52] The *Anacortes American* published a brief story about *Wawona*'s pending homecoming. Loved ones waved at the fishermen as *Wawona* approached the dock.[53]

Meanwhile, in the Rofico office, the staff scrambled to open the safe and get money ready for the crew's $100 advances against catches, tons of dressed fish, or wages, in the case of the monthly men. They'd get their full wages a few days later, after *Wawona* was unloaded.

Wawona arrives in Anacortes after a cod fishing trip. Note the crew at the forepeak.
(Northwest Seaport)

As the dockworkers caught the mooring lines tossed by *Wawona*'s crew, a few cheers went up in a taciturn Scandinavian way. Men on the dock called to the fishermen as if they'd left only a few days before. The gangplank was set in place, and crew began to depart, duffels over their shoulders, hugging and kissing wives, girlfriends, and children. Later in the day, if former crewmen happened to meet on the street, they would shake hands as if they had not seen each other for months.[54] Perhaps the enthusiastic gesture was recognition of shared experience, or a silent request for forgiveness of shipboard slights, or an embrace for men who love one another, but cannot say it. It's a fair bet that McInturf picked up Diane in his strong arms, nuzzled her with his red beard, and kissed Irene's mouth with passion. He never sailed again.

✳   ✳   ✳   ✳

Once the fish were counted on shore, and the count checked against the onboard count, each of the fishermen and the dress gang received the balance of their wages. Haugen's four dollars a ton worked out to $1,696.39, corrected to 424.1 tons, although his check at the dock was less, because of deductions for telegrams, slop chest purchases, and draws against his wages by his wife Anne. Several women asked for advances against their men's wages while the men were at sea.

Berger Jensen, the first mate, was highliner. He caught 19,416 fish, worth $1,169.33. Ed Field earned the smallest amount, $180. Don McInturf, in addition to about $425 in wages, caught 2,007 fish, grossing $537.52.[55] Orvia Parker was highliner of the dress gang, catching 3,121 cod from *Wawona*'s rail, and when added to his pay for cleaning fish, he received a check for $286.71. Many fishermen would blow their pay in town within a week, sometimes less.[56] Because Bagger was a frugal man, *Wawona* came home with extra food stores. Robinson Fisheries sold the food to the fishermen at half the retail price, selling some enough butter, salami, flour, sugar, and other basics to last until the following fishing season.[57]

McInturf, like the men in the forecastle, was now unemployed. Shortly after *Wawona*'s arrival, Robinson Fisheries' hired him to skin codfish in preparation for packaging. He was paid 40 cents per hundred pounds. Some men could skin 1,000 pounds a day, which amounts to $4 for a day's work.[59]

McInturf grew tired of the work and quit. He found a job in the new industry of commercial aviation, helping pilots as an emergency radio operator for United Air Lines in Medicine Bow, Wyoming. He moved his family to Utah, then Nevada. In November, 1939, he caught a cold, which went into his lungs. He died on November 28, 1939 of acute pulmonary edema.[60] He was 35 years old.

Captain Thorsten Haugen took *Wawona* to the Bering Sea five more times before war broke out with Japan on December 7, 1941. The next year, the U.S. Army requisitioned *Wawona* for the war effort. The government cut down her masts and her bowsprit, renamed her *BCS-710*,[61] and loaded her with lumber for Boeing Company warplanes. She also carried supplies to Army bases in the Aleutians, where she was attacked by the Japanese. An Imperial Japanese warplane drop two bombs near the barge as she was anchored at Attu Island. Both bombs missed.[62]

Cod Processing on Shore

Women prepare salt cod for packaging, removing small bones with tweezers.
(Photo courtesy Ed Shields Collection)

Shortly after *Wawona* was tied up, a work gang of two dozen or so men, including some of the newly arrived fishermen, began unloading *Wawona*. Workers swung a boom with a hanging cargo net over *Wawona's* hatch and lowered it inside. Men pughed salted cod into the sling, and the boom lifted the sling onto the dock. The fish were washed of excess salt, sorted into small, medium and large piles, and dumped into large troughs of 100 percent brine solution, where they stayed for as long as a year. Unloading took ten days to two weeks. In the summer, as preparation for the final steps in the process, the cod fillets were laid on "flakes," long outdoor tables with slats spaced about one inch apart, where they dried. In the winter months, the fish were dried in a dryer, a room with steam coils and a rotating fan.

Now that the fish were on shore, women took on the tasks of preparing the cod for market. First, a male worker tore off the skins and tore out belly cavity tissue, saving the waste for rendering into glue. He also trimmed off bones left by the dress gang. Then a female worker carefully pulled out each of the fish's small bones with a pair of pliers or tweezers. This allowed salt cod producers to label the fish as "boneless." A motion picture of the work shows a mature woman peering closely at the fillet while she picked out small bones and cartilage. A photograph of a processing plant interior shows three women in a large room working on fillets with only bare light bulbs above them. Tiny bones and bits of skin are scattered on the floor around their wooden chairs. After picking out the bones, other women removed blemishes and dead parasites. As they worked, the women would share community news and just plain gossip.

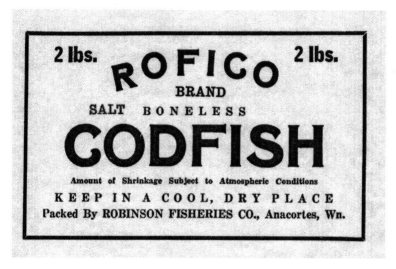

A tissue wrapper for salt cod packed by Robinson Fisheries. (Northwest Seaport)

Women and men worked together on the final packaging. Whole cod fillets were stacked and trimmed by large knives into one or two pound blocks. A female worker wrapped the rectangular blocks in parchment paper and inserted the block into a cardboard carton. Another woman wrapped the carton in cellophane before putting several cartons into a corrugated box for shipment to grocery wholesalers. Most of the women workers were single and childless, or their children were old enough to allow mothers to work part-time. One of the largest employers in the area, the cod processing plant in Poulsbo employed 40 workers at its peak and 10 to 12 all year. Some of the year-round workers were women. A circa 1930 photograph of the plant crew shows 31 individuals. Seventeen are women. One of the women is Asian. Three of the men are Asian. Poulsbo is located near Bainbridge Island, which had a large Japanese community.[58]

Robinson Fisheries re-acquired *Wawona* in 1945, refitted her with new masts and bowsprit, and installed a small refrigeration unit under the main cabin. But Haugen, once again in command, filled her hold with only 228 tons of cod in 1946[63] and 168 tons in 1947.[64] No one could explain the poor catches, but Robinson Fisheries would not send her north again. Haugen went on to master diesel-powered halibut vessels. He died in July, 1980, aged 93. "He never made a lot of money, but he loved his job, and he loved that old schooner," his widow Anne said. She scattered his ashes near Cape Flattery, where *Wawona* would begin her journeys north.[65]

In the fall of 1947, very near the 50th anniversary of her launch in Humboldt Bay, California, after sailing hundreds of thousands of miles from the Bering Sea to the Fiji Islands under five captains and perhaps a hundred sailors, Robinson Fisheries laid up *Wawona* in Lake Union, where she idled with other obsolete windjammers. The last sailing ship to fish for cod in the Bering Sea was the *C.A. Thayer*, which made its run in 1950. Shortly after, the salt cod business on the west coast died.[66]

But fishermen and their families kept the memory of *Wawona* and the cod fleet alive. "Looking back from the end of my working life at all of the things I have done, and if I could go back and pick an hour from any of the things I did when working," fish dresser and fisherman Orvia Parker wrote, "I would take an hour at the wheel of *Wawona* when there was plenty of wind and the sea is pretty rough. It is a thrill that is different than anything else."[67] Though *Wawona*'s working days were over, her story was not.

CHAPTER 8

▼

SAVING THE BIG SHIP

Thursday, July 25, 1963
City Hall, Seattle

At 5:30 p.m. on a Thursday during Seattle's six-week summer, a group of eight men and women, including a novelist, a newspaper writer, a magazine publisher, and a socialite, most in their thirties and forties, listened to Seattle City Councilman Wing Luke. They gathered in Luke's modest City Hall office on Fourth Avenue, a mile or so from *Wawona*'s berth in Lake Union, to talk about a dream for a maritime museum.

A half-mile from *Wawona*, the Space Needle, barely a year old, towered over the ageing piers and sagging warehouses of the central waterfront. The graceful 600-foot structure, looking like a flying saucer on three white bandy legs, symbolized Seattle's new vision of itself as a forward-thinking, high-tech metropolis, ready to take on the challenges of the Space Age. The successful and profitable 1962 World's Fair, dubbed the Century 21 Exposition, for which the Space Needle was built, lifted the city out of a post-World War II dullness and it infused the half-million residents with an almost prideful optimism. It was their coming out party.

Flush with a can-do attitude, Luke and the eight people in his office chatted about ways to resolve a persistent and annoying problem, the slow dribbling away of the city's maritime past. The dwindling inventory included the last working codfish schooner, the *C.A. Thayer*, which left Puget Sound in 1957 for the San Francisco National Maritime Historical Park, the *Wapama*, a steam schooner that also wound up in the Bay Area, and the *Falls of Clyde*, an 1878 square-rigger.[1] The losses pricked at Seattle's deep-seated insecurity about its relationship to the glamorous megalopolises to the south. The group in Luke's office knew that people outside Washington State eyed *Wawona*, the Northwest's last floating maritime relic in good condition, as the next target. [2]

Sensing a good issue, Luke dusted off an old proposal for a Seattle maritime museum and put *Wawona* at its center. He went before the city parks board and suggested that an old natural gas plant on the north end of Lake Union, which the city was about to take over, would be a good site.[3] Meanwhile, the *Seattle Times* took phone calls and published letters from readers supporting the proposal. But his idea failed to catch fire with the Seattle Parks Department, especially after Luke said bringing the *Wawona* to the park would cost around $100,000. Luke argued that other cities, namely San Francisco, were benefiting from the ships as tourist attractions. City officials were unmoved, but Luke did not give up easily.[4]

Luke, though popular, had little pull in city government. Born Wing Chong Luke on February 25, 1925 in Guangzhou, China, he emigrated with his parents to America at age six. During World War II, Luke's fellow high school students elected him to student body president, and the White House invited him to a conference on juvenile crime. Joining the Army in 1944, he came home with six combat stars. He earned a law degree from the University of Washington and litigated civil rights cases as an assistant state attorney general. In 1962, leading a group of 1,000 young volunteers, and flashing his trademark smile under large eyeglasses, he earned a seat on the city council with an overwhelming majority, despite accusations of Communist sympathies.[5] Described as a modest man with good leadership qualities, Luke was a rising star at age 38, and he took *Wawona*'s cause to heart.

Everyone in the July meeting waited for Luke to explain his next move. John Ross contributed his views, though he was a newcomer to the city and a stranger to most of the group. A Boston native, Ross was a 38-year-old Harvard-trained teacher and lawyer. He'd served in the Navy during the war, and he loved to sail.[6] He was tall, balding, with a narrow jaw, an easy manner, and a touch of the disciplinarian. He'd recently arrived on Puget Sound on a cruising ketch, and he called up friends on Mercer Island, a wealthy neighborhood east of Seattle. He had recently broken up with his wife, and he did not have a full-time job.[7] The friends introduced him to local historians and sailors who told him stories about

H.D. Bendixsen, Matt Peasley, Charles Foss, and Tom Haugen. They also introduced him to Wing Luke. Ross visited *Wawona*, and he paced her deck.[8]

Luke announced to the others in his office that it was time to buy *Wawona*, and make her the centerpiece of a Pacific Northwest maritime museum. Ross leaned forward in his chair, and Luke looked at him. "I think you might be the man to do it," Luke said to the New Englander. "I indicated I would help," Ross wrote years later, and Luke asked him to join the leadership of the group, called Save Our Ships. Luke's brand of quiet charisma had touched Ross, who was inspired by the task. "I was a thousand miles offshore," he wrote in an unpublished memoir, "seeing, in the mind's eye, the curve of mains'l against an azure sky, feeling the gentle reaching breeze on the cheek, the friendly pressure of a wheelspoke on the palm."

*   *   *   *

One of the women in the SOS group, Anne Wagner, a Coast Guard captain's daughter whom Ross described as "attractive and thirtyish," volunteered to drive to Montana and track down *Wawona*'s owner, William P. Studdert, a crusty ex-fisherman, cattle rancher, and experienced businessman in his sixties who hung out with movie stars and cultivated Hollywood connections. "The word was...that Mr. Studdert loved his old ship and would sooner see her fall apart where she lay on Lake Union than be ignominiously misused by the impractical do-gooders who knocked on his door."[9]

Cruises and Cattlemen

William Studdert bought *Wawona* in 1953 for $10,000 from Capt. Ralph Pederson, a would-be cruise operator, who had purchased the laid up ship from Robinson Fisheries. Pederson painted the hull white and the forecastle pink ("shocking pink" in some accounts), and he advertised $950 excursions to the South Seas. The project died when the Coast Guard ordered thousands of dollars worth of safety and communications equipment installed, which never happened. Studdert reportedly planned to refit *Wawona* as a cargo vessel for carrying 5,000 Hereford cattle to Russia's Kamchatka Peninsula. Press reports said Studdert was in negotiations with the Russian

---

government and the State Department, but other rumors said *Wawona* would be a floating base for Aleutian Island hunters and fishermen. Whatever Studdert's plans, they fell through, because *Wawona* never left Lake Union. John Ross suspected the whole scheme was a "tax dodge."[10]

With Luke's blessing and a gift of beer, Ross got into Wagner's car, gassed it up, crossed the Cascade Mountains at Snoqualmie Pass, dipped down into the scrub desert of eastern Washington, crossed the Idaho border, climbed up the western slope of the Rocky Mountains, traversed the Great Divide, and wound their way through the dry valleys and wet mining towns of western Montana. The drive lasted all-day, all-night, and part of the next-morning. "I remember little of the drive for I was exhausted and it was hot," Ross wrote. They passed through the gate of Studdert's T-Bar-Three ranch, approached the clapboard house, and inquired after the owner. He was gone, but he might be in Anaconda, said the cook. "Truly this had all the earmarks of a fine lark," Ross said. They found Studdert's Anaconda home, but he wasn't there either. The travelers decided to take rooms at the historic Marcus Daly Hotel, which local preservationists had saved from demolition.[11] The stack of Anaconda Copper Mining Company's smelter puffed dun-colored smoke into the summer heat.[12]

Studdert heard Ross and Wagner were looking for him. He called the hotel and asked the visitors to meet him in the bar. Ross described Studdert as tall, craggy and courtly, like "the colonel in Owen Wister's *Virginian*."[13] Studdert told them he wasn't sure he wanted to sell *Wawona*. For one thing, his friend Gary Cooper the actor might want to sail her or maybe use her in a movie.[14] If that's so, Studdert said, I can't sell her. "He assured us he was interested in our idea," Ross wrote. "But that was as far as he would go."[15]

Disappointed with the visit, but impressed with Studdert, Ross and Wagner started west for Seattle. But they noted that the rancher had not refused to deal. Twenty-three miles from the Idaho border, Ross talked Wagner into returning to Anaconda for a second try. Wagner dropped Ross off in Missoula and returned to Seattle, while Ross hopped a bus for a room at the Marcus Daly. Back in town, "I talked to anyone who would listen to my tale about trying to acquire *Wawona* for Seattle," he said. "I could sense curiosity about what I was doing just hanging around Anaconda." The easterner from west of the Rockies stuck out like a sore thumb, but Ross kept up his politicking, and people began to see his point: Studdert didn't need the ship; SOS did, so why not sell it to them?

Studdert discovered that friends in Hollywood might buy the vessel. But he confided to Ross that it might be just talk. "Bullshit and whiskey," Studdert called it. He added that preservationists in Portland had expressed interest in the ship. Studdert said he would have to pursue the Hollywood interest further. The two parted. As Ross read it, Studdert had again left the door open to a sale.[16]

Ross decided to "investigate the Hollywood scene" for himself. He returned to Seattle, and drove his bug-eyed Austin-Healey Sprite sports car, called "Snug," to the Bay Area.[17] Ross was directed to actor Sterling Hayden in Sausalito, who greeted his visitor in a full beard with manuscript in hand.[18] Hayden said he once had an option to buy *Wawona*, but he would offer support to Ross with a letter to Studdert.[19]

Then Ross made a connection to Deane F. Johnson, a partner in the tony Beverly Hills law firm of O'Melveny and Myers. The Cooper Estate had no claim on *Wawona*, Johnson said, and he "had talked with Jimmy Stewart, John Wayne, and others and neither they nor he were at all interested in using *Wawona* for a movie or for a South Seas cruise."[20] Johnson offered his own letter of support to Ross and SOS.

With California competitors out of the way, and learning that Portland had dropped out of the competition, Ross had to crack Studdert. He was optimistic as he drove Snug up U.S. Highway 101 along Oregon's wild coast. "I could almost see *Wawona* scudding through the mist as I squinted in the rain from Cape Foulweather," he wrote. Wing Luke wrote to Studdert telling about SOS's need to "continue our momentum" and asking for "prompt action."[21] Letters came in from museums on both coasts supporting the SOS cause. Ross remembered the lessons of the departures of *C.A. Thayer, Wapama,* and *Falls of Clyde*: "In the right place and in the right hands and done in the right way, *these craft have value.*"[22]

Back in Seattle Ross followed *Wawona*'s paper trail, and he discovered that the ship was the sole asset of a Studdert "shadow" corporation called the North American Trading Corporation of Seattle. Ross and Wagner, armed with $1,000 in cash,[23] a price ceiling of $20,000, and a plan to purchase all NATCS shares, left for Montana.[24]

*   *   *   *

Arriving in Anaconda, Ross handed the rancher a framed painting of *Wawona* as a goodwill gesture.[25] But Studdert put him off for a day, adding that he had one or two things to straighten out. "What could be the matter now?" Ross wrote. Studdert headed to Seattle, promising to return quickly. Ross waited in Montana, again talking up the potential sale to townspeople.

When Studdert returned to Anaconda a few days later, he announced he had a bid for *Wawona*, paired with the steamer *Sierra*, tied up next to *Wawona* in Lake Union. The bid was $35,000. Taken off guard, Ross offered Studdert $37,500 for both vessels, believing *Sierra* could be sold quickly. Studdert gave the other bidders a chance to counter.

A day turned into two, then three. Studdert, a gracious host, got Ross up at 3:30 a.m. for breakfast and a jeep ride across his ranch. "My bones were thoroughly shaken up," Ross wrote. "I don't know about my leathery companion." Studdert let out that his Seattle friends hadn't responded to Ross's bid. Ross and Studdert would also chat about the ship. "But the conversation would always return to the minutiae of pure-bred Hereford ranching: loading and unloading hay bales, repairing fences, caring for sick calves and cattle, carpentry, automotive repairs, etc."[26]

Ross's patience wore thin. He asked Studdert if the price were settled. Nope, it's now $40,000 for the two ships. That's the bid Studdert expected from his Seattle contacts. Unfazed, Ross asked, what if SOS offered $40,000? Studdert liked the idea, as long as SOS bought both vessels. Ross phoned Luke, and the SOS president authorized Ross to raise the SOS bid. Ross called Studdert's cards, and the rancher said he would sell the ship to the first person who put $40,000 into his hands. Then the prickly ex-fisherman said he didn't want to talk about the ships any more.[27]

At dawn the next day, Studdert arrived at the Marcus Daly in his Cadillac, offering Ross the wheel of the luxury car. He also handed Ross a sheet of paper, which the Bostonian ignored. Instead, Ross launched into a discussion of transaction details.

"The wrath of Job erupted," Ross recalled. "Vituperation assumed magnificent proportions and from his tirade I gathered that the trouble, time and fussing around—I put it mildly and without his artistic cussing—made him sick of the whole deal. It was off! Forget it! Let the damn ships rot where they lay."

Studdert took back his piece of paper and stuffed it in his pocket.

Hurt by Studdert's attack, Ross loosed his own invective for a minute or two: "It, too was moderately profane and also dealt with procrastination. I wound up by saying that I was tired of it all and I might as well go back to the hotel." Ross slowed to turn the Caddy, but Studdert grabbed the wheel and said, "Keep going." Ross kept going.

The two men rode in silence, though the anger was muted. "I sensed a new element in our relationship, something approaching mutual respect," Ross wrote.[28] Studdert turned to Ross and again handed him the sheet of paper. This time, Ross opened it. It was a fifteen-day option to buy the *Wawona* and *Sierra* for $40,000 "as is where is." The deal was done. In the Marcus Daly Hotel, Ross put an arm around Studdert's shoulder and told him, "You're a lovable old bastard," and Studdert beamed.[29]

With only fifteen days to act, SOS did not have time to raise money through a public campaign. Ross decided to "buy the blooming ships myself then worry about disposal and transfer later." Like an Old West card player, he gambled that Wing Luke and SOS could find the money to buy the boats from him. "'What the hell,' I thought, 'You don't often get a chance to do something really worthwhile in this old world.'" Ross made a few phone calls and raised the money, probably through personal loans, though the sources are unclear. On November 12, after five months of "heartache, worry, and exhilaration," Ross handed Studdert a check and shook the old man's hand.[30]

∗　　　∗　　　∗　　　∗

Wawona was in the hands of a preservationist, but she was not yet saved for Seattle. As 1963 turned into 1964, SOS[31] faced the awkward tasks of raising money to buy something Ross owned, *Wawona*, while the Bostonian was on the SOS payroll as executive director.[32] SOS was open about the arrangement. It told the media that despite offers from others, Ross wanted to sell *Wawona* to SOS, if the community could come up with the money "within a reasonable length of time."[33]

The media became the project's biggest booster. A radio station called for donations.[34] Both dailies, most of the neighborhood-based weekly newspapers, a few papers outside Seattle, and *Marine Digest*, a maritime trade magazine, printed articles about the announcement. Wing Luke had his picture taken aboard *Wawona* and published. The *Seattle Post-Intelligencer* editorialized for the project, and they sent a reporter to interview a retired Tom Haugen. "It would be wonderful," he said of the restoration plan. "That's what they should do with her. She's the last of her kind."[35] A former *Wawona* fisherman wrote a letter to the editor complaining about his treatment by Capt. Charles Foss, but he donated $10.[36]

While the public relations campaign kept the SOS effort in the public eye, the organization faltered behind the scenes. Friends with influence in Seattle's elite seemed few. SOS gaffed when it published a long list of key establishment people as members of a finance committee without asking their permission. Even the local maritime heritage community was divided over whether *Wawona* should be saved. Wing Luke and John Ross asked for the blessing of Horace McCurdy, a fixture in Seattle's maritime industry, a supporter of the Puget Sound Maritime Historical Society, and a board member of Seattle's leading museum, the Museum of History and Industry. "No, it's a sink hole," he said. "Just a way to throw your money away."[37]

Tensions appeared in SOS. Ross tried to resign in early 1964, though the reason is unclear.[38] The SOS board refused Ross's resignation, extending him "a complete vote of confidence." Later in the year, probably at the request of Ross, who had a $40,000 debt over his head, the board voted to give the executive director a down payment for *Wawona* of $1,000. It also gave itself a deadline of June 16, 1964 to exercise an option to buy the vessel for $28,500.[39]

In April, Ross again handed in a resignation letter, and this time the board accepted, but it rehired him as "interim consultant" until the option to buy *Wawona* expired. The attempts to resign suggest a conflict of interest question may have been raised because of Ross's positions as executive director and a member of the board and his ownership of *Wawona*, which SOS was trying to buy from him. No one directly accused Ross of a conflict, and there's no indication in the minutes, other documents, or press reports of anything underhanded. But it may have looked odd to outside observers.

Pressure mounted on SOS. *The Seattle Times* reported that "interested parties in California" would buy *Wawona* if SOS did not come up with the money.[40] One story said the parties were in San Pedro, California, adding that SOS had raised so little cash, that it "doesn't want to talk about it."[41] In late May, Wing Luke dressed up as an 1890s-style waiter at a fundraising event. Attendees paid a dollar to hear Luke and other city council members sing for *Wawona*. The event raised $622.[42]

Two weeks before the deadline, SOS was short $23,000, and no one was willing to lead the fundraising effort.[43] There was some good news: A dry dock survey found no problems below *Wawona*'s waterline. Her "better-than-expected condition" meant that estimated restoration costs fell from $100,000 to $75,000. However, the ship needed new masts and rigging. The board also released program plans for *Wawona*, which would be "historical and educational in nature."[44]

With six days to go, one of Seattle's most prominent citizens spoke his mind. Ivar Haglund, a restaurateur who hyped his seafood joints with octopus wrestling, folk singing, and slogans such as "Keep Clam," held a "rump caucus" at his

Ivar's Acres of Clams on the central waterfront's Pier 54. A master self-promoter, he released a statement in eccentric, fractured language that proclaimed his support for the SOS effort. He urged "gifts, donations, pledges, admissions (to the vessel), [and] affairs sponsored by those who love the '*Wawona*' for what it really means," referring to the schooner as a symbol of Seattle's status as a great port city. He also suggested mooring the vessel next to his restaurant.

On June 16, the deadline, SOS had $6,695.16 in its purchase account, plus an extra $213.00 in contributions that day. Subtracting its $1,000 down payment to Ross and the contributions, SOS was $20,591.84 short.[45] Haglund proposed a solution. He would loan SOS $10,000 without interest or term, provided *Wawona* was berthed at Pier 54. A board member then reported another loan of $11,000 by an anonymous donor, "given because of the wide support of the project by the community and the extensive participation by children."[46] At the last moment, community leaders had come through, and *Wawona* was saved for Seattle.

✳   ✳   ✳   ✳

Wawona was riding high on a sea of publicity, visitors swarmed the ship, now docked at Pier 54 on the central waterfront, and volunteers donated thousands of hours. But SOS was losing money, spending little time on raising the $75,000 needed for restoration, and it owed John Ross back pay. He stuck it out from the summer of 1964 through the spring of 1965, when the board received terrible news. On May 16, Wing Luke was killed in a plane crash. The pioneering politician, the first Asian-American to hold an elected position in a large city, often mentioned as a potential mayor of Seattle or congressman, died when his small plane went down in the Cascade Mountains. He was 40 years old. Luke inspired the initial efforts to save *Wawona*, pushed them forward, and when he died, the spirit nearly left Save Our Ships. The organization never found a leader to match him. "If he hadn't died," *Wawona* supporter Kay Bullitt said, "I think we could've made it."

The next month, SOS lost its other leader, John Ross.[47] He left for good, citing the failure of SOS to pay his salary, "and the fact that the decisions made by the board had not always been binding." A short time later, Ross took a job at Mystic Seaport running a maritime training program and a sailing program for children. He also taught people how to build furniture. He never led another not-for-profit group.[48]

After Wing Luke's death and John Ross's departure, SOS drifted, hoping to find meaning for itself and set goals beyond a vague target of "restoring the Old Girl."[49] In 1970, *Wawona* was named to the National Register of Historic Places, the first ship so designated.[50] But restoration work on *Wawona* crawled. New masts were finally installed in 1972.[51] SOS changed its name to Northwest Seaport and hired a new curator, letting her go a few years later when the organization ran out of money.[52] Cared for by a few hard-core volunteers, *Wawona* was losing a battle with time.

*   *   *   *

On December 2, 2004, 57 years after *Wawona*'s last working voyage, a cod fisherman boarded the ship at South Lake Union Park in Seattle. Dave Wright stepped onto the aluminum gangplank, his bent hands grasping the tubular railing as he steadied himself on the incline. At the beginning of three seasons in the early 1940s, the 85-year-old man had mounted a wooden ramp to fish from a dory in the Bering Sea. On this day, a television crew videotaped him remembering old times.

Once on board, Wright crept down the steep companionway from the poop deck into the main cabin, where Haugen, Foss, and Peasley once wrote their reports to their owners. Each piece of millwork inside the cabin reflected the care of H.D. Bendixsen's joiner crew. Gray light from the cabin skylight illuminated the green floor paint and brown paneling. Passing by the radio room occupied by Don McInturf in 1936, Wright emerged onto the deck. He saw the rigging loose, plywood covering holes in the deck, the wood in the rail dissolving into brown, crumbly dust moist and matted from a rain, and paint lifting from the topside planking.

Then he saw memories: "That table wasn't here, it was over there. I think that tub was bigger. Yes. Did I tell you that story about Big Bill Woodruff? Well, Woodruff had saved a bottle of whiskey for a stormy day. We wouldn't go out in the dories in bad weather. When a stormy day came, he drank that whiskey. But he wasn't finished. He went into the galley and drank all the sourdough starter. It had alcohol, you see. But he wasn't done yet. No, sir. He found all the extracts, you know, the flavorings. Well, Bill drank all those up, the vanilla extract, the almond, everything. I ran into Bill and he put his arm around me and said I was a great guy and he loved me and his breath *stank* of almonds. To this day, I can't eat anything flavored with almonds."[53]

Wright told his story in a neighborhood around *Wawona's* Lake Union berth[54] that barely resembles the days when she was laid up for the winter. South Lake Union has changed from a grimy twentieth-century industrial hub to a revitalized twenty-first century center for the nascent business of biotechnology. Microsoft and dozens of spin-off companies now define the region's identity as powerfully as Boeing and maritime once did. Millions of new residents have no connection to the city's maritime past.

Seattle is a different city now, unimpressed by nostalgic appeals to an insecure civic culture that passed away with the construction of Interstate 5 and Interstate 90, the globalization of trade, the corporatization of ownership that diluted a sense of responsibility to local communities, the transformation of information into 1s and 0s that have no boundaries, and the drive to judge everything by its market value and ability to create wealth. Underneath the apathy and disinterest is *Wawona's* dirty little secret: She is irrelevant to the great majority of Seattleites. The challenge for her current owners and future supporters is to make her matter to the people who live in Seattle today.

Despite everything, *Wawona* remains. She *was* saved for Seattle, after all, and she still floats in Seattle, her home more than half her working life. That's the great accomplishment of Wing Luke and John Ross and *Wawona* supporters over the years. But other regions continue to best Seattle in the maritime heritage field: The *Falls of Clyde* is afloat and restored at the Hawaii Maritime Center in Honolulu; the *Wapama* is out of the water in Sausalito and out of danger of hull-destroying shipworms; the *C.A. Thayer* has undergone a $12 million restoration funded by the federal government. While *Wawona* is afloat, the cruel irony is that if she had left Seattle, she would very likely be in better shape than she is today. Seattle can catch up and surpass her competitors, and put *Wawona* at the center of a world-class maritime museum. But every day that passes makes the prospect more expensive and less likely. In 2006, her crumbling 1972 masts were removed, and the ship closed to visitors indefinitely for safety reasons.

For now, *Wawona* carries the memories of Dave Wright. He is one of the last people who remember her as she was, and when he thinks of the chance that she might be gone, he declares, "It's a crying shame." When he is gone, *Wawona's* last cargo will be stories told by others, and if she exits the stage, the stories will remain, in archives, photograph albums, and books, waiting for discovery.

Appendix A

▼

Saga of the *Wawona*

Jack N. Healey sailed aboard the *Wawona* on her first trip to the Bering Sea as a cod fishing boat in 1914. Forty-seven years later, he wrote a poem about the ship and his experience. He called the poem "Saga of the *Wawona*." He sent it to Captain Thorsten "Tom" Haugen in 1964, *Wawona*'s last master, along with a letter. "I was a young fellow [in 1914]," Healey wrote to Haugen, "big and husky and [I] had my nineteenth birthday in the Bering." Captain Charles Foss commanded the first voyage, and Healey remembered Foss "as a fine skipper who cared well for his ship and his crew." Foss would later hire Haugen as mate. Foss died at the *Wawona*'s wheel in 1935, leaving Haugen in charge.

Healey sailed only once on *Wawona*. He later worked as a railroader and a logger. In his retirement, he penned poetry for the local newspaper in Sedro Woolley, Washington. Healey had heard about efforts to preserve the *Wawona*, and he tried to get his poem published, but it's not clear if he succeeded. Healey died in 1966, and his family donated the poem to Northwest Seaport, *Wawona*'s current owner.

Saga of the *Wawona*
Jack N. Healey

I'll spin ye a tale of a ship that sailed far to the northern seas.

It's done every day, but that way. Just bear with me, if you please.

A story of a wooden ship with a crew of iron men.

A tale of old like you've been told and it won't be told again.

We are not a sea-farin' people? I beg to differ with you.

From Skagit County she sailed away, a white-winged ship of an earlier day,

With Sedro-Wolley men in her crew.

Ever hear of Pete Uphouse, first white child in Sedro born?

They gave him a couple of lots as a prize, he's long gone now, I fear,

But he walked that deck, a seaman by heck, haven't seen him in fifty year.

So we are a sea-farin' people, all set for great enterprise,

And the Skagit will be, it seems to me, proud of the way it lies.

From up where the glorious ramparts stand tall, there in the eastern sky,

Down to the mightiest waters of all, down where the gray gulls fly.

This is of increasing importance, increasing as each year rolls by,

That the Skagit runs free to roads of the sea, the roads that the great ships ply.

Now this is a story that's hard to plan, a right tough job for a writin' man,

To cut the corners on which to speak, to tell the half would take a week.

So I'll make a try, my word to apply, to the ship, the sea, and the ocean sky.

We sailed far out on the ocean blue, just like the poets say,

But I was on the ship a solid six months and that ocean was oftener black, or gray.

We didn't sail to the southern climes. The blue may hold true down there,

But we pointed her nose to the Bering ice floes,

If we pointed our own, we'd get 'em froze, quick, in that icy air.

We were heading north but the wind pushed south, and sailing ship were we,

So when we had left De Fuca's mouth, beyond Cape Flattery,

We had to drive west and south of west if we really wanted to "go".

We had to get out in the fast traffic lane, out where the trade winds blow.

When I said fast, that's what I meant, for a sailing ship, 'tis true,

Fourteen knots in a fresh fair breeze and when the wind in the riggin' hit High C, man, we fairly flew.

Over two thousand miles in seven days, we couldn't go straight like a plan.

But give the *Wawona* a bone in her teeth, she'd put many a steamer to shame.

Her name, the *Wawona* of Indian lore, a mystic Indian princess was she,

A name that in California will live, in the mighty *Wawona* redwood tree.

She was a princess, to that I'll lay, no stauncher ship ever breasted the sea.

Built in Eureka by master hands, with solid fir timbers in every knee.

That means every rib reinforced against storms, braced against endless attacks from the sea,

Was hewn from natural, curving fir forms, as master shipbuilders willed them to be.

Surely her builders "went for broke", that she, a princess would remain,

With only timbers of finest fir at every point of strain.

When she was launched and building had ceased, they dressed on her sails and sent her to sea.

They found they'd created a masterpiece of shipbuilders' art, and I quote a real authority.

Our Russian first mate was a sailor born. Every port in the world he had seen.

He'd sailed the world over, ten times round the Horn, and he called the *Wawona* a queen.

To point this up, though he never would boast, he'd sailed in the America's Cup of Lipton's time,

It still was a fact known all over the coast, and the America's Cup was the greatest, the sailing race of all time.

I was in his watch and lucky I found it to be. He seemed to take pleasure in having a try at making a sailor out of me.

He was a quiet, kindly man, no bucko mate was he.

He'd give me an order, then walk on by like he was about to forget,

But I knew darned well that on the sly, his eye was on me yet.

I learned that well the very first day when he said, "Take that bucket of sludge.

Go up and grease the main gaff jaws." My feet would hardly budge.

But I'd read a little of Maritime laws. I had to give it a try.

As I looked up at the swaying spars, or was it a swaying sky?

He just stood there, a solid man, with a twinkle in his eye.

Then he told me, most carefully, of every danger on the way.

How to go up and how to come down, how to live another day.

Well, I went up and greased those jaws, and I came down again.

But I'll bet my fingerprints on those steel lines of the *Wawona* will remain.

After the first time, it was fun, if chance came when the weather was fair,

I'd back up there on the run. Why, I half lived up there!

Often and often I'd grab a book, times when my watch was off,

And scoot up there to the swaying truck, my favorite perch aloft.

The wind in the riggin' seemed to strum under the swinging sky,

Music from Heaven or Mandalay, there, by my nest on high.

Then I'd look down upon the deck, 'twas ninety feet and more.

She seemed so narrow that the swaying masts must tip the whole works o'er.

The mate kept showing me little things a sailor man should know,

And soon I made a fair sailor's hand, all aloft and alow.

One of the things he patiently told and show most carefully

Was the artist's touch upon the wheel that guides a ship at sea.

A sailing vessel, of course I mean, dependent on the wind.

From every quarter comes that wind, and "Don't let her fall off to the lee."

He showed me the slightest touch, a quarter spoke starboard, then port again,

A ship like the *Wawona* would respond like a thoroughbred to the reign.

And then there were the sails to watch, the ripple and the flow.

"Get those things straight and sure as fate in any winds that blow,

I promise you that you'll drive her true, as an arrow from a bow."

Of all on board, when the great winds roared, across the raging sea,

Only a few were called to steer, and one of the few was me.

A truckload of books were sent along. I read 'em all, through and through.

They were filled with romance, adventure and song, then I must tell them all to the crew.

I suppose some could read, of that there's no doubt, but I learned there's much child in a man.

When I told 'em the first one, their eyes bugged out, they must hear every word, "Was he hero or lout?" I became the *Wawona's* Saga Man.

For we were forty, alone on the sea, for better than half a year,

And the government boats that were to call on us, three times all summer came near.

No power, no letters, no radio, no airplanes, no nothin' but sea and man.

The first world war was three months old before we ever knew it began.

Once in Dutch Harbor the very first week to pick up some water and oars.

Once more in midsummer to some wild rocky cape, to fill up with water once more.

For the rest, never close that fifty miles out, we cruised nigh from Nome to Japan.

We sailed for six months through fog and through storm without setting foot on land.

Many have seen this land and this sea with machines of the second world war,

But they'll never know how it was long ago, with the few who had been there before.

That cape where we went for water, it was four hundred miles from anywhere,

But littered with tracks, they were two feet long, and figgered a Sedro-Woolley logger must be shacked up around there,

But after scoutin' around we found, they were tracks of the big brown bear.

Sure we did some fishin', caught a whole shipload, packed 'em in tight as a board.

At last we came home with over five hundred tons, our wages a scanty reward.

At three in the mornin', over the side, in twelve hours our day'd just begun.

Twenty-five dories out with the tide, for our hearts they were young and our shoulders wide, under the Midnight Sun.

Twenty-five dories, one man in each, out from one to ten miles,

And if you were forced to land on the beach, you'd find only one—the "Beach of the Paradise Isles".

We'd throw out a handline with a ten-pound lead, it averaged forty fathoms there.

We'd pull up a cod and clobber his head, most times we pulled up a pair.

We'd haul out his gizzard and put him to bed in three hundred tons of salt.

Yep, salted him down from his tail to his head, if he "spiled", it wasn't our fault.

But they didn't spoil, they kept just fine, each mornin' we'd pump out the brine.

To associate the *Wawona* with fish still makes me feel wan and pale,

But steam had at last come on to displace those beautiful ships of sail.

There's a light that lies in those northern skies, the Aurora with banners unfurled,

And the stars and volcanoes that glow in the night make a sight that is out of this world.

But August has gone and our holds they are full, and we long from the lights of home.

But we are heavy and low at the waist, before we can see them we're sure gonna taste an awful lot of Pacific foam.

So, like the voyage, I must begin to close this story, tho the Lord only knows it's not half here.

So much can happen at sea, all in a full half year.

I could tell of the German cruisers that lay off the cape, ready to clobber all who couldn't escape

Till the ships of his British Majesty trailed 'em south o'er the surging sea,

Caught up with 'em down where the Falklands lie and sunned their bottoms to the sky.

Of how we were caught in a dead flat calm, right in the traffic lanes, dice in God's palm.

Of the might freighter that through the murky night, came like a ghost, full speed, never showing a light.

For this was war. Of shouts and yells, clangin' of bells, prayer and curse, as the great engines went into reverse.

Close? Well, let me relate, as she slid by, we could spit on each plate.

Then a wind came up, we were on our way back to old Anacortes Bay.

She seemed to smell "Home", she flew like a gull, with a bone in her teeth and spray on her hull.

With her wings spread wide to the racing tide, we have the home folk a shock.

Some came to meet us and though it's seldom done, we sailed her right up to the dock.

In Anacortes, the Skipper said, "We'll lay but a little while.

Then we'll wash her down and clear her away to seas where the flying fishes play and the beautiful "Wahine" smiles.

We'll load her with copra to make her pay in the Polynesian Isles."

But we were destined for the beach, our romantic plans all shot,

By some half-remembered Warlord who prated of "Me unt Gott."

Now let me tell, and I proved it well, as did millions who smelled that South Sea foam,

That smiles more fair than any there were waiting right here at home.

The best remembered thing of all, of those years so long ago,

Was to stand the midnight watch at the wheel, along on a peaceful sea,

While the ocean breathes low of things you should know and you get the feel that Heaven is real and Peace lies near to Thee.

At such a time there's a Heavenly chime in the breezes through the shrouds,

While the stars at the masthead brilliantly glow and nodding night winds softly blow and the sails look like silver clouds.

Ageless mystery walks over the sea, let one has the soul of a clod,

That sound on the water you silently hear gives a feeling of glory near, and the ripples are the footsteps of God.

I've often thought as the years go by, to have missed it I'd be loathe.

That the winds that sweep an ocean sky like those that speak in the mountains high,

Are cleanest, and that all should try to know a little of both.

So some men lived and some men died and the Bering claimed their bones.

Some never returned from their first dory ride, now they all sit yarning side by side, on the locker of "Davey Jones".

Of all the ships that ventured forth, some were ill-fated, others ill-run.

An Angel rode the *Wawona* north, and she brought back every one.

Brought back her cargo and her crew, unchallenged her cargo record runs.

For her speed and class, both still hold true, more than five hundred dead weight tons.

This was the *Wawona* fifty years ago, after those years and a million miles.

She was in Lake Union ready to go on a trip to romantic South Sea Isles.

Maybe she went and maybe she stayed, this ship with the Royal Indian name.

With the "Two-Spot"[1] she joins the "Big Parade". They had what it takes to play out the game.

---

1. The "Two-Spot" is a logging locomotive which sits in Sedro-Woolley' Harry Osborne Park. It was responsible for hauling out most of the logs in the nearby mountains in the 1930s and 40s.

APPENDIX B

▼

Wawona CREWING
HISTORY 1929-1941

Approximately 156 men shipped on *Wawona* from 1929 through 1941, according to records of Robinson Fisheries, *Wawona*'s owner in those years. The following table shows which crew member shipped during a particular year. The table is based on data compiled by Harriet DeLong for Northwest Seaport, *Wawona*'s current owner. Some men were listed by slightly different names in different years. The author has attempted to account for the duplicates. Records for 1932, 1933, and 1939 are lost.

Key: 1st = 1st Mate; C = Cook; Cn = Captain; DG = Dress Gang; F = Fisherman; Fl = Flunkey; R = Radioman; W = Watchman

Last	First	Position	1929	1930	1931	1934	1935	1936	1937	1938	1940	1941
Anderson	Bill	F			x	x	x	x	x			
Anderson	Frank	DG		x	x	x	x	x	x	x		
Anderson	Harry E.	DG										x
Arnhold	Harry	W								x		
Arthur	D.E.	F							x			
Bagger	Jean	C				x	x	x				
Balks	John	DG	x									
Benson	Peter	F										x
Berg	John	F				x	x	x		x	x	x
Blondin	Eugene	DG	x									
Brandin	Harry	DG										

Last	First	Position	1929	1930	1931	1934	1935	1936	1937	1938	1940	1941
Bridges	Fred	DG		x							x	
Caldwell	Lonzo	F							x	x		
Carlson	George	F									x	x
Collins	Horace	R			x							
Commons	Merle	DG								x		
Cook	Lewis	DG	x									
Coolin	Jack	F	x									
Cowdin	Roy	Fl			x							
Craig	A.	F							x			
DeJong	Irvin	DG	x									
DeMars	Ed	DG				x						
Eide	John	F		x	x	x	x	x	x	x	x	x
Ellingson	John	F		x	x	x						
Erick	Ed	F	x									
Felsted	Tom	F									x	x
Fickley	Earl	DG				x			x	x		
Field	Ed	DG						x			x	x
Field	Maurice	DG				x	x					
Field	Nick	F, 1st	x	x		x	x	x	x	x	x	x
Floren	John Tracy	DG								x		
Forgerg	Lars	DG				x						
Foss	Charles	Cn	x	x	x	x	x					
Fox	Mitchell	DG								x		x
Frost	Charles	DG	x									
Gilles	A.C.	F	x		x							
Gress	Alex F.	DG						x				
Gustafson	Oscar	F				x	x					
Haagenson	Anton	F	x									
Haagenson	Olaf	F	x			x	x	x	x	x	x	x
Haejn	Elmer	F					x	x				
Hamill	Alex	F						x				
Hamuel	A.	F				x	x		x	x		
Hamul	Alarick	F	x		x						x	x
Hansen	Fred	F	x									
Hanson	Chester	DG										x
Hanson	Harold E.	DG										x
Harry	Brandon	F							x			
Haugen	Tom	1st, Cn	x	x	x	x	x	x	x	x	x	x
Herron	George	DG			x							
Hogmire	Clifford	DG										x
Holeman	Clyde	DG			x							
Hollard	Cornelius	F							x			
Hornus	John	Fl		x								
Howard	Ed	DG								x	x	
Hughes	Gordon	DG							x			
Iverson	Martin	F										x

Last	First	Position	1929	1930	1931	1934	1935	1936	1937	1938	1940	1941
Jacobsen	Perry	DG		x	x	x	x	x	x	x	x	x
Jacobsen	Peter	F	x									
Jani	Izerne	DG								x		
Jason	William	F	x									
Jensen	Berger	F						x	x	x	x	x
Johansen	Einar	F						x				
Johansen	Joseph	DG	x	x	x	x	x	x				
Johansen	Otto	F				x	x					
Johnsen	J.R.	F			x							
Johnson	Alex	DG			x		x			x		
Johnson	Charles	F				x			x	x	x	
Johnson	Charles H.	F										x
Johnson	Walter	DG							x	x		
Johnson	Willard I									x		
Johnson	Woodrow	DG							x			
Kaland	John	C									x	x
Kangas	Charles	F	x	x	x	x	x	x	x	x	x	x
Kenney	Fred	DG		x	x	x						
Kenney	Sydney	DG		x	x							
Korpe	Dan	DG		x								
Korpi	Matt	F		x	x	x	x	x	x			
Korpin	Dan	DG	x									
Koskinen	George	F			x							
Kydell	Otto	C		x	x							
Laakso	Charles	F	x	x	x	x	x	x		x	x	x
Lacey	Ed	DG						x				
Largo	John	F	x	x								
Larsen	Tony	F	x									
Lundall	Maurice	DG						x				
Lynch	Bob	DG		x	x							
Mack	Jack	F	x			x	x					
Macki	Gust	F				x	x	x	x			
Marino	C.	DG						x				
Martinson	Sverre	DG							x			
Maser	Herman	F	x		x	x	x	x				
Mattson	Tobias	F	x									
McInturf	Don	R						x				
McKay	Angus	DG		x	x							
McNeary	Jim	DG			x	x	x	x	x	x	x	x
McNutt	Jack	DG	x									
Moller	Charles	DG		x								
Myron	William	F							x			
Nelson	Carl	Flunkey									x	
Nelson	Charles	DG			x							
Nelson	Hugo	DG	x	x		x	x	x	x	x	x	x
Nelson	Nels	F		x								

Last	First	Position	1929	1930	1931	1934	1935	1936	1937	1938	1940	1941
Nicholas	James	DG										x
Nielsen	Ivan	R				x	x					
Noble	Cecil	F	x	x	x				x	x	x	x
Nordlund	Marvin	DG	x									
Olsen	Hans E.	F		x	x							
O'Neil	Floyd	DG				x	x					
Palmer	Ted	DG			x							
Panger	Arnold	DG	x									
Parker	O.F.	DG						x	x	x		
Paulsen	Arthur	DG						x	x	x	x	x
Paxton	Orville	DG					x	x				
Paxton	R.C.	DG				x						
Pearson	Carl M.	F						x				
Peters	Alvin	R		x								
Potter	Ralph	DG		x	x							
Press	Ray	F	x	x	x							
Robert	Nels	DG									x	
Rydell	Otto	DG							x			
Ryder	Bob	DG		x								
Ryer	Conrad	DG	x			x	x					
Salo	Hans	F	x	x	x							
Sandager	M.	F				x	x					
Sandgren	Gust	F		x								
Schlertmieir	Marvin	DG		x	x							
Schloesser	Michael	DG				x		x	x	x		
Schloesser	Nick	DG					x					
Shrewsbury	J.B.	F							x			
Simpson	I.	DG						x	x	x		
Smith	Harry	DG							x			
Smith	W.E.	DG	x									
Snow	Charles	DG									x	x
Snow	Robert	DG				x	x	x	x	x		
Stockwell	Walter	DG				x	x	x	x	x	x	
Stuckey	Fred	F									x	x
Sunde	Knut	F					x					
Taylor	Sterling	DG	x									
Thorsen	Hans	F										x
Todnem	Alfred	F	x	x							x	x
Tomko	Michael	F					x			x	x	
Treffen	Nicholas	DG					x					
Tyres	James											x
Van Horn	Willis	DG				x	x					
Van Orsdale	C.	DG						x				
Vanamo	Reino	DG								x		
Wallin	Dick	F					x			x	x	x
Wang	Lawrence	DG								x		

Last	First	Position	1929	1930	1931	1934	1935	1936	1937	1938	1940	1941
West	Soren	F		x							x	x
Wicks	Albin	DG									x	
Wicks	Olaf	F	x					x	x	x	x	x
Winter	Axel	F		x								
Wirtaner	John	F		x								
Woodruff	Bill	DG								x	x	
Wright	Dave	DG									x	x
Wright	Ralph	DG									x	x

Appendix C

▼

Wawona Crew Wages
FOR 1936

Robinson Fisheries divided its pay schedule in three ways: by the ton at the dock for the captain and the fish dressers, by the pound at the dock for fishermen, and by the month for the radio operator, cook, and cook's helper. Most of the dress gang and monthly men fished from the mother ship after completing their assigned jobs. The company paid $.0175 (one and three-quarter cents) per pound of cod, based on the average trip weight of 2.92 pounds for each dressed fish. Mates were paid $.020625 (two and one-sixteenth cents) per pound.

The following figure shows the final gross pay of each *Wawona* crew member in 1936, based on Robinson Fisheries 1936 account books. The information was first compiled by Harriet DeLong for Northwest Seaport, *Wawona's* current owner.

Name	Job	Wages	Fish Caught	Total Wages
Anderson, Frank	dresser	.30/ton	702	163.11
Anderson, William	fisherman	.0175/lb	12,462	636.81
Bagger, Jean	cook	150/month	—	725.00
Berg, John	fisherman	.0175/lb	18,924	967.02
Eide, John	fisherman	.0175/lb	11,226	573.65
Field, Ed	dresser	.30/ton	1,052	180.00

Field, Nick	2nd mate	.020625/lb	17,350	1,013.24
Gress, Alex F.	header	.325/ton	3,014	291.83
Haagensen, Olaf	fisherman	.0175/lb	11,593	592.41
Hamul, Alex	fisherman	.0175/lb	14,090	720.00
Harju, Elmer	fisherman	.0175/lb	15,396	786.73
Haugen, Thorsten	captain	4.00/ton	424.098 tons	1,696.39
Jacobsen, Perry	dresser	.30/ton	1,961	227.44
Jensen, Berger	1st mate	.020625/lb	19,416	1,169.33
Johansen, Einar	fisherman	.0175/lb	8,709	445.03
Johansen, Joseph	watchman	.325/ton	3,556	319.55
Kangas, Charles	fisherman	.0175/lb	16,680	852.36
Korpi, Matt	fisherman	.0175/lb	11,619	593.72
Laakso, Charles	fisherman	.0175/lb	17,872	913.26
Lacey, Ed	dresser	.30/ton	1,265	191.88
Lundell, Maurice	dresser	.30/ton	1,060	181.39
McInturf, Donald	radio operator	90/month	2,007	537.55
McNeary, Jim	1st splitter	1.475/ton	2,884	772.91
Macki, Gus	fisherman	.0175/lb	12,835	655.87
Marino, Carmine	header	.325/ton	835	180.50
Maser, Herman	fisherman	left Wawona due to illness		
Nelson, Hugo	1st salter	1.475/ton	3,506	804.71
Parker, Orvia F.	dresser	.30/ton	3,121	286.71
Paulson, Arthur	fisherman	.0175/lb	12,532	640.38
Paxton, Orville	2nd salter	1.375/ton	2,315	701.43
Pearson, Carl	fisherman	.0175/lb	10,531	538.14
Schloesser, Michael	cook's helper	50/month	2,640	376.58
Snow, Robert	fisherman	.0175/lb	12,448	636.09
Stockwell, Walter	2nd splitter	1.375/ton	2,855	729.03
Van Arsdale, Albert	dresser	.30/ton	1,157	186.35
Wallin, Dick	fisherman	.0175/lb	14,815	757.05
Wicks, Olaf	fisherman	.0175/lb	17,893	914.34

Glossary

Aft: Toward the rear or stern of the vessel.

Amidships: Along a vessel's center line; the middle of the vessel.

Apron: A timber which is part of the stem assembly of a ship.

Articles: The contract which binds a seaman to the voyage and sets the pay rate.

Assistant keelson: A timber bolted to the keel and keelson to provide additional strength.

Bald-headed: A schooner mast with no topmasts.

Ballast: In most vessels, stones, lead weights, or water in the lowest part of the ship that keeps the vessel upright. However, *Wawona*'s hull was so heavy, she did not carry ballast.

Bank: A shallow underwater area, often near the shore.

Barkentine: A three-masted sailing ship, of which only the foremast is square-rigged, the others all being fore-and-aft rigged.

Beam: The measured width of a vessel at its widest point.

Belaying pin: A wooden pin used to secure a line in a pin rail.

Bend: The act of attaching a sail to a mast, boom and gaff.

Berth: The place where is ship is moored; a seaman's bunk; a fishing spot.

Bitt: A single or double post on a deck for securing mooring lines and towlines.

Block: An assembly containing a sheave which is used for gaining extra purchase or leverage with a line.

Blowing out the stink: Hanging laundry from booms and letting wind and rain wash them.

Boom: In a gaff-rigged sailing ship, the boom is a long spar extending from a mast holding the foot or lower edge of a sail.

Bow: The leading edge of a vessel.

Bowsprit: An extension of a ship's bow, to which the stays of the foremast are fastened.

Brig: A two-masted sailing vessel square-rigged on both masts.

Bucko: A sadistic officer.

Bulwarks: Part of the ship's hull above the waterline.

Capstan: A drum on the deck, often part of a winch, which is used to weigh anchor or move a ship toward a dock..

Capsize: Turn a boat over so that the hull is out of the water.

Casting a lead: A method for determining depth and sea bottom conditions using a lead weight attached to a long line. Seamen could see general bottom conditions by viewing sand or mud attaching itself to a sticky substance on the lead weight.

Checkers: Pine planks laid on end in a checkerboard pattern to manage newly landed fish.

Chronometer: A highly accurate clock used to determine longitude.

Clamp: A timber that strengthens the shelf.

Cleat: A fitting to which lines are attached.

Ceilings: Interior planks which cover the hull frames.

Copra: The raw material for coconut oil.

Counter: The overhang of the stern above the waterline.

Cradle: A timber assembly holding a ship as it slides down the ways into the water.

Crimp: A person who obtains crew for ships, often corrupt.

Cutter: A type of fast patrol vessel favored by the U.S. Coast Guard.

Davit: A small, movable crane on a ship.

Deadwood: Solid timbers in the bow and stern assembly that add strength.

Deckhouse: A small enclosure holding a steam or gasoline engine used to raise sails or hoist equipment.

Deck load: Cargo stowed on deck.

Desertion: Leaving a ship before the end of its voyage.

Discharge: Unload.

Dog watch: The period of time between 1600 and 2000 (4 p.m. and 8 p.m.), split into two smaller periods, called the first and second dog watches.

Donkey engine: A small steam engine and winch assembly used to raise sails or hoist equipment.

Donkey's breakfast: Straw used to make a mattress for a seaman; goat's nest

Dory: A small, narrow, flat-bottomed boat with high sides and a sharp prow.

Drag hawser: When launched a ship down a ways, a drag hawser, attached to an anchor or heavy weight, keeps the vessel from traveling too fast into the water.

Dress gang: Two teams of fisher dressers each consisting of a splitter, a header, two idlers, a spare man, and two salters.

Dresser: A worker aboard a fishing vessel that guts and dresses fish.

Drift: An iron bolt joining two or more large timbers.

Dubber: A workman who ensures that planks lay flush against frames.

Eulachon: Smelt.

Fathom: Six feet.

Fiddlehead: A carved piece of wood similar to a figurehead.

Flakes: Outdoor tables for drying fish.

Forecastle: The living quarters for crew below officer rank, also called the fo'c'sle.

Foremast: The mast nearest the bow in a sailing ship.

Fore: Towards the front or bow of a vessel.

Forepeak: A compartment directly under the bow of a ship.

Frame: A structural rib of the hull attached to the keel.

Futtock: Separate timbers that, when joined, form a frame.

Gaff: In a gaff-rigged sailing ship, the gaff is a long spar extending from a mast holding the head or upper edge of a sail.

Gaff-rigged: Rigged with trapezoidal sails that lie along the center line of a vessel and are raised by gaffs.

Gadus macrocephalus: A species of cod found in the North Pacific and North Atlantic.

Gale: A high wind; storm.

Galley: Kitchen.

Gangplank: A ramp from the shore to the vessel for passengers and crew.

Garboard: The first plank on the outer hull next to the keel.

Great schooner: Any of numerous late nineteenth century large schooners with more than three masts.

Gripe: A timber that is part of the stem assembly of a ship.

Gurdy: A small capstan or reel that takes up or pays out medium line often attached to a small anchor.

Gurry: Fish guts.

Gurry boils: A skin infection on the hands and wrists caused by contact with salt water and fish gurry.

Halyard: A line used to raise or lower a sail or another object, such as a flag.

Handline: Fishing gear that is raised or lowered by hand without a pole.

Hatch: An opening in the deck for reaching the cargo area.

Hawse pipe: An opening in the bow above the waterline through which the chain to the anchor is hauled.

Hawser: A heavy line used for secure a ship to another object.

Half-hull: A model used by shipwrights to show the shape of a hull.

Haul out: Removing a ship from the water for repairs and maintenance.

Head: Toilet.

Header: A fish dresser who removes the head.

Helm: The wheel and associated steering gear of a ship.

Helmsman: The seaman assigned to steer the ship; quartermaster.

Highline: The boat and fisherman who catches the most fish.

Hold: The cargo area of a ship.

Hoops: Hoops of bent wood that hold sails to masts.

Hull: The main body of a ship containing the cargo spaces, living quarters, and in powered vessels, the engines.

Idler: A member of the dress gang who moves fish around checkers and into boxes on deck.

In ballast: When a ship is sailing without cargo, it is said to be traveling "in ballast."

Jib: A type of sail attached to the jib boom. *Wawona* carried an inner jib, outer jib, and a flying jib.

Jib boom: A spar extending from the bowsprit to which jib sails are attached.

Jibe: An act that turns a vessel into the wind by coming around in a circle.

Jigging: A fishing by which the fisherman moves bait up and down with sharp motions.

Joiner: A workman specializing in fitting smaller pieces of wood.

Keel: The structural member of a ship, running lengthwise at the lowest part of the hull from bow to stern, to which the frames are attached.

Keel block: Blocks of wood under a keel when a ship is under construction.

Keelson: A timber bolted to the keel to provide additional strength.

Keelson rider: A timber that adds strength to the keelson.

Kench: A wooden, open-top box with sides attached to the hull stanchions and planking, used to store salted fish.

Knee: A heavy, shaped timber buttressing beams on which rest the deck planks.

Lay up: To idle a vessel until it is put to work again.

Lee: Downwind.

Leeward: Downwind from a vessel or the land.

Liner: A type of passenger vessel.

Lock: An enclosure on a canal that closes to control the water level, also used to raise or lower vessels that pass through it.

Log: The official journal of a vessel.

Main mast: In a schooner, the mast immediately aft the foremast.

Martingale: A permanent stay that holds the jib boom down against the pull of opposite stays attached to the foremast.

Masthead: The top of a mast.

Mate: A deck officer ranking immediately below the captain.

Messenger: A small, easy-to-throw line used to pull a heavier line or cable.

Mizzen mast: In a schooner, the mast immediately aft the main mast.

Mug up: A snack.

Nipper: A wide, thick rubber band that fits around the palm and grooved for grabbing tarred line.

Painter: A line to which small boats are attached, often in series.

Pennant: A long triangular flag flying from the masthead.

Pier: A platform over water to which ships are moored perpendicular to the shore.

Pier head jump: Boarding a vessel at the last minute without baggage or a contract to work on a ship.

Pin rail: A railing with holes to accept belaying pins.

Pitch: The rotation of a ship along its beam, felt as an up and down motion.

Planker: A workman who lays planking on the hull or the deck.

Port: Left

Pugh: A tool resembling a pitchfork with a single prong, pronounced "pew."

Quarterdeck: The after part of the upper deck, usually reserved for officers; sometimes referred to as the poop deck.

Quartermaster: Officer in charge of steering a ship; helmsman.

Reel: A metal or wooden drum that takes up and pays out line.

Rig: The assembly of hooks, lines, and other equipment that holds and presents bait.

Rigging: The lines and other equipment used to hold mast or move sails.

Roll: The rotation of a ship along its center line; swaying

Rudder: The assembly which, when moved, forces the vessel in the opposite direction.

Rudder post: The timber assembly to which the rudder is attached.

Running lights: Safety lights allowing other ships to see a vessel.

Saloon: In *Wawona*, a gathering area in the main cabin for officers.

Salter: A member of the dress gang responsible for salting fish in the hold.

Samson post: A large diameter post attached to the keel to which a tug hawser is attached.

Scarf: A joint made of two notched pieces of lumber attached end-to-end

Schooner: A fore-and-aft rigged sailing vessel with two or more masts, with the foremast usually shorter than the other masts. (In *Wawona*, all three masts are the same height.)

Sextant: A device used to determine the height of the sun or moon from the horizon.

Sheave: A wheel with a grooved rim that guides line in a block.

Sheer: The curve of a sailing ship's hull as seen from the side.

Sheet: A line attached to the lower corners of a sail.

Shelf: A horizontal timber on which deck planks are laid; a generally flat, raised underwater formation, often extending from shore.

Shipwright: A carpenter or metal-worker specially trained to construct ships.

Shipyard: A place where ships are constructed.

Shrouds: Permanent rigging that holds the masts in place.

Sight: An observation of the sun or moon used to determine position on the globe.

Single up: Order to remove all but two lines mooring a ship to a wharf or pier.

Sinker: A lead weight that holds the fishing rig below the water.

Slop chest: On-board store or commissary.

Snoot line: A gangion or leader.

Snappers: In cod fishing, juvenile cod.

Sound: A cod's air bladder.

Spanker: A type of trapezoidal mizzen sail.

Spar: A pole, such as a boom or gaff, used to support sails and rigging.

Spare man: A member of the dress gang responsible for odd jobs and counting fish.

Splice: The point at which two lines have been interwoven and attached.

Splitter: A fish dresser who splits a fish through the belly, allowing the carcass to lay flat on its back.

Spreader: A metal rod that holds two gangions.

Square-rigged: Rigged with four-cornered sails hung from yards.

Stanchion: A vertical timber that supports the deck.

Starboard: Right.

Stay: A permanent line that holds a mast in place.

Staysail: A triangular sail immediately fore of the foremast, held in place with a boom, also referred to as a jumbo.

Steam schooner: A steam-powered cargo vessel derived from the sailing schooner, often with two masts.

Stemson: A timber adding strength to the stem at the bow of the ship.

Stern: Rear of the vessel.

Stevedore: A dock worker specializing in the loading and unloading of cargo ships; longshoreman.

Steward: The crewman responsible for food and drink; cook; a leadership position in a union.

Stock anchor: An anchor with the class nautical "T" shape and curved flukes.

Swell: Undulating movement on the sea surface.

Swivel: A metal link that allows line to turn without binding or tangling.

Tack: The act of changing position of a sailing ship when heading into a wind. See jibe.

Taffrail: A railing around the stern of a ship.

Thwart: A seat or brace running laterally across a dory or small boat.

Tongue: The part of a codfish inside its jaw, considering a delicacy.

Tongue cutter: A fish dresser assigned the task of removing and packing cod tongues.

Topmast: In a schooner, a spar that extends the length of a mast. *Wawona* carried no topmasts, hence she was called "bald-headed."

Towline: The towing hawser from the tug to a vessel.

Troller: A type of fishing vessel that drags baited lines from long poles.

Trunnel: A thick wooden dowel fastening together two or more pieces of wood; tree nail.

Turnbuckle: A threaded metal device for tightening stays or other rigging.

Ways: A structure used to hold a ship during construction and launch it when completed.

Watch: A shift board a vessel, usually four hours. See dog watch.

Weigh anchor: To raise the anchor.

Wharf: A platform over water to which ships are moored parallel to the shore.

White horses: The foam blown off the tops of waves by wind.

Winch: A device which boosts hauling power when raising or trimming sails or moving objects, such as an anchor.

Windward: Toward the wind.

Wireless: Refers to the ship's radio.

Principal Sources

Books, Articles and Manuscripts

Broderick, Henry. *The 'HB' Story: Henry Broderick Relates Seattle's Yesterdays With Some Other Thoughts by the Way.* Seattle: Frank McCaffrey Publishers, 1969.

Carranco, Lynnwood, and Labbe, John T. *Logging the Redwoods.* Caldwell, Idaho: The Caxton Printers, Ltd., 1975.

Carse, Robert. *The Twilight of Sailing Ships.* New York: Galahad Books, 1965.

Cobb, John N. *Pacific Salmon Fisheries.* Washington, DC: Government Printing Office, 1917.

Cox, Thomas R. *Mills and Markets: A History of the Pacific Coast Lumber Industry to 1900.* Seattle: University of Washington Press, 1974.

Crooks, Jimmy. "Sailing Conditions During the Depression," *The Sea Chest.* 8: 6-9

DeLong, Harriet Tracy. *Pacific Schooner* Wawona. Bellevue, Wash: Documentary Book Publishers Corp., 1985.

Charles Desmond. *Wooden Ship-Building.* New York: The Rudder Publishing Company, 1919.

Hale, Frederick, ed., *Danes in North America.* Seattle: University of Washington Press, 1984.

Hiscock, Barbara A. Wawona: *The Heritage of Sailing in the North Pacific.* c.1965.

Hvidt, Kristian. *Danes Go West*. Copenhagen: Rebild National Park Society, 1976.

Hughes, John C., and Beckwith, Ryan Teague. *On the Harbor: From Black Friday to Nirvana*. Aberdeen, Washington: *The Daily World*, 2001.

Hughes, Ronald L. Wawona—*A Research Paper with Supplementary Notes*. Seattle: Northwest Seaport, c.1964.

Huycke, Capt. Harold D. 1981. "The *Wawona* is Waiting (Part I)." *Sea History*, Summer.

Huycke, Capt. Harold D. 1981. "The *Wawona* is Waiting (Part II)," *Sea History*, Fall.

Gardner, John. *The Dory Book*. Camden, Maine: International Marine Publishing Co., 1978.

Jones, Gordon. "Matt Peasley and the *Vigilant*." *The Sea Chest* 5.

Jones, Gordon P. 1966. "Cod Bangers to Alaska," *Alaska Sportsman*, March.

Irvine, Leigh H. *History of Humboldt County, California*. Los Angeles: Historic Record Company, 1915.

Kline, Mary, et al., *All Aboard: An Educational Curriculum*, Seattle: Northwest Seaport, 1997.

Kyne, Peter B. *Cappy Ricks, or the Subjugation of Matt Peasley*. New York: Curtis Publishing Company, 1915.

McInturf, Don. *Diary of the 1936 voyage of the* Wawona. Seattle: Northwest Seaport. Portions published in 2004.

Newell, Gordon. *The H.W. McCurdy Marine History of the Pacific Northwest*. Seattle: Superior Publishing Co, 1966.

Phegley, John W. 1959. "H.D. Bendixsen—Shipbuilder" (unpublished paper). Eureka, California: Humboldt County Historical Society.

Preston, LaVerne. 1918. "Shipbuilding" (unpublished paper). Eureka, California: Humboldt State University.

Robinson, W.F. 1908. "The Codfish Industry," *The Coast*, November.

Ross, John. *To Buy a Schooner—Montana Fashion* (unpublished manuscript). Seattle: Northwest Seaport, 1988.

Sargent, Shirley. *Yosemite's Historic Wawona.* Yosemite, California: Flying Spur Press, 1979.

Story, Dana. *Frame-Up! The Story of the People and Shipyards of Essex, Massachusetts.* Gloucester, Massachusetts: Ten Pound Island Book Company, 1986.

Shields, Capt. Ed. *Salt of the Sea: The Pacific Coast Cod Fishery and the Last Days of Sail.* Lopez Island, Washington: Pacific Heritage Press, 2001.

Shields, Capt. Ed. 1981. "Captain J.E. Shields (Part I)", *The Fisherman's News*, November.

Shields, Capt. Ed. 1968. "Fresh Water in the Bering Sea," *The Sea Chest*, March.

Shields, Capt. J. Edward. "Captain John Grotle, Codfisherman," *The Sea Chest*, 30.

Trott, Harlan. *The Schooner That Came Home: The Final Voyage of the* C.A. Thayer. Cambridge, Maryland: Cornell Maritime Press, 1958.

Van Syckle, Edwin. *They Tried to Cut It All.* Seattle: Pacific Search Press, 1980.

Archives and Collections

Aberdeen Museum of History

Aberdeen Public Library

Anacortes History Museum

Andover Historical Society

Coos Bay Historical Society

HistoryLink

Humboldt County Historical Society

Humboldt State University Library

King County Public Library

Museum of History & Industry

Puget Sound Maritime Historical Society

Seattle Room, Seattle Public Library

Special Collections, University of Washington Libraries

Wawona Collection, Northwest Seaport

Interviews and Private Papers

Katherine "Kay" Bullitt

Diane Colson

Paul Douglas

Fern Hill Cemetery, Aberdeen, Wash.

Janice Deweyert

Linda Haakenson

Graham L. Peaslee

Louise Shields

Colleen Wagner

Publications

Aberdeen Daily World

Anacortes American

Boston Globe

Fisherman's News

Humboldt Times-Standard

Mains'l Haul

Marine Digest

Northwest Seaport newsletters

Sea Chest

Sea History

Seattle Post-Intelligencer

Seattle Times

Seattle Star

Tacoma News Tribune

Other Sources

Historic Seattle

National Oceanographic & Atmospheric Administration

U.S. Census

U.S. Coast Guard

Notes

Chapter One: The Sturdy Dane

1 Handwritten notes provided by the Humboldt County Historical Society, possibly by Harriet DeLong, that appear to be an 1885 property description of the Bendixsen residence. Fay Avenue is not on modern maps of Fairhaven. The name "Fay" may have come from the G.M. Fay & Brother firm, which owned the property before Bendixsen.

2 "Ship-Building on Humboldt Bay: 1875—1918" (unpublished paper). 1967. Humboldt State University, 8. The paper is located in the Humboldt County Historical Society archives.

3 Irvine, *History of Humboldt County, California*, 810.

4 Trott, *The Schooner That Came Home: The Final Voyage of the* C.A. Thayer, 9.

5 Irvine. The father is identified as "F.C.", and the mother is identified as "Mariane von Mehren." A search of genealogical records at http://www.family-search.org/on Nov. 2, 2004 revealed the full names. The Danish records spell the surname "Bendixen."

6 DeLong, *Pacific Schooner* Wawona, 13.

7 Translation of a Danish newspaper clipping headlined "Det regner Guld over Thisted" dated Dec. 14, 1954 in the archives of Humboldt County Historical Society.

8 Genzoli, Andrew. "Bendixsen's sailing vessels helped make bay important," *The Times-Standard* (Eureka, Calif.), Jan. 6, 1975, 5.

9 Genzoli.

10 Bendixsen left his country at the beginning of a wave of emigration that would reduce Denmark's population over the next 40 years by a greater amount in percentage terms than Germany, Russia, and Italy during the same period. In Denmark, as in the rest of Europe, industrialization, population growth, high fertility rates, and overworked land forced Danish peasants to the cities. In 1864, Den-

mark lost a war and two provinces, Holstein and Schleswig, to Prussia, driving Danish refugees to the overcrowded cities. The population of Copenhagen more than doubled during the last half of the 19th century. The population of Aalborg tripled. The unemployment rate reached 50 percent during the winter in Copenhagen. "Their answer to the black misery," wrote historian Kristian Hvidt, "was internal migration in search of work—or emigration to America and Australia." Three hundred thousand Danes left the country between 1860 and World War I. Some would hand over as much as a year's pay to reach New York and purchase a homestead. Sixty percent of the emigrants were men, mostly independent tradesmen, craftsmen, professionals, students, clerical workers, shop assistants, civil servants, journeymen, and apprentices. Many couldn't compete in the new industrial economy. Hvidt, *Danes Go West*, 152-154. Hale, *Danes in North America* xi, xiii.

11 "Ship-Building on Humboldt Bay: 1875—1918", 1.

12 Genzoli, Andrew M. "Hans Bendixsen Created Living Beauty in Sailing From Sturdy Humboldt Pine!" *The Humboldt Times* (Eureka, Calif.), April 27, 1952, 5.

13 DeLong, 13.

14 Genzoli said Bendixsen arrived in Humboldt Bay in 1865. The anonymous author of the "Ship-Building on Humboldt Bay: 1875—1918" paper said he arrived on April 1, 1867.

15 Irvine refers to the *Fairy Queen* as a topmast schooner. Trott calls her a topmast river schooner.

16 Genzoli, "Bendixsen's sailing vessels helped make bay important." The reader should note that the anonymous writer of "Ship-Building on Humboldt Bay: 1875—1918" quotes a 1965 Genzoli article which said that Bendixsen began independent shipbuilding at a site at the foot of Sixth Street, "in what was later to become known as the Mathews Shipyard." Bendixsen may have leased space at one shipyard before setting up his own with his partner Thomas McDonald. But the first ship attributed to Bendixsen is the *Fairy Queen*.

17 DeLong, 14.

18 Phegley, "H.D. Bendixsen—Shipbuilder," 7. Genzoli in "Bendixsen's sailing vessels helped make bay important" added that the Fay brothers came from Connecticut. And in his 1952 article, Genzoli said Bendixsen made a brother a partner in his firm before moving operations to Fairhaven. But this is the only mention in the available records of any blood relative with an interest in his shipyard.

19 Trott, 113.

20 Phegley, 5.

21 Cox, *Mills and Markets: A History of the Pacific Coast Lumber Industry to 1900*, 63, 65. Carranco and Labbe, *Logging the Redwoods*, 14-16.

22 DeLong, 14.

23 Irvine.

24 Emma was Bendixsen's second wife. "His first marriage," Irvine writes, "which was of but short duration, united him with a lady from the vicinity of his old home in Denmark." No other record mentions his first marriage.

25 Trott.

26 Phegley, 11-12. Phegley cites page 49 of John Mathewson Eddy's *In the Redwood's Realm*, published by D.S. Stanley Company of San Francisco in 1893.

27 Roberts, Earl G., "A Story of Industry: Bendixsen at Fairhaven," newspaper clipping in the Humboldt County Historical Society archives, possibly *The Humboldt Times*, February, 1945.

28 DeLong, 13.

29 Phegley, Appendix III.

30 Map labeled "H.D. Bendixsen Ship Yard" in the archives of the Humboldt County Historical Society.

31 Genzoli, "Hans Bendixsen Created Living Beauty in Sailing from Sturdy Humboldt Pine." See accompanying photos.

32 Genzoli, Andrew, "Redwood Country," (column), *The Humboldt Times*, July 6, 1971, 6. Genzoli quotes from a *Humboldt Times* article dated March 25, 1892.

33 Vaughn, 347.

34 Trott, viii.

35 Vaughn, 348.

36 "Ship-Building on Humboldt Bay: 1875—1918", 4.

37 Northwest Seaport records.

38 Majority owners of ships often sold minority interests to investors to spread risk. This was the ownership of *Wawona* at enrollment in government records on October 4, 1897: John Dolbeer, 32/96 (33 percent); William Carson, 32/96 (33 percent); H.D. Bendixsen, 20/96 (20.83 percent); Capt. Olaf Isaaksen, 6/96 (6.25 percent); A Cavner, 3/96 (3.125 percent); J. Lundstrom, 3/96 (3.125 percent). In the late nineteenth century, ownership interests were delineated in fractions. DeLong, 19. See photograph of Certificate of Enrollment.

39 Probably the 341-ton *Hueneme*, launched in 1897 about the time of *Wawona*. See Trott, 141.

40 Trott, 9.

41 "Ship-Building on Humboldt Bay, 1875-1918," 11.

42 In 1901, *Wawona* delivered lumber to Honolulu and returned to Puget Sound with a load of household furniture. See letter and enclosed statements from William G. Mugan to R.E. Peasley, May 25, 1901, *Wawona* Collection, Northwest Seaport.

43 Captains sometimes complained about the deck loads; heavily laden ships had as little as 18 inches of freeboard. Mill men replied, "Hell, its just lumber. You've never seen wood sink, have you?" Cox, 245-248.

44 "Ship-Building on Humboldt Bay, 1875-1918," 4.

45 "Ship-Building on Humboldt Bay, 1875-1918," 4. It is possible the writer may have transcribed the word 'ceiling' as 'sealing,' since it's not clear the writer was expert in ship-building terms. For this work, he is given the benefit of the doubt.

46 Preston, "Shipbuilding," unpublished paper in the Humboldt State University library. A copy is held in the archives of the Humboldt County Historical Society. In 1875, the San Francisco Board of Marine Underwriters rebuffed the easterners by promulgating rules governing the use of Douglass-fir in ships. Eventually, the easterners came around. A table in a 1919 shipbuilder's reference book published in New York suggested that Douglass-fir from the ancient forests of northern California and the Pacific Northwest was lighter than oak while nearly matching its strength. Desmond. *Wooden Ship-Building*, 18.

47 Genzoli, "Hans Bendixsen Created Living Beauty in Sailing from Sturdy Humboldt Pine." Genzoli referred to the *C.A. Thayer*, a three-masted baldheaded schooner which Bendixsen built in 1895. Her timbers are "of the finest Humboldt pine taken from the Freshwater area," he wrote. *C.A Thayer* is now at the San Francisco National Maritime Park.

48 Genzoli, "Redwood Country."

49 Genzoli, "Redwood Country."

50 Genzoli, "Redwood Country."

51 In New England shipyards, once a frame was ready, someone would yell "Frame up!" and everyone would drop what they were doing, lift the frame to perpendicular, and manhandle it onto its place on the keel while others set up temporary supports. As ships grew bigger, a donkey engine did the heavy lifting, pulling wire rope run through a block at the top of a vertical spar. Story, *Frame-Up! The Story of the People and Shipyards of Essex, Massachusetts*.

52 Fimrite, Peter. "High-seas skeleton sails in red ink," *San Francisco Chronicle*, November 5, 2004. The article concerns the restoration of *Wawona*'s sister ship, *C.A. Thayer*.

53 Huycke, "The *Wawona* is Waiting (Part I)," 26. Other dimensions as described by the text were measured by the author.

54 Author Dana Story in his book about the Essex, Massachusetts shipyards tells the tale of John Wetmore, a dubber who did not take care of his tools. "He would bang away with the thing getting duller and duller until out of sheer desperation or exhaustion he had to stop," Story wrote. One day, Wetmore's boss grew frustrated with Wetmore's carelessness. When Wetmore put down his adze and went to lunch, the boss found a large rock in the weeds and "gave the adze a few healthy belts on the edge of the blade. Then he put it back where he found it. Upon coming back from dinner, John picked up his adze and eyeing it ruefully he disappeared to the grind stone where he remained the rest of the afternoon grinding out those awful nicks. He later took more pains with his adze after that." Story, 23.

55 Trott, viii.

56 "Ship-Building on Humboldt Bay, 1875-1918," 4.

57 Trott, viii.

58 Joiners are highly skilled artisans. Unlike wood in homes, which generally runs straight and square, wood in ships runs along curves and rarely butts against another piece squarely. Even today, in some vessels, the joiner has to find a unique matching angle for every piece of wood.

59 "Ship-Building on Humboldt Bay, 1875-1918," 3-4.

60 Trott, 8.

61 Irvine.

62 Trott, 36.

63 This description of *Wawona*'s launch is a composite of various accounts of other launches from sources listed in these notes. The only known account of *Wawona*'s launch comes from DeLong, who quotes the September 12, 1897 edition of the *Humboldt Standard*.

64 Huycke, "The *Wawona* is Waiting (Part II)," 9.

65 Trott, 114.

66 Sargent, *Yosemite's Historic Wawona*, 13.

67 The yard kept Bendixsen's name through several owners until it was sold to James "Sunny Jim" Rolph, Jr., owner of Rolph Navigation and Coal Company, mayor of San Francisco, and governor of California from 1931 to 1934. As wooden shipbuilding disappeared, so did the Fairhaven yard and the little community that surrounded it. The only reminder on modern maps is the name Fairhaven and a street named "Bendixsen." "Bendixsen Shipbuilding Co. Is Sold

to Mayor Rolph, Jr.," *Humboldt Standard*, Feb. 17, 1917; MapQuest, http://www.mapquest.com, Oct. 22, 2004.

68 DeLong, 16.

69 DeLong.

70 Trott, 8, perhaps using the same source, spells out the names as "Matson, J.D. Spreckels, E.K. Wood, Eschen & Minor, Rolph, Charles Nelson and A.P. Lorentzen."

71 Gonzoli, "Bendixsen's sailing vessels helped make bay important."

72 DeLong, 16.

73 Irvine.

74 "Det regner Guld over Thisted."

Chapter Two: Master, Manager, and Infinite Yankee

1 William G. Mugan to R.E. Peasley, July 31, 1899, plus enclosure, *Wawona* Collection, Northwest Seaport. Mugan added, "You will understand that the above is not said in any fault-finding spirit, but with the desire, which we hope will be always between you and this office, of point out frankly anything that we think should be remedied."

2 Ninety percent of the lumber carriers visiting Puget Sound were wind-powered. Cox, 293.

3 Lumber order for Schooner *Wawona*, transcribed by Harriet DeLong from Port Blakely Mill Company papers, University of Washington, transcription in *Wawona* Collection, Northwest Seaport.

4 Trott, *The Schooner That Came Home: The Final Voyage of the C.A. Thayer*, 86.

5 Posting on GenForum by Graham Peaslee, "Re: Ralph Peasley-captain of Pacific-1920s," April 25, 2002, http://genforum.genealogy.com/peaslee/messages/261.html. Also, e-mail from Graham Peaslee to the author, November 14, 2004.

6 Jones, "Matt Peasley and the *Vigilant*," 142.

7 Van Syckle, Edwin, "Captain Matt Peasley," handwritten manuscript in the archives of the Aberdeen Museum of History, Aberdeen, Wash.

8 Van Syckle, "Captain Matt Peasley"

9 Norton, Wilda, "Matt Peasley Here to Pilot Moran Cruise," *The Seattle Post-Intelligencer*, September 18, 1930, 8.

10 Graham Peaslee posting.

11 Seath, Irvine, "Captain Matt Peasley Marks 81st Birthday," newspaper clipping in the Ralph Peasley biography file at the Aberdeen Public Library. The

cousins are identified as William McKay of Burlington, and Austin M. Smith and Charley Look of Montesano.

12 Hughes and Beckwith, *On the Harbor: From Black Friday to Nirvana*, 62.

13 Jones, 143.

14 Kyne, *Cappy Ricks, or the Subjugation of Matt Peasley*, dedication. Kyne said the incident occurred on *Louis'* maiden voyage, but the ship was built in 1888 in Coos Bay, Ore. by Asa Mead Simpson, and it seems unlikely a conservative man probably would have given first command of this ship to a 22-year-old. Van Syckle in his draft article (see note 7) said the incident occurred in the spring of 1896. He said Peasley celebrated his thirtieth birthday on the voyage.

15 Asa Mead Simpson, founder of one of the first major timber companies on the west coast, came from Brunswick, Maine. He was a sea captain by training, and he served as master in some of his own lumber carriers. He built the *Louis* at Coos Bay, Ore. John Dolbeer of Dolbeer & Carson hailed from New Hampshire, and his junior partner, William Carson, was born across the Maine/US border in the Canadian province of New Brunswick.

16 William G. Mugan to R.E. Peasley, July 17, 1901.

17 Email from Graham Peaslee to the author, November 14, 2004.

18 Dolbeer & Carson statements of Peasley's account in *Wawona* Collection, Northwest Seaport.

19 Handwritten notation on a photograph in the *Wawona* Collection, Northwest Seaport.

20 Records of the Whiteside Undertaking Company, Aberdeen, Washington.

21 1903 Polk Directory for Aberdeen, Wash.

22 The exact date of the marriage is unclear, though it appears to be in the latter part of 1903.

23 Van Syckle, *They Tried to Cut It All*, 253. The number was Peasley's own estimate. See "Death Ends Career of Captain Ralph Peasley" in Ralph Peasley biography file at the Aberdeen Public Library.

24 The wallet is in the *Wawona* Collection of Northwest Seaport.

25 Van Syckle, *They Tried to Cut It All*, 250.

26 "Fact Sheet" describing *Wawona's* specifications, probably written in the 1960s as part of the first effort to preserve her, Northwest Seaport archives. Peasley apparently followed the common practice of masters of giving their own names to sails. In a letter dated December 29th, 1902 regarding a repair, Mugan asks for a clarification "stating how you name the sails on your vessel, to avoid any confusion as to the sails you desire us to send." A 1937 fishing crewman reported that *Wawona* had a square yard and sail attached to her foremast to take

advantage of following winds, but evidence for this is scarce during her lumber carrying days. Her fishing crew would also rig a small, triangular "fisherman's" sail on the mizzen mast and boom to hold her into the wind while she rode at anchor.

27 Hughes and Beckwith, 62-67.

28 When he made this remark in 1924, Peasley wasn't alone in clinging to sail. Robert Dollar, a powerful pioneer lumberman and shipping magnate in California, shipped lumber by sail as late as the 1920s. Hughes and Beckwith, 64.

29 Alexander Beattie, a master who shipped as Peasley's first mate in *Wawona* for two years, hoped to get his own command with Dolbeer & Carson. Peasley put in a good word for Beattie with Mugan, who responded, "[We] do not question but he is a steady and capable man and trust that some time we may see our way clear to secure a vessel for him. Such good men are in demand." Mugan added in a following letter, "It speaks well of yourself and the vessel that you have retained him." The letter also congratulated Peasley on getting his license as master of sailing vessels on any ocean. "Such license may be of considerable use to you hereafter," Mugan wrote. In another letter dated February 3, 1902, Mugan expressed relief that Peasley decided against a job offer from another firm. William G. Mugan to R.E. Peasley, December 29, 1900; William G. Mugan to R.E. Peasley, January 3, 1901; William G. Mugan to R.E. Peasley, February 3, 1902.

30 A statement accompanying the letter of June 27, 1899 contains a $10 line item noting an "amount collected from the tug *Annie* to cover damage to *Wawona's* chain plate in collision off Meiggs Wharf at San Francisco about June 1898." This is the first record of damage to the ship while she was working. William G. Mugan to R.E. Peasley, June 27, 1899, plus enclosure, *Wawona* Collection, Northwest Seaport.

31 William G. Mugan to R.E. Peasley, Sept. 16, 1902; William G. Mugan to R.E. Peasley, Oct. 3, 1902.

32 Invoice from C.F. Meyer & Company (ship chandlery), Seattle, Jan. 5. 1901. *Wawona* Collection, Northwest Seaport.

33 In November, 1899, a heavy gale drove Wawona into Barclay Sound in Canadian waters off British Columbia and damaged several other ships along the coast. Peasley sought refuge behind Cape Beale, and received assistance from "Thomas Patterson of the Cape Beale lighthouse." Peasley wired Mugan: "*Wawona* wants mainsail, forestaysail, flying and outer jib. Will you send these?" Mugan wrote a letter dated November 29, 1899 acknowledging the wire. "We knew you had been blown into a safe anchorage at Barclay Sound and had wired for a tug. You must have had a very rough trip of it. Other vessels along the Coast have been

suffering and we are glad to know that you are safe and that the vessel was carried through all right, though with the loss of sails." Mugan goes on to say that San Francisco sail makers Simpson & Fisher are "very busy and working overtime." But Mugan is doubtful Peasley will get all his sails quickly.

In the meantime, Peasley limped to Port Blakely under tow. The large sails were shipped on a steamer heading north, but on December 11, Mugan wired Peasley to say that the two jibs wouldn't arrive for three weeks. "Can you secure jibs there or manage with present sails until you reach Newport [Calif.]?" Mugan asked. In a following letter, Mugan told Peasley that "the sail makers are working night and day" and "they have orders ahead of them to keep them busy for six months."

Peasley took Mugan's cue. He wired Mugan on December 12 after getting Mugan's bad news. "Having sails made," Peasley said, "Finished Friday." Mugan is pleased. In his answer letter of December 12, Mugan said, "We are glad you have been able to have the new sails made as the Sound at this season of the year is hard on even the best canvas." A year later, *Wawona* suffered through another bout of stormy weather, and apparently came through safely. "We think you did well to wire us of your arrival at the Sound as there is, of course, a certain amount of anxiety felt among ship owners when the weather is as rough as it has been of late," Mugan wrote.

At one point in the correspondence about the 1899 storm, Mugan refers to Peasley's financial exposure: "We do not think others are insured beside yourself." Peasley's personal account statements contain regular $27.00 charges to Fireman's Fund Insurance, which may be for a policy against his financial interest in *Wawona*. Mugan's letter said the vessel was insured "at the rate of $30,000." *Wawona* had to sustain $2,000 or more damage to recover on the loss. Mugan's letter also notes that *Wawona* did well financially on the voyage "in spite of her disaster." William G. Mugan to R.E. Peasley, December 8, 1899; William G. Mugan to R.E. Peasley, November 29, 1899. William G. Mugan to R.E. Peasley, December 29, 1900; Western Union telegram from William G. Mugan to R.E. Peasley, December 11, 1899; William G. Mugan to R.E. Peasley, December 11, 1899; William G. Mugan to R.E. Peasley, December 12, 1899; William G. Mugan to R.E. Peasley, January 28, 1904.

34 William G. Mugan to R.E. Peasley, April 28, 1899. Mugan is constantly correcting Peasley's arithmetic throughout the seven years of correspondence.

35 Burrie Dalton Peasley to R.E. Peasley, June 8, 1904, *Wawona* Collection, Northwest Seaport.

36 Hughes and Beckwith, 62-67.

37 Van Syckle, 253.

38 Genovera Eloisa Y de Braun (?) to R. Peasley, January 9, 1920.

39 The incident occurred in Honolulu in 1920. The documents are held in the *Wawona* Collection at Northwest Seaport in Seattle.

40 Crooks, "Sailing Conditions During the Depression," 6-9. For a readable academic work on the history of maritime labor struggles, read Bruce Nelson's *Workers on the Waterfront: Seamen, Longshoremen, and Unionism in the 1930s*, published by the University of Illinois Press.

41 Trott, 39.

42 Huycke, "The *Wawona* is Waiting (Part I)," 27.

43 Huycke, "The *Wawona* is Waiting (Part II)," 10.

44 This is an estimate based on a *Wawona* crew list under Conrad Scheel, Peasley's successor. See following note.

45 This conclusion is based on a number of crew lists gathered by Harriet DeLong from the first decade of the twentieth century and the 1920s and 30s. The pay amounts are from DeLong's *Pacific Schooner* Wawona, 51. It should be noted that Orvia Parker, a *Wawona* crew member in the 1930s, remembers a Japanese cook named "Tommy" in the 1938 and 1939 voyages of *Wawona* as a fishing vessel. "I had always been partial to rice as a food and Tommy was an expert on different ways of cooking it," he said in written descriptions of the voyages in Northwest Seaport archives. However, no Japanese surname appears in the 1938 crew list, and the 1939 crew list is missing. Furthermore, a crew member by the name of "Lawrence Wang" appears in the 1940 crew list. His country of origin is listed as the United States.

46 Nelson, 62-63.

47 Trott, 39.

48 William G. Mugan to R.E. Peasley, April 22, 1903. Mugan added, "Not hearing anything from you in the matter, we are inclined to think the report has no foundation." The nameless man was one of hundreds of seamen who died every year in their trade. Capt. Harold Huycke, a marine surveyor and historian, says names of dead sailors were printed every week in a union newspaper. The toll was "accepted and anticipated," given the hazards of the work. "They drowned, fell from aloft, committed suicide, or died of heart failure, alcoholism, consumption, or perhaps were murdered in the normal course of their calling." Huycke, 28.

49 DeLong, 56.

50 The only trace of direct conflict with an officer while Peasley captained *Wawona* is referenced in a letter from Mugan dated January 3, 1901. Mugan wrote, "We saw in the paper where you lost your mate and were confident that it

must have been from just the cause to which you attribute it." The mate may have been lost in a storm referenced in the letter's preceding paragraph, but the matter-of-fact tone makes the author wonder whether there's more to the story.

51 Van Syckle. *They Tried to Cut It All*, 249.

52 William G. Mugan to R.E. Peasley, March 14, 1902.

53 William G. Mugan to R.E. Peasley, October 18, 1901.

54 William G. Mugan to R.E. Peasley, November 27, 1901. See accompanying statements.

55 DeLong, 69. It is possible the crew may have been on Peasley's side during the dust up; they wanted to maintain an historic right to work cargo. A history of the Sailors Union of the Pacific singles out the lumber trade, because of its specialized nature, relatively small size, and limitation to the Pacific Coast, as critical to the success of union organizing efforts. "In the lumber trade," the author of the history writes, "the ship owners have consistently supported the seamen against the longshoremen." The SUP and the lumbermen shared common interests, though from different perspectives. The union wanted to control who worked the ships; the owners wanted to keep costs down by using its seamen for dock work. Paul S. Taylor, *Sailors Union of the Pacific*, 1923, 169.

56 William G. Mugan to R.E. Peasley, June 4, 1904.

57 The author found virtually no information on Scheel, except that he mastered *Wawona* from 1906 to 1913.

58 Newell, *The H.W. McCurdy Marine History of the Pacific Northwest.*

59 "Attempt Is Made To Intimidate Witness," *Grays Harbor Washingtonian*, May 4, 1910, 1. Transcribed notes from the original in the Ralph Peasley biography file of the Aberdeen Public Library.

60 The *Wawona* Collection at Northwest Seaport has a British gun license with Peasley's name dated July 22, 1921. He likely bought the license on his second trip aboard *Vigilant*, in which he carried coal from Port Angeles to Newcastle, Australia.

61 The photos, probably from the 1920s, are in the *Wawona* Collection of Northwest Seaport in Seattle.

62 Norton, Wilda, "Matt Peasley Here to Pilot Moran Cruise," *The Seattle Post-Intelligencer*, September 18, 1930, 8.

63 The *Aberdeen Daily World* published this poem as part of a package celebrating the memory of the famous Aberdeen resident. The author is unknown, although the paper said it was "most likely" Charley Grant.

64 Peasley's last command anticipated an industry of two generations later The *Seattle Sunday Times* reported that Peasley would take a group of students and

teachers up Alaska's Inside Passage to Glacier Bay and Mt. Fairweather. The group would shoot reels of motion picture film and take still photographs of finback and blue whales, and collect specimens of marine life. The group "is not the least bit interested in whale oil, whale bone," or fertilizer made from whales, the paper said. "They are going to hunt whales with a camera and not a harpoon gun." The paper called the trip "a whaling expedition with a modern flavor." A modern writer would have called it a whale-watching cruise. The trip, which started on July 1, 1931 and ended a month later. The vessel was the forty-five-foot auxiliary sloop Linda. It was the first and last time Peasley ever piloted a boat with an engine, something he swore he would never do. "Captain Peasley, Scientific Party to Study Whales," *The Seattle Sunday Times*, May 24, 1931, 14.

65 Author interview with Bill Jones, Aberdeen, Wash., November 10, 2004. Bill Jones is the son of Bliss Jones, who took numerous photographs of Peasley and Grays Harbor shipping.

66 "Peasley Discusses State Liquor Control," newspaper clipping in Ralph Peasley biography file, Aberdeen Public Library.

67 Newell, 410.

68 Hughes and Beckwith, 64.

69 Hughes and Beckwith.

70 "Capt. Peasley, 75, Ready to Fight Japan," *The Seattle Times*, December 8, 1941, 21.

71 Records of the Fern Hill Cemetery, Aberdeen, Washington.

72 Van Syckle, 254.

73 See notes labeled "Captain Ralph E. Peasley," in Ralph Peasley biography file of Aberdeen Public Library.

74 Seath, Irvine, "Captain Matt Peasley Marks 81st Birthday," newspaper clipping in Ralph Peasley biography file, Aberdeen Public Library.

75 Peasley commanded the five-masted *Vigilant*, the last large wooden schooner built on the west coast, from its launching at Aberdeen in 1919 to 1930. At the time of her wreck, she was called the *City of Alberni*. Hughes and Beckwith, 62-67. Gibbs, James A. Jr., 1949. "Capt. Matt Peasley Passes Away in the Wake of His Old-Time Command," *The Marine Digest*, January 1, 14.

76 "Capt. Ralph E. Peasley," *The New York Times*, December 14, 1948, 29. The *Times* said his age was 83. He was actually 82. Peasley was buried at Fern Hill Cemetery, the grave marked with a small red granite stone carved with the device of the Brotherhood and Protective Order of Elks. Peasley was survived by three

sisters, Mrs. Evelyn P. Sawyer, Mrs. Margaret Moody, and Mrs. Annetta Van Atta, all of Auburndale, Florida.

77 "Cod Schooners Ready to Sail," *The Seattle Times*, April 3, 1940, 12.

Chapter Three: Captain's Last Bed

1 Hughes, "*Wawona*—A Research Paper with Supplementary Notes," 44.

2 Hughes.

3 As far as can be determined, Foss is not related to the family which started the famed Foss Maritime Company of Seattle.

4 One census taker lists his home country as Sweden. But subsequent counts list his country of origin as Norway.

5 1900 Census, City of Skagway, via USGenWeb, http://ftp.rootsweb.com/pub/usgenweb/ak/skagway/census/1900/1900a.txt.

6 The 1935 Seattle City Directory lists the couple's address as 1545 12th Avenue South, as does the 1920 census. The 1910 census lists the address as 1545 22nd Avenue South, which the author believes is an error.

7 The 1910 census lists the following people in Foss' household: Charles Foss, age 42; Marian S., 27; Marian N. Haskell, 67; Ethel M—, 34; William Gillman (father-in-law), 55; May [Gilman], 50. Marian S. and all the additional people in the household are from Maine, except for two Canadian lodgers, possibly sailors, Harvey Rogers, 39, and Michael Keating, 30. By the 1920 census, only Foss' mother-in-law remained, besides Marian.

8 For an official history of North Pacific codfishing, read Cobb's *Pacific Salmon Fisheries*.

9 Robinson, "The Codfish Industry," 365.

10 Cobb, 477. See also Newell below.

11 "City served as busy cod port," *Anacortes American*, Oct. 29, 1980, 6; DeLong, *Pacific Schooner* Wawona, 89-91.

12 Newell, 211.

13 The last lumber schooner, called the *Oregon*, was constructed in Prosper, Oregon by E.H. Heuckendorf in 1905. However, some shipbuilders built schooners for European buyers during World War I. West coast shipbuilders turned to steam schooners, which were wooden vessels powered by steam, or iron and steel steamships, or they went out of business. The existing lumber schooners, such as *Wawona*, still plied their trade. But owners didn't replace them when damaged or wrecked, and in the slow economic years before World War I, they started selling them off. Huycke, "The *Wawona* is Waiting (Part II)," 10-12.

14 Trott, *The Schooner That Came Home: The Final Voyage of the* C.A. Thayer, 31-33.

15 In 1929, the company also added a 32-volt electrical system run off batteries charged by a gasoline engine. Crews now had safe and steady electric light, replacing the kerosene lamps. "Seattle's Codfishing Fleet Heads for Northern Waters," *The Seattle Star*, April 22, 1935, 1.

16 Letter from John F. "Jack" Healey to Captain Thorsten "Tom" Haugen, February 1, 1964, *Wawona* Collection, Northwest Seaport, Seattle.

17 Healey letter.

18 Cobb. See also Newell.

19 Workers rushed to get her ready for the 1919 fishing season, and they had a big job on their hands. Copra was usually infested with copra beetles and their eggs, which hatched on the way from the tropics. "They were into everything, and were worse than ants in their ability to escape from the hold and invade the living quarters," wrote Ed Shields. "After discharge, it was necessary to fumigate the vessel to get rid of these creatures." Shields, "Captain John Grotle, Codfisherman," 163-164.

20 Huycke, 12.

21 "Seattle Schooners Set Canvas for Ocean Race to the North," *The Seattle Star*, April 12, 1934, 1, 3.

22 Certificate of Naturalization for Maikel Maitak, *Wawona* Collection, Northwest Seaport, Seattle; "Account of Wages and Effects of a Deceased Seaman," U.S. Dept. of Commerce, Sept. 14, 1917, *Wawona* Collection, Northwest Seaport, Seattle.

23 Ellsworth Trafton, the son of *Wawona*'s owner.

24 "Sailing Ships at Last Off on Long-Delayed Race North," *The Seattle Star*, April 16, 1934. See also Hiscock (note 30), and Hughes, 41-43.

25 Much of the following life history of Thorsten Haugen is drawn from a typewritten manuscript written about 1980 titled "Mrs. 'Tom' Haugen's Nautical Scrap Book" in the *Wawona* Collection of Northwest Seaport in Seattle. Most of the manuscript was published in the *Anacortes American*.

26 In the 1925 off-season, Haugen survived his own shipwreck, when an unidentified vessel went down near Coos Bay, Oregon.

27 Orvia Parker recollections, *Wawona* Collection, Northwest Seaport, Seattle.

28 "Wawona—An important chapter in Anacortes history," *Anacortes American*, October 15, 1975, 6.

29 Schooner *Wawona* to Trafton, Robinson Fisheries, Federal Telegraph Company, April 28, 1935, *Wawona* Collection, Northwest Seaport. Foss later pur-

chased three "Lowell" dories at $120 each at Dutch Harbor. See telegram of April 29, 1935.

30 Hiscock, Wawona: *The Heritage of Sailing in the North Pacific.*

31 Schooner *Wawona* to Robinson Fisheries, Federal Telegraph Company, August 12, 1936, *Wawona* Collection, Northwest Seaport.

32 Hughes.

33 "*Wawona* 'alumni' recall sailing ship era," *The Seattle Times*, October 15, 1988, B1.

34 Interview with Dave Wright, April 27, 2004. This story was passed down to him by other fishermen who witnessed the incident.

35 Schooner *Wawona* to Cutter *Chelan*, Federal Telegraph Company, August 13, 1936, *Wawona* Collection, Northwest Seaport.

36 USCG Cutter *Chelan* to Schooner *Wawona*, Federal Telegraph Company, August 14 (?), 1936, *Wawona* Collection, Northwest Seaport. The date on the telegram is August 14, but the author believes this is an error.

37 Schooner *Wawona* to Commander, Cutter *Chelan* (1), Federal Telegraph Company, August 13, 1936, *Wawona* Collection, Northwest Seaport.

38 Schooner *Wawona* to Commander, Cutter *Chelan* (2), Federal Telegraph Company, August 13, 1936, *Wawona* Collection, Northwest Seaport.

39 USCG Cutter *Chelan* to Master, Schooner *Wawona*, Federal Telegraph Company, August 13, 1936, *Wawona* Collection, Northwest Seaport.

40 Schooner *Wawona* to Trafton, Robinson Fisheries, Federal Telegraph Company, August 14, 1936, *Wawona* Collection, Northwest Seaport. The date on the telegram is August 14, but the author believes this is an error.

41 USCGC *Chelan* to Master, *Wawona*, Federal Telegraph Company, August 13, 1936, *Wawona* Collection, Northwest Seaport.

42 Schooner *Wawona* note to Kielhorn, Commander, Cutter *Chelan*, Federal Telegraph Company, undated, *Wawona* Collection, Northwest Seaport.

43 This interpretation is based on photographs taken at the burial site. The photographs are in the Northwest Seaport *Wawona* Collection.

44 *Anacortes American*, October 15, 1975.

45 Hughes, 45.

46 Photograph, *Wawona* Collection, Northwest Seaport, Seattle.

Chapter Four: May You Wet All the Salt

1 Author interview with Diane Colson, March 13, 2004.

2 Diane McInturf Colson to Paul J. Douglas, November 23, 1976. Author's collection. Diane Colson is the daughter of Don McInturf. Paul J. Douglas is a former member of the board of Northwest Seaport, Seattle.

3 Kline, *All Aboard: An Educational Curriculum*, 14.

4 Photo "Men Inside Skid Road flophouse, Seattle, 1950," Museum of History & Industry collection.

5 Caption for photo "Edwin Hill repairing roof of shack in Hooverville, Seattle, November 1939," *Seattle Post-Intelligencer* staff photographer, 1939, Museum of History & Industry collection.

6 Caption for photo "Men scavenging in garbage dump, Seattle, 1937," Seattle Post-Intelligencer staff photographer, 1937, Museum of History & Industry collection.

7 Photo "Public employment office exterior showing men looking at listings, Seattle, 1936," Museum of History & Industry collection.

8 Broderick, Henry. *The 'HB' Story: Henry Broderick Relates Seattle's Yesterdays With Some Other Thoughts by the Way*," 143. See photo.

9 Interview with Dave Wright, January 11, 2005.

10 Carse, *The Twilight of Sailing Ships*, 121, 138, 150-153. On the west coast, the number of operating sail-powered general cargo vessels was reduced to three, including the *Vigilant*, the *Commodore* and the steel-hulled bark *Kaiulani*. "Last of the Sailing Ships," *Seattle Post-Intelligencer*, April 2, 1937, 23.

11 "Codfish Schooners To Sail In April," *The Seattle Sunday Times*, March 15, 1936, 14.

12 Shields, *Salt of the Sea: The Pacific Coast Cod Fishery and the Last Days of Sail*, 211.

13 "A Sailor Job That's Vanishing," newspaper clipping dated March 20, 1936 in the *Wawona* Collection, Northwest Seaport. The clipping is probably from *The Seattle Star*.

14 Krantz, Ray, "Ship's Cook Busy Man in the Morning," *The Seattle Star*, March, 1936.

15 "Tom Haugen Schooner's New Master," newspaper clipping dated 1936 in the *Wawona* Collection, Northwest Seaport.

16 "Safety First," newspaper clipping dated 1936 in the *Wawona* Collection, Northwest Seaport.

17 Shields, *Salt of the Sea: The Pacific Coast Cod Fishery and the Last Days of Sail*, 68. This account is adapted from Shields' account of preparations of his father's ship, the *Sophie Christensen*.

18 Undated (November, 1976?) letter from Diane Colson to Paul J. Douglas, given to the author.

19 The family lived at 3716 Angeline Street, about a half block off Rainier Avenue, which had a street car at the time.

20 Shields, *Salt of the Sea: The Pacific Coast Cod Fishery and the Last Days of Sail*, 75.

21 Shields. The meat may have been pork in some years. The meat was probably beef in 1936, because McInturf mentions the cook serving T-bone steaks a few days into the voyage.

22 Shields, *Salt of the Sea: The Pacific Coast Cod Fishery and the Last Days of Sail*, 76.

23 This scene is based on a recollection in Shields, page 77.

24 The tug *Challenge* was owned by Robinson Fisheries. McInturf said *Valencia* towed *Wawona* to sea. See McInturf diary, April 15.

25 Log of the *Wawona*, April 15, 1936, *Wawona* Collection, Northwest Seaport.

26 Van Syckle, *They Tried to Cut It All*, 229.

27 An invoice authorized Robinson Fisheries to deduct the cost of the supplies from McInturf's wages at the end of the trip and pay the chandler. Total bill: $22.75. Sunde & d'Evers receipt for D.W. McInturf, April 14, 1936, *Wawona* Collection, Northwest Seaport.

28 Parker, Orvia F., "Crew Routine Aboard the *Wawona* when Sailing To And From The Bering Sea: Years of 1936—1937—1938—1939," *Wawona* Collection, Northwest Seaport. Parker wrote down much of his information in 1986 as accompaniment to a number of donated photos.

29 McInturf, *Diary of the 1936 voyage of the* Wawona, April 20.

30 Agreement For Codfishing Voyage, 1931, Schooner *Wawona*. Robinson Fisheries. *Wawona* Collection, Northwest Seaport.

31 "Wawona Crew, 1936," spreadsheet compiled from Robinson Fisheries account book by Harriett DeLong for Northwest Seaport. *Wawona* Collection, Northwest Seaport.

32 "Wawona Crew, 1936."

33 Sunde and d'Evers Company receipt for Robinson Fisheries, April 14, 1947, *Wawona* Collection, Northwest Seaport.

34 Fisheries Supply Company receipts for Olav Wicks, April 13, 1936, and April 14, 1936; Pacific Marine Supply Company receipt to Robinson Fisheries ("O. Wick, Schooner *Wawona*"), April 11, 1936 (2), April 13, 1936. *Wawona* Collection, Northwest Seaport.

35 McInturf, April 15.

36 Schooner *Wawona* to Coast Guard Station Neah Bay, Western Union, April 16, 1936 (1), *Wawona* Collection, Northwest Seaport.

37 Schooner *Wawona* to Coast Guard Station Neah Bay, Western Union, April 16, 1936 (2), *Wawona* Collection, Northwest Seaport.

38 Schooner *Wawona* to Coast Guard Station Neah Bay, Western Union, April 16, 1936 (3), *Wawona* Collection, Northwest Seaport.

39 The next day, a Seattle newspaper reported the rescue, adding information about the mercy flight by seaplane to the Marine Hospital. The reporter noted the irony of a modern plane flying a windjammer sailor to the hospital. "Coast Guard Saves Sailor," newspaper clipping dated April 17, 1936 in the *Wawona* Collection, Northwest Seaport. The clipping is probably from *The Seattle Star*.

40 McInturf, April 17.

41 One of the men who would stand his watch at the wheel was Orvia F. Parker, a member of the dress gang on his first trip. He had been inspired to go to sea by Peter Kyne's *Cappy Ricks* books.

42 Log of the *Wawona*, April 17, 1936. *Wawona* Collection, Northwest Seaport.

43 J.E. Trafton to Thorsten Haugen, June 18, 1936, *Wawona* Collection, Northwest Seaport.

44 McInturf, April 30.

45 McInturf, May 1.

46 Log of the *Wawona*, May 1, 1936.

47 McInturf, May 1.

48 Log of the *Wawona*, May 2, 1936.

49 McInturf, May 2.

50 Log of the *Wawona*, May 2, 1936.

51 McInturf.

52 Alaska Volcano Observatory, http://www.avo.alaska.edu/avo4/atlas/volc/shish/activity.htm, November 17, 2004.

53 Five men lived at the lighthouse, one of the loneliest in the Coast Guard's lighthouse service. Their nearest neighbor for many years was a trapper 10 miles away. Families were not permitted to live at Scotch Cap and the lighthouse at Cape Sarichef, 17 miles away on the island's northwestern edge. The isolation drove some people batty. And the safety of solid land was deceptive. Nine years and 11 months after McInturf's first sight of Scotch Cap Light, on April 1, 1946, a 100-foot tsunami destroyed the lighthouse and killed its entire crew. Alaska Light Stations, http://www.uscg.mil/hq/g-cp/history/WEBLIGHTHOUSES/LHAK.html, November 16, 2004.

54 *Assessment of the National Ocean Service's Tidal Current Program*, NOAA Technical Report NOS CO-OPS 022, National Oceanographic and Atmospheric Administration, April, 1999, 11.

55 McInturf, August 24.

56 *Wawona* also carried a yard, square sail, and spare boom to take advantage of a following wind, but it was rarely raised. Orvia F. Parker, a member of the 1936, 1937 and 1938 crews, said it was used on the homeward bound leg of the 1937 voyage. See notes accompanying "Picture 101: The Schooner *Wawona*" in the *Wawona* Collection, Northwest Seaport.

57 McInturf, May 3.

58 Log of the *Wawona*, May 3.

59 McInturf.

60 McInturf.

61 McInturf.

62 McInturf.

63 Though the engine in 1936 was fueled by gasoline, it followed the same principle as Wawona's original coal-fueled steam donkey. Other sails were raised by hand. In an interview with the author, fisherman Dave Wright recalled an incident related to ship's discipline and sail raising. When the crew failed to lower a sail fast enough in a storm, the mate jumped forward and cut the halyard with a knife, bringing the sail down to the deck. The sailors were then told to splice the line. Fishermen also raised and lowered dories with the deck engine. Orvia Parker says that after 1935, *Wawona*'s spanker did not have a gaff. Two or three men could raise the gaff-less spanker without the deck engine.

64 McInturf to 3716 Angeline St., Seattle, Federal Telegraph Company, May 4, 1936, *Wawona* Collection, Northwest Seaport.

65 McInturf, May 5.

66 McInturf, May 5 ("add").

67 Haugen to 22 John Street, Seattle, Federal Telegraph Company, May 5, 1936, *Wawona* Collection, Northwest Seaport.

68 Schooner Wawona to Juanita Whyte, Federal Telegraph Company, May 5, 1936, *Wawona* Collection, Northwest Seaport.

69 Mrs. Orville Paxton, Anacortes, Federal Telegraph Company, May 5, 1936, *Wawona* Collection, Northwest Seaport.

70 Schooner Wawona to Robinson Fisheries, Federal Telegraph Company, May 5, 1936, *Wawona* Collection, Northwest Seaport.

71 Captain Thorsten Haugen to J.E. Trafton, May 6, 1936, *Wawona* Collection, Northwest Seaport.

72 Letter from Captain Haugen to J.E. Trafton, May 6th, 1936, *Wawona* Collection, Northwest Seaport, Seattle.

73 "I used to get nine or ten letters at a time," she remembered years later. "I would number mine and he would number his as they were written." Headline unknown, *Seattle Post-Intelligencer*, January 1, 1964 (?), 16. Haugen is pictured studying a painting of his old command.

74 Photograph, *Wawona* Collection, Northwest Seaport.

75 McInturf, May 7.

Chapter Five: Snaffling the Codfish

1 Throughout his diary, McInturf misspells Jean Bagger's first name "Gene." The error is corrected throughout the text to maintain clarity.

2 McInturf, *Diary of the 1936 voyage of the* Wawona, June 19, May 7.

3 McInturf, April 22.

4 Shields, "Captain J.E. Shields (Part I)", 32. The articles were taken from a memoir published privately by the family.

5 Image from a 1950 color film taken by Capt. Ed Shields aboard the schooner *C.A. Thayer.*

6 McInturf, April 23.

7 Orvia F. Parker said *Wawona* was short a spare man on the port side team.

8 Shields, *Salt of the Sea: The Pacific Coast Cod Fishery and the Last Days of Sail,* 117.

9 Cod eat pretty much any living or mildly dead thing it can swallow, including pollock, sculpin, salmon, herring, capelin, halibut, sand launce, and mackerel. Biologist John N. Cobb found three ducks in the belly of one cod. Adult cod also eat their young. John N. Cobb, *Pacific Cod Fisheries* (Washington, DC: Government Printing Office, 1927), 390.

10 McInturf, May 23.

11 McInturf, May 10.

12 Cobb, 388.

13 McInturf, June 14.

14 Ed Shields, writing in a Kitsap County Herald on October 5, 1950, said catches of 300 to 350 fish in three or four hours was not unheard of. He said the single day's record was 1,002 fish. The single day's ship record was held by his father's vessel, the *Sophie Christensen.* Its 22 dories once brought in more than 17,000 cod, the equivalent of 180,000 pounds of fresh fish.

15 McInturf, May 23.

16 McInturf, May 13, May 14, May 24.

17 McInturf, June 11.

18 McInturf, May 24.

19 McInturf, May 5, June 2.

20 Log of the *Wawona*, June 2, 1936, *Wawona* Collection, Northwest Seaport.

21 The tallies are based on entries in the official 1936 voyage log of the *Wawona*, *Wawona* Collection, Northwest Seaport.

22 Kline, *All Aboard: An Educational Curriculum*, 13.

23 Parker, Orvia F., "Picture No. 105: On Way Home from the Bering Sea in 1936," notes accompanying a photo, *Wawona* Collection, Northwest Seaport.

24 Shields, *Salt of the Sea: The Pacific Coast Cod Fishery and the Last Days of Sail*, 122.

25 Narration from a 1950 film of the codfish schooner *C.A. Thayer* taken by Captain Ed Shields.

26 McInturf, June 14.

27 Thorsten Haugen to J.E. Trafton, June 8, 1935, *Wawona* Collection, Northwest Seaport.

28 Gardner, *The Dory Book*, 37. Gardner also says a version of the *batteau* was used in Oregon to ferry lumber. See page 24.

29 McInturf, June 2.

30 In 1914, the schooner *Fortuna* attempted to use 12 motorized dories with little success. Most fishermen did not understand them and so neglected maintenance and repair. And they complained the motor took up capacity they'd rather fill with fish. Cobb, 424. See also Jones, "Cod Bangers to Alaska," 12.

31 Early manufacturers included Evinrude and Johnson Engine. Shields, *Salt of the Sea: The Pacific Coast Cod Fishery and the Last Days of Sail*, 59-60

32 *Wawona* fisherman and dress gang member Orvia F. Parker, who documented much of *Wawona*'s daily working life, credits Olaf Wicks and John Berg with much of the design changes to the dories. Both were in *Wawona*'s 1936 crew.

33 Parker, "Picture No. 105."

34 Shields, *Salt of the Sea: The Pacific Coast Cod Fishery and the Last Days of Sail*, 59-60.

35 Shields, 20.

36 Joe Haberstroh, "*Wawona* 'alumni' recall sailing-ship era," *The Seattle Times*, October 11, 1988, B1.

37 Shields, "Captain J.E. Shields (Part I)", 32. See also Orvia F. Parker, "Picture No. 105."

38 Interview of Dave Wright by the author, January 16, 2004.

39 McInturf, June 6.

40 McInturf, June 11.

41 McInturf, May 28.

42 McInturf, June 11.

43 Orvia Parker, "Picture No. 102: Jimmy McNary," notes accompanying a photo, *Wawona* Collection, Northwest Seaport.

44 McInturf, May 24.

45 Cobb, 436. Cobb uses slightly different titles from Orvia Parker, who said the above deck gang member titles were "splitter," "gutter," "header," "idler," and "spare man." The names may reflect slight differences in procedures on each shi-Cobb also noted that Atlantic cod companies used a mechanical device similar to the "iron chink" used by salmon fishers to dress their catch. But there's no mention of this machine in any writing by Pacific Coast cod companies. They may have felt that the fish would spoil before they could be transported to Puget Sound or San Francisco for processing.

46 Shields, "Captain J.E. Shields (Part I)".

47 Narration from 1950 film taken by Ed Shields.

48 Parker.

49 Parker, "Picture No. 103."

50 Cobb, 436-437.

51 Cobb, 437.

52 Parker, "Picture No. 103." The difficult and inefficient work of hand line fishing was hard on the men, but it was easier on the fishery than trawling methods that become popular after World War II. Environmentalists have criticized bottom trawling, which scoops up tons of immature fish, unwanted fish species, or other creatures than inhabit the sea floor. The late Capt. Ed Shields argued that the hand line method used by his men "far exceeded modern conservation efforts."

The hook-and-line method of catching fish resulted in few other species being taken. In fact, it was normally a problem to catch enough fish of other species to provide the required amount of bait. Further, the hook-and-line did no damage to the bottom. Today, by contrast, the large trawlers towing their heavy nets with cables and otter doors literally plow up the bottom, causing considerable ecological damage.

Ed Shields, 134-135.

53 Shields.

54 McInturf, June 23, 24, 25.

55 McInturf, April 29.

56 Gus Dagg, "Codfishing in the Bering Sea," *The Spanker*, newsletter of Northwest Seaport, September/October, 1979.

57 Schooner *Wawona* to Ships Doctor, Coast Guard Cutter, Federal Telegraph Company, May 28, 1935, *Wawona* Collection, Northwest Seaport.

58 Dagg.

59 Log of the *Wawona*, May 9.

60 "He saw pink elephants." Wright interview, November 24, 2004.

61 Hiscock, Wawona: *The Heritage of Sailing in the North Pacific.*

62 "Trying to get out of the top bunk on a three-tiered set is no easy task when your hands are tied, but he did it, and landed on his head. He was a Norwegian though, so no damage was done." Jack Healey, quoted in Hiscock.

63 McInturf, June 19.

64 McInturf, June 29.

65 McInturf, June 20.

66 Capt. J. Edward Shields, "Captain John Grotle, Codfisherman," *The Sea Chest*, Puget Sound Maritime Historical Society, Vol. 30, 156-157.

67 Shields, 22.

68 Dagg.

69 McInturf, May 17.

70 McInturf.

71 McInturf, June 29.

72 J. Edward Shields, 161.

73 The author could not identify the species.

74 Orvia F. Parker, "Picture No. 108: Easter Sunday, 1938," notes accompanying a photograph, *Wawona* Collection, Northwest Seaport.

75 Kline, 9.

76 Ed Shields, "Captain J.E. Shields (Part I)", 32.

77 McInturf, July 3. Wick may have provoked the whale. McInturf notes in his May 24 entry that Wick hit the whale with an oar when the animal came too close for comfort.

78 McInturf, May 24.

79 Log of the *Wawona*, May 22, 1936, *Wawona* Collection, Northwest Seaport.

80 Orvia Parker, "Picture No. 103: Part of the Dress Gang in 1937," notes accompanying a photo, *Wawona* Collection, Northwest Seaport.

81 McInturf, June 19.

82 McInturf, June 22.

83 McInturf, June 20.

84 "Codfish Ship Has Poor Year; Mate Is Lost," *The Seattle Times*, September 4, 1941, 28. See also Hugh McCaffrey, "Journal of *Sophie Christensen*," *Wawona* Collection, Northwest Seaport, May 27 and May 28, 1941.

85 Wright interview.

86 Parker, "Picture No. 105."

Chapter Six: The *Wawona* Brewing Society

1 Log of the *Wawona*, 1936, *Wawona* Collection, Northwest Seaport.

2 Parker, Orvia F., "Routine Aboard the Wawona When Fishing in the Bering Sea," *Wawona* Collection, Northwest Seaport.

3 Shields, *Salt of the Sea: The Pacific Coast Cod Fishery and the Last Days of Sail*. The crew spent four or five weeks preparing the ship's larder as it lay docked in Seattle. Much of the information for Bagger's requisitions comes from this memoir, which recounts voyages of the *Sophie Christenson*, a four-masted sister ship of the three-masted *Wawona*. The *Sophie Christenson* accompanied *Wawona* on the same 1936 voyage. The author assumes that many of the needs of *Wawona* were similar, although *Wawona* carried a crew of 36, as opposed to the *Sophie Christenson*'s 45.

4 The temperature of the Bering Sea water outside the hold hovered just above freezing.

5 DeLong, *Pacific Schooner* Wawona, 106. Some owners purchased several tons of hard wheat flour from Alberta, Canada.

6 "Requisition Supplies for Schooner _____," Robinson Fisheries Company, *Wawona* Collection, Northwest Seaport, Seattle. The form lists 215 items.

7 DeLong says 30 cases, *Pacific Schooner* Wawona, 106.

8 Parker.

9 Shields, *Salt of the Sea*; Author interview with Louise Shields, widow of Captain Ed Shields, January 2, 2005.

10 DeLong

11 Shields, "Captain J.E. Shields (Part I)", 29.

12 Parker, Orvia, "Crew Routine Aboard the Wawona When Sailing To and From the Bering Sea: Years of 1936—1937—1938—1939." *Wawona* Collection, Northwest Seaport, Seattle.

13 Parker.

14 Parker, Orvia, "Picture No. 108: Easter Sunday 1938." *Wawona* Collection, Northwest Seaport, Seattle. Haugen's place at the table was a break from long-standing tradition. Normally, officers eat separately from the rest of the crew. It's unclear why Haugen broke this tradition.

15 Shields, "Captain J.E. Shields (Part I)", 29.

16 Don McInturf, *Diary of the 1936 voyage of the* Wawona, June 19.

17 Shields, "Captain J.E. Shields (Part I)", 30.

18 Shields, "Fresh Water in the Bering Sea," 36.

19 Shields, "Fresh Water in the Bering Sea."

20 Gus Dagg, "Codfishing in the Bering Sea," *The Spanker*, newsletter of Northwest Seaport, September/October, 1979.

21 Handwritten caption on a fisherman's photo, *Wawona* Collection, Northwest Seaport.

22 Ed Shields, "Fresh Water in the Bering Sea."

23 Dagg.

24 Gus Dagg later claimed he had more hair at 73 than he did at 20.

25 Hiscock, Barbara A. Wawona: *The Heritage of Sailing in the North Pacific*, 1965.

26 Orvia F. Parker, "Crew Routine Aboard the *Wawona* when Sailing To And From The Bering Sea: Years of 1936—1937—1938—1939," transcribed(?) letters, *Wawona* Collection, Northwest Seaport.

27 McInturf, April 30, May 15.

28 Kline, *All Aboard: An Educational Curriculum*, 13.

29 McInturf, July 6.

30 Schooner *Wawona* to Radio Inspector, Federal Building, Seattle, Federal Telegraph Company, July 6, 1936, *Wawona* Collection, Northwest Seaport.

31 McInturf, July 10, Aug. 17.

32 Jean Bagger, Letter to Robinson Fisheries, October 6, 1936.

33 Ray Krantz, "Ship's Cook Busy Man in Morning," *Seattle Star*, March or April, 1936.

34 Shields, "Captain J.E. Shields (Part II)," 40.

35 Parker, "Crew Routine."

36 Parker, "Routine Aboard the Wawona."

37 McInturf, June 8.

38 McInturf, May 24.

39 McInturf, May 17.

40 McInturf, July 9, 10, 11.

41 Parker, "Crew Routine."

42 Crooks, Jimmy, "*Wawona* Drive Recalls Codfishing," *The Seattle Post-Intelligencer*, Feb. 2, 1964.

43 Robinson Fisheries accounts, *Wawona* Collection, Northwest Seaport.

44 "Typhoid Ties Up Towns," *The New York Times*, July 27, 1936, 17.

45 McInturf, May 8.
46 Author interview with Diane Colson, March 13, 2004.
47 McInturf, June 19.
48 McInturf, June 19.
49 McInturf, June 19.
50 See 1936 account books and handwritten orders for furs in *Wawona* Collection, Northwest Seaport.
51 McInturf, May 5.
52 Parker, Orvia F., "Picture No. 109: Dories on the Beach," *Wawona* Collection, Northwest Seaport.
53 Steel tanks above and below the main deck stored fresh water on *Wawona*. The owners coated the inside of the tanks with Portland cement every three to five years. When the new coat dried, the captain filled the tanks with fresh water at the dock, flushed them, then filled them again just before departure. Baffles and splash plates inside the tank kept the water from sloshing around too much when the ship rolled, while keeping the water aerated and fresh-tasting. Shields, "Fresh Water in the Bering Sea," 39.
54 McInturf, June 11.
55 McInturf, June 10.
56 McInturf, June 11.
57 McInturf, June 27.
58 McInturf, July 3.
59 McInturf and others on *Wawona* made no less than four kegs of wine by the time they returned to Anacortes in early September.
60 McInturf, June 28.
61 McInturf, July 4.
62 McInturf, July 5.
63 Fisherman Dave Wright told the author that the captain and the mates (as well as the radio operator) relieved themselves over the stern. A visitor to the Wawona today sees a commode near the captain's cabin. But Wright believes it was added in the early 1950s by Captain Ralph Pederson. (See chapter 8.) Wright's claim fits with McInturf's comment about "sitting on a towing bitt," two of which were astern near the main cabin.
64 McInturf, July 7.
65 McInturf, July 24.
66 On the other hand, Captain J.E. Shields, one of the best known captains of the cod fleet at the time, regarded alcohol with suspicion. His son, Ed, suggests that on sailing day, the vast majority of fishermen and fish dressers had spent the

previous night at a tavern, a bootlegger joint, or sleeping off a binge in jail. Ed Shields, *Salt of the Sea*, 75-82. For Shields, father and son, it seemed that seamen had only two goals in mind, getting drunk and staying drunk. In one memoir, Ed Shields laments the stereotypical Scandinavian weakness for white lightning. "This one item was the downfall for most of them when ashore," he wrote. "Probably this fact accounted for them following the sea and fishing. Here they were away from the alcohol for months at a time and they could enjoy life, hard as it was at times. On shore, there was only the one lifestyle, that of consuming more alcohol than they could handle." Shields, "Captain J.E. Shields (Part II)," 41.

67 McInturf, July 26. Nearly 40 years later, Haugen told a Seattle historian about McInturf's rotgut, recalling it "with amusement." De Long. *Pacific Schooner Wawona*, 151.

Chapter Seven: The Smallest Man on Board

1 Don McInturf, *Diary of the 1936 voyage of the* Wawona, April 18.

2 McInturf, April 24.

3 McInturf, April 26.

4 McInturf, May 24.

5 Parker, Orvia F., "Picture No. 110: *Wawona* on the Way Home in 1936," transcribed notes accompanying a photograph, Northwest Seaport, 1986; Author conversation with Dave Wright, December 2, 2004 at Northwest Seaport, Seattle.

6 Thorsten Haugen to J.E. Trafton, Robinson Fisheries, June 8, 1936.

7 Author interview with Diane Colson, March 13, 2004.

8 McInturf, May 23. His reference to the "engine room" is unclear; Wawona was never propelled by anything other than wind. He's probably referring to the deck house.

9 McInturf, June 12 and 13.

10 McInturf, June 14.

11 McInturf, June 16.

12 McInturf, June 17.

13 McInturf.

14 Colson interview.

15 Parker, Orvia F., "Picture No. 104: Donald McInturf—Wireless Telegraph Operator," transcribed notes accompanying a photograph, Northwest Seaport, 1986.

16 Colson interview.

17 McInturf, May 28.

18 McInturf, May 18. Fisherman Orvia Parker had a different opinion of Bagger. "He was an expert, a hard worker, and very dedicated to his profession," he said. "Everything he cooked, like the plain every day food, was very appetizing." Orvia F. Parker, "Crew Routine Aboard the Wawona when Sailing To And From The Bering Sea: Years of 1936—1937—1938—1939," *Wawona* Collection, Northwest Seaport.

19 McInturf, June 7 and June 11. The milk is either condensed or powdered.

20 McInturf, July 7.

21 McInturf, July 9, 10, 11.

22 McInturf, July 15, 16, 17, 18, 19.

23 McInturf, July 25.

24 McInturf, July 24.

25 McInturf, July 26.

26 Parker, Orvia F., "Picture No. 107: Towing the Wawona With Dories Through Unimak Pass," transcribed notes accompanying a photograph, Northwest Seaport, 1986. The incident happened in 1938.

27 McInturf, July 9, 10, 11.

28 McInturf, August 1.

29 McInturf, August 2.

30 McInturf, August 4.

31 McInturf, August 7, 8.

32 The smell of Bagger's home-canned meat suggests spoilage.

33 Log of the Schooner *Wawona*, Northwest Seaport, Seattle.

34 McInturf, August 14.

35 McInturf, August 15.

36 McInturf, August 16.

37 Log of the *Wawona*.

38 McInturf, August 17.

39 Schooner *Wawona* to Robinson Fisheries (Rofico), Western Union, August 19, 1936, *Wawona* Collection, Northwest Seaport.

40 Log of the *Wawona*.

41 McInturf, August 18.

42 McInturf, August 26, 27, 28, 29, 30; September 1, 2.

43 McInturf, September 3, 4, 5.

44 "Seattle Fish Boat Battles Arctic Gale; Navy Speeds Aid," *Seattle Post-Intelligencer*, August 26, 1947, 1; "Battered Seattle Ship," undated, and "Lusty Sea

Atmosphere As *Wawona* Comes Home Again," September 25, 1947, newspaper clippings in *Wawona* Collection of Northwest Seaport.

45 McInturf.

46 Schooner *Wawona* to Rofico, Western Union, September 7, 1936, *Wawona* Collection, Northwest Seaport.

47 Schooner *Wawona* to 22 John St., Seattle, Federal Telegaph Company, September 7, 1936, *Wawona* Collection, Northwest Seaport.

48 Robinson Fisheries to Haugen, *Wawona*, Western Union, September 8, 1936, *Wawona* Collection, Northwest Seaport.

49 Author interview with Louise Shields, widow of Captain Ed Shields, January 2, 2005.

50 Robinson Fisheries to Mrs. Tom Haugen, Western Union, September 8, 1936, *Wawona* Collection, Northwest Seaport.

51 Robinson Fisheries to Mrs. D. McInturf, Western Union, September 8, 1936, *Wawona* Collection, Northwest Seaport. The address indicates that Irene and Diane moved to a house, possibly a rented room, during McInturf's voyage.

52 Parker, "Picture No. 104."

53 Although no record of the *Wawona*'s 1936 arrival survives, a photograph from a later arrival shows Mrs. Bob Snow waving at the ship as she is towed to the dock at Robinson Fisheries in Anacortes. "Home from the Sea," newspaper clipping in the *Wawona* Collection, Northwest Seaport.

54 Nast, Stan, "[Unknown Headline]", *Seattle Post-Intelligencer*, February 1, 1964, 16.

55 Spreadsheet created by Harriet DeLong from Robinson Fisheries account books, *Wawona* Collection, Northwest Seaport.

56 Hiscock, Wawona: *The Heritage of Sailing in the North Pacific*, 1965.

57 Parker, Orvia F., "Routine Aboard the *Wawona* When Fishing in the Bering Sea," notes accompanying photos, *Wawona* Collection, Northwest Seaport. Also author interview with Louise Shields, January 2, 2005.

58 Shields, *Salt of the Sea: The Pacific Cod Fishery and the Last Days of Sail*, 181-190. Some of the details were supplied by Louise Shields and the film of the 1950 voyage of the *C.A. Thayer* and subsequent fish processing. Ed Shields filmed the final voyage of the *C.A. Thayer* and the fish processing in 1950. The color film is owned by the family.

59 Parker, "Picture No. 104."

60 Diane McInturf Colson to Paul J. Douglas, November 23, 1976. Author's collection.

61 DeLong, *Pacific Schooner* Wawona, 134.

62 Wright interview. The fishermen spent the war years in the Army Transport Service and witnessed the attack.

63 Robinson Fisheries installed a small refrigeration unit under her cabin that year.

64 "Lusty Sea Atmosphere As *Wawona* Comes Home Again," September 25, 1947, newspaper clipping in *Wawona* Collection, Northwest Seaport.

65 Sherman, Bruce, "'He Had Respect for the Sea,'" *Seattle Post-Intelligencer*, August 18, 1980, A4.

66 The Union Fish Company of San Francisco, the last Bay Area cod company, disappeared before World War II. The Poulsbo-based Pacific Coast Codfish Company, owner of the *C.A. Thayer*, got out of the cod business in the early 1950s, opting for the growing Alaska crab fishery, but the company eventually closed down. Robinson Fisheries also gave up cod around 1950, and the business closed its doors in 1969.

67 Parker, "Picture No. 110."

Chapter Eight: Saving the Big Ship

1 Krenmayr, Janice, "Seattle Still Has Two Windjammers," *The Seattle Times*, February 24, 1963. Shortly after the story was published, the mastless hulk was purchased for $26,000 by a maritime museum in Hawaii, now called the Hawaii Maritime Center, and towed to Honolulu, where it was restored. "Windjammer Will Find Haven in Museum," *The Seattle Times* (?), June 26 (?), 1963. Newspaper clipping in scrapbook, *Wawona* Collection, Northwest Seaport.

2 Luke was lobbied by Katherine "Kay" Bullitt, the community-minded wife of businessman Stimson Bullitt. One of her interests was historic preservation. At a party, Kay brought up the *Times* article to newly elected city councilman Wing Luke. Author interview with Kay Bullitt, January 7, 2005.

3 Willix, Douglas, "Lake Union Park Proposed as Sailing-Ship Museum Site," newspaper clipping in *Wawona* Collection, Northwest Seaport, dated February 26, 1963. The land was later redeveloped into Gas Works Park, without a museum.

4 "Hopes Fade for Display of Old Ships," *The Seattle Times*, June 18, 1963, 12.

5 Wing Luke Biography at HistoryLink, http://www.historylink.org, December 30, 2004.

6 "John Ross, 77; was teacher, sailor, and furniture maker," *The Boston Globe*, December 25, 2002.

7 Interview with Kay Bullitt, January 7, 2005.

8 Ross, *To Buy a Schooner—Montana Fashion*, 1-3.

9 Ross, 3.

10 "New Owner of Wawona Proud of Purchase," magazine clipping in *Wawona* Collection, Northwest Seaport, March 15, 1952; "An Opportunity to Those Who Are Interested in Sailing: Windjammer 'Wawona,'" promotional brochure in *Wawona* Collection, Northwest Seaport.

11 The hotel was named for Marcus Daly, who founded Anaconda's main industry, copper mining and smelting.

12 Ross, 5.

13 Ross, 6.

14 Cooper made his reputation in the 1940s and 50s playing cowboys and western lawmen. The Montana native died in 1961. Ross may have meant the Cooper Estate.

15 Ross, 7

16 Ross, 10.

17 Ross doesn't say how his car suddenly turns up in Seattle. In the Bay Area, he first visited Karl Kortum, director of the San Francisco Maritime Museum, who counseled patience, reminding Ross that years had passed between initial contact and final purchase of the square-rigger *Balclutha* for his organization.

18 Hayden would soon play cigar-chomping, bodily-fluid obsessed General Jack D. Ripper in *Dr. Strangelove, or How I Learned to Stop Worrying and Love the Bomb.*

19 Ross, 11.

20 Ross, 14.

21 Wing Luke to William Studdert, September 16, 1963, Northwest Seaport Archives.

22 Ross, 16.

23 The cash was donated by Kay Bullitt. Author interview with Kay Bullitt, January 7, 2005.

24 Ross said a male Wagner friend, whom he didn't identify, accompanied himself and Wagner on this trip.

25 The painting was by Seattle marine artist Hewitt Jackson.

26 Ross, 20.

27 Ross, 20-21.

28 Studdert had an Old West kind of gallantry and sense of honor. When Anne Wagner drove out alone to meet Studdert while Ross was in California, Studdert gave Wagner two tires to replace ones she had worn out on the trip.

29 Ross, 24.

30 Ross, 25.

31 Save Our Ships incorporated on January 20, 1964.

32 Minutes of SOS Meeting, December 9, 1963, Northwest Seaport Archives. His salary was set at $7,000 a year.

33 "Press Conference: Schooner Wawona," announcement and handout, January 7, 1964, Northwest Seaport Archives.

34 MacIntosh, Heather, "Save Our Ships! An Interview with Kay Bullitt," Preservation Seattle, http://www.cityofseattle.net/commnty/histsea/preservationseattle/youngvoices/defaultjune3.htm, June/July, 2004. See also SOS minutes for June 16, 1964.

35 The story was accompanied by a photo of Haugen touching a painting of his old command. Haugen had visited her at South Lake Union, and he thought one of the masts "seemed soft." He had installed the mast in 1945. Nast, Stan, "[Unknown Headline]", Seattle Post-Intelligencer, February 1, 1964, 16.

36 Crooks, Jimmy, "Wawona Drive Recalls Codfishing," The Seattle Post-Intelligencer, Feb. 2, 1964.

37 MacIntosh.

38 The minutes suggest some sort of issue raised by Capt. Adrian Raynaud, the main source for the newspaper story a year before that sparked the effort to save Wawona. SOS minutes, January 28, 1964.

39 Minutes of SOS Meeting, June 3, 1964, Northwest Seaport Archives. See also minutes for April 17. The discrepancy between the Studdert price of $22,000 ($40,000 minus the projected Sierra price of $17,500) and the $28,500 SOS price on June 3 is not explained. However, a newspaper report said that "interested parties in California" would purchase the ship if SOS did not. The $28,500 figure may have been their bid. Ross eventually sold the Sierra to a man who planned to turn her into a floating restaurant. Northwest Packet, Northwest Seaport newsletter, probably 1974. Sierra's owner at the time was Mart Liikane.

40 Krenmayr, Janice, "City Has 3 Weeks to Save Wawona," The Seattle Times, May 24, 1964, 42.

41 "Outside Interests Gaze Lovingly at Wawona," Seattle Post-Intelligencer (?), undated newspaper clipping in Wawona Collection, Northwest Seaport.

42 "Public Officials to Sing for Wawona," The Seattle Times, May 27, 1964, 42. "Hundreds Jam Blue Banjo to Help Save Wawona," The Seattle Times, May 28, 1964, 24. "Save Our Ships Rally Set at Pioneer Square," The Seattle Post-Intelligencer, May 28, 1964, 25. "Luncheon Adds to Ship Fund," (photo caption), The Seattle Times, May 29, 1964, 33. Special lyrics were composed for the event. The lyrics are transcribed in a scrapbook in the Wawona Collection at Northwest Seaport.

43 SOS minutes, June 16, 1964.

44 "Museum-Ship Plans Disclosed," *The Seattle Times*, June 9, 1964, 28. "$75,000 Would Be Cost of Restoring Schooner Wawona," undated newspaper clipping in *Wawona* Collection, Northwest Seaport.

45 SOS also reported $1,830 in pledges, but pledges don't always turn in contributions, so SOS couldn't apply this figure to its contributions total.

46 SOS minutes, June 16, 1964, Northwest Seaport Archives. The donor was later identified as Dorothy Stimson Bullitt, founder of a local broadcasting empire and the mother-in-law of SOS board member Kay Bullitt. See MacIntosh.

47 SOS had rehired him as executive director shortly after the organization purchased *Wawona* from him.

48 *Boston Globe* obituary.

49 SOS acquired other vessels, including a lightship, a tug, and a salmon troller, which fit its overall dream of a destination maritime heritage site. One of its ships, the ferry *San Mateo*, was lost to British Columbia.

50 The nomination form is in the Northwest Seaport Archives. The plaque is on her main cabin.

51 *Mainsail*, Northwest Seaport newsletter, September, 1972.

52 Curator Mary S. Kline worked for Northwest Seaport from 1973 to 1980.

53 Wright told this story to the author on November 18, 2004, then retold it for the television producer.

54 She also spent a number of years at a berth in Kirkland, a suburb of Seattle on Lake Washington.

Index

·

978-0-595-41833-
0-595-41833-3

Printed in the United States
66930LVS00003B/115-189